Introduction

From the time my husband, Jack Yunits, first mentioned he was thinking of running for mayor of the city of Brockton, MA—an old industrial city whose claim to fame was once the "Shoe Capital of the World," as well as the birthplace of boxing great, Rocky Marciano—I was fearful of what would befall our family. He had never run for office before and Brockton was sinking fast.

But Jack believed that if he could re-create the Brockton "of old," where "Industry, Education and Progress" distinguished the city's intent as written by the city's forefathers, then its citizens could once again live up to Brockton's nickname "City of Champions."

For ten years Jack did just that, with help from hundreds of friends, supporters, elected officials, our four kids and myself, who worked harder than we probably preferred because Jack urged us all to follow his lead, to work with him, to team up together, and to bring back Brockton pride. We didn't let him down, nor he us, resulting in a renewed spirit and dozens of physical structures to prove that his vision wasn't all talk.

People started hoping again, and hope, I believe, is our single most cherished feeling. Jack said to me once, "If a city full of loving families and dozens of neighborhoods can't be saved, then who or what is worth saving?" I couldn't agree more.

CHAPTER 1

"If you can accept losing, you can't win."
—*Vince Lombardi*

In a home hair salon near the downtown area of Brockton, Massachusetts, the odor of perm chemicals filled a room of a three-family home as a hairdresser got ready to work her magic. She chatted with an elderly customer while the stylist applied the mix. The talk revolved around the man who had recently been inaugurated as Brockton's newest mayor—my husband, Jack Yunits. The customer remembered him from the previous summer when he knocked at her door.

"When he showed up at my house," the client recalled, dabbing a stray drip of a hair mixture with a towel, "his white shirt was drenched from the heat. Short guy, kind of Italian-looking, and he had on these dress shoes I can't imagine could have been that comfortable. He seemed sincere about wanting to help the city."

"Yeah, I heard about that," the hairdresser agreed, swishing a small brush into the mixing bowl. "He spoke at our crime watch meeting, too. Good luck to him. Tough job."

"I don't know what he can do around here," the elderly woman murmured, squirming a bit in her plastic seat. "The city is changing. In my day you could walk from the north side to the south side at any hour of the day or night and feel safe. No more. Too bad. I voted for him anyway."

Yeah, me, too," the hairdresser responded, putting down the empty bowl. "Now, why don't you come sit over here before I wash you out." The hairdresser motioned to a tufted maroon easy chair.

Her home on Warren Avenue wasn't in the worst section of town, although that area of Brockton, known as Campello, had seen better days. With the amount of traffic that moved up and down Warren Avenue, the woman's hair salon seemed well situated for business. People could be seen going in and out the side door on a regular basis. I drove by the triple-decker every day on my way to work at my husband's law firm. He stopped working there when he became mayor. But I continued as the bookkeeper and Jack's law partner, John McCluskey, now runs the business. Secretaries and a couple of other lawyers keep the place hopping.

Shortly after the grandmotherly customer left the home salon dolled up in her curly perm, a stranger entered the room easily. He lifted a gun and shot a bullet through the hairdresser's body. The force threw her back against the sink killing her instantly.

I was at work when I got the news from Jack. The atrocity shook everyone up. "What is going on around here?" one secretary asked, staring out the window. Her view took her past the big Lutheran church and up Main Street, where the ambulance was shrieking away to the scene of the crime. She, like most of our staff, was born and raised and is still living—happily, for the most part—in Brockton. This new wave of violence was unnerving, though, and repeating itself too often for anyone's comfort.

The following morning, several Boston TV stations called our house looking for Jack's reaction. Even though the ringing phone made me jump, I was growing accustomed to the 5 a.m. calls. "Hello?" I answered, stretching my face so that my eyes would pull open.

"Mayor Yunits, please," a reporter requested.

"May I ask what the issue is?" I said, pulling myself to a sitting position, even if I was fairly sure I knew the answer.

Soon, after hurriedly downing a cup of black coffee, Jack left for the police station and the District Attorney's office, in an attempt to calm everyone's fears. The flood of calls to City Hall from concerned citizens overwhelmed Jack's new staff. His lovely secretary, Lillian Pilalas, remained composed, though. She knew half the callers by name and understood how frightened they were by the thought of a deranged individual on the loose. Lillian placated them. "Yes, the mayor is working on it. Yes, love, I will tell him you called," she said, delicately pushing a strand of her hair away from her face. Lillian was the anchor in the midst of the storm.

Radio talk show hosts emphasized the fault of leadership, and people hurried home from work to lock themselves behind their doors. Jack's voice was heard on the radio, reassuring the angry public that everything possible was being done. He put all policemen on alert, drove to hastily arranged ward meetings, and met with crime watch groups. He implored people not to panic, that the police would find the perpetrator.

What failed to come out in the news report until days later was that the hairdresser was a heroin addict. Oh, boy, I wondered which was worse—the fear of random home invasions, or realizing that one among us, a supposedly innocent hairdresser, had fallen victim to hard drugs. It seemed everything about Brockton lately had become a sad mystery.

Jack verbally slammed the District Attorney's office and the police for keeping quiet about the drug connection. He'd had to deal with a completely terrorized population, when a full disclosure of the nature of the crime might have kept the citizens' fears more contained.

Not that anyone felt better about the woman's death. But you could almost hear the giant sigh of relief from the public, "Oh, thank God, she was a heroin dealer." Drug-related crimes were somewhat easier to come to terms with in a city. The disheartening thing was that Brockton wasn't like that when we first moved in.

Barely a week went by before a church-going, independent woman, wearing a tweed overcoat had her purse ripped from her shoulder in the Shaw's supermarket parking lot, was pulled to the pavement, dragged across the dirty tar and suffered a heart attack. She later died as a result. The citizens mourned collectively as another cruelty to humans ravaged the city.

Jack and I hurried from a high school football banquet in time for the citizens' rally for the elderly victim, being held in the same parking lot where she was attacked. I was wobbly on high heels when we met up with Mary Waldron, Jack's Chief of Staff. She's short, like Jack, which positions the two of them eye-to-eye. They talked as I stared out at the gathering crowd. Even if the sun was shining, it was a cold afternoon. Although the crowd was respectful there were many angry, disappointed people wondering what role government played if the majority of the general public didn't feel safe. Jack took to a makeshift wooden stage and spoke briefly. Mary and I stayed planted on the asphalt. Her red hair flared a bit from static, my blonde hair likewise. The boards creaked underneath Jack's feet as he apologized, saying he was sorry that he hadn't been able to prevent the crime and subsequent death. He felt the weight of responsibility. I reminded him afterwards that he'd been mayor for less than two months. But this was on his watch; it was his city now.

Again, he reassured the public that the police were working on the case, and that the officials would prevail. Most of the onlookers shook their heads and stuck their gloved hands into coat pockets. Mary rubbed the back of the slain woman's relative. These folks had heard it all before—politicians with empty promises. No one cared about Brockton anymore, they whispered. Like hundreds of other old manufacturing cities, when the industries fall away, the populations are left straddling some tough waves. Look at Lowell, Massachusetts, for instance, which once thrived as a textile center, or Scranton, Pennsylvania, a once booming coalmining town. Brockton's industry was shoes—specifically, fine men's shoes. It was why the city was once called the

"Shoe Capital of the World." But that was a long time ago and now, as Jack began his first term as mayor, the bare shells of hundreds of abandoned shoe factories reminded us of what the city once was.

The day after the rally, the culprit who caused the death of the grandmother was caught. "Thank you, God. There is hope. Jack can make a difference," I thought. From then on, Jack made sure that a security guard in a car with flashing lights had a presence at every large supermarket and department store in the city. It was the first step—a tiny beginning to the turnaround that Brockton had long awaited.

Still the feeling persisted citywide that if murders were now taking place at the supermarket, what about our schools? Our neighborhoods? Would common citizens still be able to enjoy a pizza at the Cape Cod Café, a/k/a the "Cod," or ziti at the Italian Kitchen? Or would more crime and fear facilitate more departures? Already we were seeing families picking up and moving out to the suburbs.

On a personal front, I wondered what our family was in for. Our four kids ranged in age from six to fourteen. Should we be exposing them to this gritty life? I knew Jack had amazing energy and incomparable sincerity. I believed that he would do what he set out to do. But I kind of envisioned our lives carrying us in a direction where maybe we might one day enjoy a summer home at the Cape. That dream seemed to be fading. Selfishly I wondered why it had to be our family that led the charge to save the city. I was, after all, in addition to being a mother and bookkeeper and now First Lady, trying also to be a creative musician. Jack's world and mine seemed to be on a collision course.

"Growing up as the mayor's son brought with it certain responsibilities. It was my duty as a student to lobby dad for more snow days and longer summer vacations. Unfortunately, dad wasn't taken by special interests. He always made decisions with the long term in mind. In the long term, Brockton became a much better place to live and I got an education. Thanks dad."

—John Breckinridge "Breck" Yunits

CHAPTER 2

*"Champions aren't made in the gyms.
Champions are made from something they have
deep inside them—a desire, a dream, a vision."*
—Muhammad Ali

Jack and I purchased our first home, as a married couple, in the city of Boston, specifically Dorchester. Moving day happened to coincide with our second child's due date. I dragged my awkward body down the stairs the next morning to tell Jack that I was in labor. "Honey," I said, moving some bubble-wrap off of a wooden kitchen chair so I could sit down, "I'm having contractions and I think they're pretty serious."

He was bustling around the red and orange kitchen, putting things away. "Just one more box," he said, matter-of-factly, hurrying into the tiny pantry to stack plates.

"But the pains are getting intense," I pleaded, rubbing my belly.

Jack had been hanging pictures and putting dishes into cupboards since we arrived. He never has much patience, always wanting things done yesterday. "John," I said, using his formal name.

"One more box," he repeated, crushing the one in his hands and adding it to a growing pile on the back stoop. A few hours, and several bumpy roads later, our daughter, Casey, burst into the world, making her one-year-old brother, Conor, a "big boy." I returned home from the hospital to be greeted by several well-wishers anxious to see both the new house and newborn baby. Our festive celebration landed me with a hangover the next day. But that's the way our lives were. We had close friends, promising times, and carefree energy. Jack worked as a fledgling attorney in the city of Brockton, about thirty miles away, and I sometimes earned money entertaining by singing with my guitar. The day after I came home from the hospital, Jack drove off to work in our white station wagon. Paternity leave, of any sort, happened to be a foreign phrase to him.

My new life meant that I could stay home during the day, while giving guitar lessons and teaching my kids how to talk.

"Where does daddy work, Conor?" I asked, balancing him on the couch to look out the window as Jack drove away.

"Court!" he squeaked, the word making his little body stand-up straight.

"Who does he see there?" I questioned

"The judge!" he said, baby teeth clenching.

The homes on our street were owner-occupied and we lived in a friendly ethnically diverse neighborhood. Our street seemed peaceful. Until one night when unbeknownst to Jack and me, a group of troublemakers followed our car home from a Boston Pops Christmas concert.

Jack pulled the car in front of our house and left it running while he ran up the short staircase to get the sitters. I'd agreed to drive them home. Jack had been in court all day and was unusually exhausted. I slid from the passengers to the driver's side and buckled myself in. When I readjusted the rearview mirror, four men appeared there, walking towards the car. Instinctively, I locked the driver's side door. But I failed to lock the passenger's side and in a blink one of the men was sitting next to me. He grabbed a hunk of my long hair and tried to pull me out of the car, but the seatbelt wouldn't let him. I recalled that in times of trouble you should make noise, so I laid on the horn and shrieked, "Johhhhhhhnnnn! Johhhhhhhnnnn!"

"Get the bitch off the horn!" the new passenger yelled, over and over. We struggled in a tangle of bodies and hands. The ripping of my hair made my eyes water.

"Merry fucking Christmas!" I hissed, thinking he'd come to his senses and stop the madness. But I knew, with a stab of fear, that these were not regular people. The creep next to me kept yelling. At the same time, he was panicking because the honking was sure to wake the sleeping neighbors.

The driver's side door suddenly opened. That intruder punched me in the face. I saw stars. I saw red. I kicked out at him with my high-heeled boots. He struck me again. This can't be happening. My purple dress tangled around my legs. Through my bangs I saw him pulling a knife out of his boot. Shit. Finally the seatbelt retracted.

"Take the fucking car," I cursed in his face when I stood up. You win, asshole.

What I didn't know until I came around the back of the vehicle, was that Jack was lying on his back on the sidewalk wrestling with one of the others, struggling to keep a knife away from his face. Every time Jack tried to shove the guy off, someone kicked him in the head or stomach.

"Get inside, Lees! Get inside!" he yelled. Like I had any intention of leaving him alone. Just then our next-door neighbor, José, appeared at the top of his steps, brandishing a large Spanish sword and his Doberman Pinscher, which took off like a bullet. The four dirt bags ran away down the street, hopped into a vehicle and sped off. We figured Jack had inflicted some damage—afterwards we found a clump of hair lying on the ground. In sad disbelief, I also picked up a Red Sox hat.

"José, thank you," Jack huffed, bending over and placing his hands on his knees, getting his breath back. José slid the decorative sword back into its sleeve. He called to his dog as the babysitter's parents arrived to pick the girls up. Twenty minutes later, a police car pulled near the curb. An officer took a few notes, collected the retrieved objects and departed. Afterwards in the house, Jack touched a warm spot on the back of his thigh and discovered a knife wound. His only pair of suit pants ruined. That's how tight our budget was. I was almost more distraught about the pants. José stayed with Conor and Casey, while Jack and I drove over to the Carney Hospital. A nurse x-rayed my head and a doctor attended to Jack's wounded leg.

As word got around to our friends and neighbors the next day, dozens arrived with presents, casseroles, Christmas decorations—the generosity was unbelievable. It felt reassuring to remember that most people are kind.

Eventually, Jack and I identified two of the men through photographs and a ring of "holiday" thieves was busted. The group had been terrorizing shoppers, mostly, stealing bags of gifts and pocketbooks. Court proceedings followed and two of the men who attacked us were found guilty and sent to jail. As harrowing as the process was, Jack's testimony on the stand impressed me—he was unbelievably fair toward the perpetrators. Someday, I thought, he might make a good judge.

As for me, I was a nervous wreck. Shortly after the trial, one of the accused called our house. I picked up the red receiver located in the tiny pantry and listened as a convicted criminal proclaimed his innocence. I hung up immediately and wondered how the authorities could let him do that. That voice in my ear fueled my constant paranoia. Every noise outside made me run to the window. I told Jack I wanted to move. I couldn't live there anymore.

A month or so went by while he and I weighed the pros and cons of leaving Boston versus staying. Then one evening I heard a metallic noise and glanced out the window in time to see two slugs jimmying the doors to our car. They were getting in before my brain registered what was going on.

"Jack! Someone's stealing our car!" I hollered, pushing away from the window. Here we go again. He ran to the door and halfway through it the thieves heard him coming. The two of them bolted from the front seat and took off running in the pitch dark. Jack was gone so long chasing them that I started to assume the worst. After that incident there was no convincing me to stay. We put our house on the market and began looking at homes on the South Shore, ruling out several suburbs, mostly because we couldn't afford the homes that realtors showed us. We took a look at Brockton, where Jack worked and offered to buy an affordable stucco house on a quiet, tree-lined street. The West Side neighborhood, we were told, was "still a good one." Some of our friends and family were surprised we chose Brockton because there was concern about the city's future. Social issues and economic instability seemed to be hovering like tiny red flags around the perimeters. But I was ecstatic at the thought of being closer to Jack's law practice and salivated at the chance of using the car once in a while.

We made the move. Our first morning, June 1, 1983, dawned bright and sunny. "Who's making the coffee?" I asked Jack, rolling over on the floor-level mattress. We hadn't had time to put together the frame, or figure out where the coffeemaker was. Moving twice in fourteen months while parenting two toddlers had been a mental and physical challenge. Moments later, I had another question: "What day is this?" Jack answered and I counted on my fingers. "What are we going to name him?" I joked. Blessed be, new house, new baby—our son, John Breckinridge, or "Breckie," was born nine months later—a good luck omen, I felt, and an indication that our move had been a fortuitous one.

Yet my newly acquired fears, coupled with the knowledge that crime happens fast, made me somewhat leery of our new surroundings. Brockton was a city of contrasts. Up and down Legion Parkway for example, in downtown Brockton where Jack's office was located, a guy was always pushing a shopping cart filled head-high with bulging plastic bags. There was a sense of rootlessness about him. Only a few business people—other than the attorneys Jack shared space with—could be seen around. Several buildings on the adjoining Main Street stood vacant. The city had seen better manufacturing days, when the now empty and dilapidated gigantic shoe factories once employed thousands of workers.

Yet, there was hope. A mile away from downtown, on West Elm Street, near our new house, the homes stood proud, the lawns groomed. My new friend, Geri Creedon, who was married to one of Jack's colleagues, lived in an attractive tudor home. Green and yellow overstuffed couches and Geri's collection of everything "duck" decorated the spacious, high-ceilinged rooms. She greeted visitors with the fragrance of potpourri simmering on the stove. Other than Geri, and some friends of Jack's from Boston College, I didn't know a soul in Brockton.

When our family moved in, though, I felt like we'd stepped into a community straight out of the movie "Pleasantville." Here was a town complete with bus transportation, a shopping mall, a movie theater, hospitals, churches, golf courses, a beautiful public park—where Jack often took long runs—and neighborhood after neighborhood of single-family homes. I was surprised to find that Brockton residents, even though there are about 100,000 of them, seemed to all know one another. Having grown up in the Air Force, my family moved every two years and I have since lost touch with every childhood friend from the fourteen different schools I attended. Here in Brockton, parents, and grandparents of people we began to meet lived nearby. High School football games on Saturday afternoons held bleachers full of alumni. Restaurant owners knew everyone by name. I relished the idea of my children planting roots and enjoying long-lasting friendships.

One memorable evening, Geri hosted a party at her house and our social circle expanded overnight. "Lees, this is Ann McCormick," Geri said, introducing me to a woman, who at my age, 29, loved music, too. Tall, brunette and gorgeous, Ann lived around the corner from me and could harmonize to anything. She and I started getting together with our kids for playgroups and spent time singing songs like "Peaceful Easy Feeling" by The Eagles, and "Twist and Shout" by the Beatles. Several other women in our neighborhood were more of the fifties generation—they liked Motown songs. "Here, talk to Suzanne O'Donnell," Geri said, pulling me over to a petite woman engaged in a lively conversation. "She knows everything about Brockton," Geri added, hurrying back to the kitchen to refresh the appetizers. The first thing I learned was that Suzanne took pride in remembering her school songs from St. Edward's Elementary and Cardinal Spellman High. Soon she was singing both out loud, her jaw quivering in the way, I assumed, her voice teacher must have taught her to activate some vibrato. Together with her humorous, taller husband, "O.D.," they also seemed to know just about every Irish song ever recorded. Soon I could strum them all.

Because of these new friends—who, among other fine attributes, also lived in some of the most elegant homes I'd ever been in—I was inspired to write many songs. One of them, "On Vacation For A Week," was a song we mastered as a group—with harmonies, kazoos and dance steps. Needless to say, we attracted others like us, and soon all of our parties—and there were many—involved singing and dancing. Our new circle of friends from Brockton offered more to my family than I could have ever imagined.

By the early 1990's, however, the atmosphere around town began drooping. Money for cities dried up at the state level, and every other day, the local newspaper, The Enterprise, ran screaming headlines about car thefts, drug busts or worse, homicides.

Wildly nervous for our children, a group of Brockton mothers, including several neighbors and myself, decided to investigate why crime was suddenly so rampant. Our first night about twenty women sat in a giant circle nibbling on cheese and crackers discussing the transformations happening in the city. We decided to call our loosely knit organization, "Mothers of Brockton," because, as mothers, we felt there had to be something we could do to protect our children. By our third gathering, however, word got around that we were married to the mob. MOB. The moniker became a loaded one—too much to bear. Then the one African-American woman in our group left. The press coverage was too much for most women. The group disbanded before we had a chance to make a difference. It was a discouraging time.

Jack's law partnership also began feeling the effects from the lagging real estate market. Customers didn't want to buy homes in Brockton. No wonder. The place was looking like a dump. Several hundred abandoned shoe factory buildings and tenements blighted the area, and the Westgate Shopping Mall was practically vacant. Soon thereafter, my friend Ann, the singer, and her family moved to Cape Cod. Another couple uprooted their three children and moved to the neighboring suburb of Bridgewater. Still others relocated to nearby Easton.

"Everyone's leaving!" I cried to Jack one afternoon, tossing G.I. Joe figurines into a wooden toy box. Sitting down on the lid to make it close I added, "Maybe you and I should think about moving, too." I had been fairly vocal about wanting a bigger house, anyway, since our fourth child, Mairi, came along. Jack finally agreed to go house hunting, but insisted he didn't want to leave Brockton. Haunted by our trauma in Boston, he adamantly refused to be chased from his home again.

"Then find me something with a view and I'll stay," I smugly suggested, not really believing there was a vista appealing enough to alleviate my concerns.

On the way up Torrey Street, however, on the far west side, we passed the pristine Thorny Lea Golf Course and Jack guided our car onto Fairview Avenue, into another of Brockton's beautiful neighborhoods.

Our blue Dodge Caravan peaked over the crest of the hilly street as half a dozen Canadian geese landed on the surface of a glimmering pond.

"Now that's a view," I said. We slowed down to take a look and there, directly across the street, stood a gorgeous house with a "For Sale" sign posted on its lawn. My neck broke out into goose bumps. The large white house looked like a castle. There was a rounded turret and a slate roof. We stared, not quite believing we had managed to find it: a unique house with a view. We couldn't get home fast enough to call the realtor. We made arrangements to see the house that afternoon.

The young owner, with perfectly polished white hair, pushed open the wooden front door and the arch of the rounded entrance caught my eye. The rest of the house took my breath away.

"Now, the foyer is quite large," the realtor began. I politely asked her not to say anything. There was an ambience to the house I wanted to feel. Two steps down to the living room—a dramatic gold-sheen fireplace beckoned at the far end. Near that, a sunroom held a bay of windows and a colorful slate floor. Already I was thinking "music room." Up two steps a dining room connected to a pantry via a swinging door. An oval bathroom nestled under one of the staircases. "This place is unbelievable," I said to Jack, running my hand along the wrought iron banister.

The house seemed a monument to wealth from a different era. Indeed, the home originally was owned by a Mr. Drake, whose success stemmed from patenting the process for mass-producing rubber soles. The only negative to the house was that sometimes there was water in the basement. Jack and I didn't see that as a major problem. But for that reason, and the fact that Brockton had become less desirable than surrounding towns, Jack and I were able to buy the 13-room, five-bedroom home for a steal. For us at the time, though, the mortgage was still a stretch. Before the closing I worried a lot. The thought of taking on a bigger mortgage, let alone vacuuming the place, kept me up at night. Not to mention wondering whether we'd be the last ones standing while everyone else left Brockton.

Soon after we moved in, however, some friends purchased the stately colonial house next door. Their extended family owns the burgeoning Magnetic Resonance Imaging Centers (or MRI centers) all over Massachusetts, and could really afford to live anywhere. That they bought a house in Brockton instead gave me a welcome boost of confidence about our own decision.

Over the next couple of years our kids and theirs skated together on Goddard's pond—named for the founder of the local Goddard Hospital, Dr. Henry Edward Goddard. We shared many dinners and social events. I began to think Brockton was going to survive after all, that the city could still attract interesting, educated people. Then rumors began circulating that our neighbors were thinking of moving again, this time to Duxbury, an affluent town by the Atlantic Ocean. My heart sank.

"Jack, what are we going to do now?" I asked. I couldn't bear the thought of our friends leaving, or our kids losing their next-door pals. Not only that, but our own Enterprise newspaper seemed to be constantly degrading everything about Brockton, as if the city had become the Massachusetts scapegoat for all things deplorable. Newscasters on the radio referred to Brockton as the place where you had to dodge bullets.

The sad thing is that they were right sometimes. And if it wasn't bullets, it was car robberies. Like ours. Again. One morning Jack was downstairs preparing to go running and found that our van was not in the driveway. The cops eventually located the Dodge Caravan by St. Casimir's School. It had been torched—when Jack went to ID it, the license plates still hung on to a skeleton of the old van.

For all of Jack's involvement as president of the Brockton Boys and Girls Club it didn't seem to be paying off in terms of righting the wrongs of Brockton. His membership with a group of businessmen—known as the 21st Century Corporation—didn't seem to be helping either. The group originated to help bring more business in to the city. But the disagreements between members were palpable. The current mayor appeared to be the problem. He had no plan for the city, yet didn't like anyone's new ideas.

In the spring, several dozen people gathered at a friend's home up the street from us after a funeral. The beer flowed and the city's Personnel Director, Maureen Cruise, and Jack started chatting. I was outside on the back steps listening through a screen door, my eyes fixed on five-year-old Mairi going back and forth on a swing. Between the creaking of the play set I heard words about the need for an intelligent person to challenge the ineffective mayor who was nearing the end of his term.

"Why don't you run, Jack?" Maureen suggested, taking a sip of beer from a frosty bottle. She had a great sense of humor. I laughed through the screen. Run for mayor? Hardly. Jack and I had our hands full raising four kids. Not to mention that I was in the middle of recording a children's Christmas album and needed his help.

Maureen's brother, Tim Cruise, a close friend who I'd sung with at parties several times, hoisted a cold Bud Light in Jack's direction. "Yeah, Jack, why not you?" he said, laughing a Fred Flintstone kind of laugh. I assumed the comments were made in jest. I mean, there was a bit of drinking going on. I turned from the screen in time to see Mairi swinging dangerously high. "Slow down, honey!" I called, waving my arms.

A cousin of theirs, Tom Kennedy, currently served Brockton as a State Representative and the family knew politics. They'd succeeded in getting Tom elected several times. Still, I couldn't make the leap to see Jack running for mayor. The talk between Jack and our friends that afternoon seemed so far-fetched I didn't give the discussion another thought.

Soon afterwards, Jack let me know that he had been mulling over the possibility of running for mayor for some time. "Since," he pointed out to me one night lying in bed, "we visited the battlefields at Fredericksburg during Thanksgiving."

"Really?" I asked, wondering why he hadn't said anything.

"Back then, our forefathers stepped up to the plate to do what they felt was the right thing. Their sacrifices make me feel I should be doing more for Brockton," Jack said, re-fluffing his feather pillow, and shoving it back under his head. But Jack had never run for any office before. I sidled up closer to him with the sheets tucked under my chin to ponder this very serious turn of events.

"Everybody loved Jack Yunits for his energy and commitment. However, in many ways he was a hard mayor to work for, because he accepted nothing as an impediment to the vision he wanted to accomplish for Brockton. Lack of money, staff, or institutional capacity, shortage of time, or even the absence of clear legal authority; each of these was simply a challenge to be overcome. But of course, overcoming these required extra commitment from many of us. But his own hard work, creativity and persuasion usually won out; very few obstacles withstood his determination. Amazingly, during his tenure one of the poorest communities in Massachusetts built three new schools, constructed a new wing for the downtown library, built a new senior center in downtown, converted a contaminated vacant "Brownfield" into the largest municipally owned solar energy complex in New England, constructed a 5000-seat baseball stadium with attached conference center, and attracted a minor league baseball team to the city. For each of these projects, most of the financing was provided by sources other than the Brockton taxpayer. Private donations and state and federal financing carried the burden. When these projects were finished, Jack always deflected praise and credit to others. There were reasons he won five terms and served more years than any other mayor in Brockton's history."

—*John A. (Jay) Condon, CFO City of Brockton*

CHAPTER 3

"I have accepted fear as part of life—specifically the fear of change . . . I have gone ahead despite the pounding in the heart that says turn back."
—Erica Jong

"Jack, how can we afford for you to run for mayor?" I asked the next night, standing at the sink rinsing a plate to be put in the dishwasher. He took the wet dish from me and placed it in the bottom section. I began rinsing another. "You know I've been counting on your support while I record my Christmas album. Your timing doesn't seem fair."

He was quiet, gripping the next slippery plate.

I continued, "You've been the one encouraging me to keep going with my music."

"I think you should."

"Yeah, but like when? Without your help I'll never get this album done," I said. I'd been writing new songs and visiting a local recording studio for some time, in between kids' sports and work at the law office. I still had several months to go.

"Oh, by the way," he added, somewhat casually, advancing so that he was directly behind me. I felt a light kiss on the back of my neck. The sensation made me tingle. "The mayor's salary, if I do run and win, will mean a forty thousand dollar pay cut."

"What?" I asked, whipping around. He squeezed me with a chuckle. He loves to tease. "Ja-ack!" I said. "Seriously! How can we live on that?" His law practice seemed to be righting itself, but we were still two months behind in our bills because of the Catholic school tuitions we were paying. Besides, I wasn't supposed to be sacrificing; I was supposed to be decorating a Cape house, and writing beautiful music. This news was discouraging.

But his passion was so convincing and his desire to clean up Brockton so strong that in comparison, my music project seemed trivial. Even so, I told him I was going to complete what I'd started, and then, I'd devote what free time I had to his efforts.

Within a short while a "meeting of the minds" was held in our living room with friends and colleagues to discuss the pros and cons of running for mayor. About a dozen people sat on antique chairs in a wide circle with the cool spring air blowing in through the tall windows. After settling in with Diet Cokes and beers, my friend Geri's husband, Rob, who makes a living as a lawyer, but whose true calling is Irish joke teller, thought the current mayor was "doing okay and might be unbeatable." I passed Doritos to one of our new neighbors, Greg Buckley, a former City Councilor and now part-time guitar player, who feared that politics might ruin Jack's good nature. Others agreed with him, including one City Councilor, James Harrington, who'd lost an election once and knew the downside of politics. Another neighbor, an attorney and graduate of Georgetown University, Rick Savignano, seemed optimistic, as did my longtime friend, Geri. Gutsy Geri. After the Mothers Of Brockton fiasco, she had run for City Council. She was now President of the political body. Geri's bright smile convinced me she thought Jack should run.

So did State Representative Tom Kennedy who once studied to be a priest. "If you've got the fire in your belly, Jack, go for it," he advised. Years before, Tom had an unfortunate fall from a window. He had served Brockton admirably for a number of years, even while being confined to a wheelchair. His cousin, our friend Tim, with the Flintstone laugh, unfolded Tom's clenched fingers in order for his hand to hold a Bud Light. I contemplated what Tom just said. I knew Jack had the fire in his belly.

My fear was what the press might do and I voiced this to the crowd. I didn't like to imagine negative stories in the newspaper about my husband. Remembering how the press slaughtered our mother's group made me shudder. I was also uneasy because the man who inspired us to hold the session that night never showed up and our next-door neighbor, Jack Shields, who offered to help raise money, arrived quite late. I questioned whether people would actually assist us in organizing a major campaign. Everyone seemed to want change in the city, but who would work for it? Everyone's lives were busy. Our cheerful friend, George Baldwin, who owned a real estate development company, felt Jack had a good chance. He offered to support the fundraising aspects and signaled his enthusiasm with two thumbs up.

The group agreed to hire professionals to conduct and analyze a phone poll to gauge voter attitudes. If the results showed that the current mayor was "vulnerable," then Jack would probably run.

On the way out the door, the Irish joke teller, Rob Creedon, said, "Just think, Jack. The worst thing that can happen is you could win!" Ooh.

When we presented our position to the kids, they had opinions early on. "Go for it!" Conor insisted. By now he was 14, already had a love of history and, being the oldest, had a good sense of responsibility. Casey, just 13, didn't think we had the money, and she was right, but offered to help with decorations and designs. We could count on her support. Breck was the one we had to convince. "Dad doesn't have the time," our eleven-year-old pointed out, preferring that his father attend his soccer games when he wasn't working at the law firm, or running for mayor. Five-year old Mairi withheld her backing too, but couldn't give a reason.

Soon Jack's work phone started ringing off the hook. Friends he went to Boston College High School with were encouraging him. His boyhood pals from Holbrook loved the idea. One owner of The Enterprise said it would be fantastic if Jack ran. I thought, "Wow! The paper supports him, too!" But I was wrong. They just wanted to sell papers and some new upstart running against the incumbent mayor would help do that.

One afternoon, still feeling unsure about the decision and what it would mean to our family, I invited my neighbor, Kathy Shields, over to discuss my options. We sat on the couch that once belonged to my grandmother. Sinking into the fluffy down cushions I offered Kathy a cold drink. She declined, but reached instead for the grapes that I had also set out. She told me that when her husband, Jack, ran for Congress a year or two earlier, she felt that if she had refrained from supporting his aspirations, he might have always held a bit of resentment towards her. I took her words to heart. I certainly didn't want to clamp down Jack's dream.

Over the next few weeks, Casey lined up friends to hold signs and Conor offered to go door-to-door with his dad. Breck told Jack he should do it after all, if that's what he wanted. Mairi dreamt she was in a house and no one could find her and she fell through a crack and lost one of her legs. Yikes. What cosmic sign was that?

The turning point for me was the realization that I loved having intelligent people in my home discussing important issues. The sense of patriotic duty, I guess you'd say, was in my blood. Both my grandfathers had been Army officers, and my great-great grandfather, John C. Breckinridge, was Vice President of the United States under President James Buchanan. In addition, my fifth great grandfather, the Reverend John Witherspoon, former president of Princeton University, signed the Declaration of Independence! Call me rich in lineage, poor in family wealth. So much for public service!

As Jack tested the waters, the days blended into one another. Our evenings turned into late night events—night after night after night. Jack was determined that if he was going to run, he was going to win. That meant thousands and thousands of people had to know who he was and what he stood for.

A typical day even before he was officially running, unfolded like this: After getting the kids off to school, in itself a Herculean effort, I'd throw in a load of laundry, race over to the recording studio, tape a few Christmas songs, return home, do some business for Jack's law office, and transfer the wet clothes to the dryer. I'd then get the kids from school, drive to soccer practice or play rehearsals, get dinner ready, supervise homework, and run another load of laundry. Then I'd slide a dress over my head and go with Jack to places like the Polish White Eagles Club, Christo's II, the Fuller Museum, or the Club National—sometimes all four establishments in the same night. There were more places to gather in, in Brockton than I ever knew existed.

Quickly I was so out of touch with the real me working myself into such frenzy that I started bumming cigarettes and drinking Black Russians. I had to do something while Jack "worked the room." He did more than shake hands. He immersed himself in people's opinions and ideas—getting to the bottom of what was ailing Brockton and conjuring his plans to fix it. I joined him like a wayward butterfly, mingling, alighting where I could and creating my own conversations. This was mostly fun, and stimulating, but after a while I found that remembering names and inventing small talk exhausted me.

I came home from work one day, thinking we'd be having a quiet family dinner to celebrate my 41st birthday, only to find dozens of children and about twenty adults crowding our backyard. Jack was happy as a clam standing at the outdoor grill cooking pounds of chicken, swordfish and steak tips. He and Casey were throwing me a surprise party. Sadly, I felt ugh. The throng of people wishing me happiness was overwhelming, immobilizing. The last thing I wanted was another social event.

"Is this what you expect?" I asked afterwards, bringing paper plates loaded with half-eaten birthday cake into the kitchen. "I'm frazzled enough without you adding more to my day. I need quiet time with my family if this is going to work," I added, running my hands under cold water. "What if I'm not the person you want me to be, Jack? What if I can't do this?"

"What if I'm not the person you want me to be?" He threw the question back at me while filling a tall plastic cup with ice cubes. I tried to figure out what he meant by that because I pretty much loved everything about him. Despite the fact that he liked to spend several hours on the golf course once in a while, he cooked, he cleaned, he was romantic. What was there to not like?

Still, keeping up with Jack's pace was challenging. "I will cherish every minute of private time with my family. From now on, please don't add anything else!" I said as we dragged our weary bodies up to bed.

The next evening, our neighbors, Frank and Ginny Middleton, who live across the street, dropped by. The two are lifelong Brocktonians—Frank owned a real estate company and Ginny, a former nurse, was his top-selling broker. I invited them out to the screened-in porch. Frank took a Rum and Diet Coke. Ginny and I clinked our wine glasses together. Jack sipped his vodka with amaretto and together the four of us hashed through the pros and cons of Brockton politics. Frank and Ginny had been around Brockton long enough to know how messy the political dealings could get. They expressed their opinions about the small-mindedness of some citizens, as well as the backstabbing that goes on. After all, being the mayor of Brockton isn't a ceremonial position like some of our nation's mayors. If Jack were to win, he'd be responsible for all union contract negotiations. He'd be President of the School Committee, accountable for the multi-million dollar budget, head of the public transportation system, graveyards, planning and procurement—a daunting task.

Jack took their words to heart, but nothing they said could deter him from his goal. At the end of the night, Frank and Ginny were assured that Jack knew what he was getting into. "All right then!" Frank said, exiting through the screen door. "We'll do whatever you want us to. Just remember you were warned," he laughed.

"Don't listen to him," Ginny piped up, pushing him through the door. "We love you two. We're just worried."

Our other good friends, Suzanne and "O.D." O'Donnell, the singers, had been reminding us all along that they, too, would always be our friends, no matter the outcome. What a blessing.

A few nights later I walked down the long upstairs hall to Conor's bedroom and found him reading a book. He was sitting in his green leather chair, his feet propped on top of the window seat. I kissed the top of his head, breathing in the fragrance of Herbal Essence shampoo, and told him I loved him. Breck was sound asleep in his room. But I kissed him anyway and rubbed his soft cheek. In a glass aquarium, his lizards, Freckles and J.T., were still, their lids partially shut. Mairi had brushed her teeth without being told and tasted like peppermint when I gave her a smooch. She wanted to sleep in Casey's bed, but Casey was moody because she found her cordless phone in the cellar window-well outside and didn't know who put it there. She softened though, as usual, and let Mairi crawl in. I straightened the quilt around them, kissed them both and told them I loved them.

After gently closing the door to our bedroom, I sat next to Jack on our king-size bed. We didn't know what was in store, but he told me that deep down inside he felt that if he were to turn back, to not run for mayor, he'd always think of himself as a quitter. I told him I loved him and was proud of him. The hair on my arms started to tingle. This was going to be an adventure. Not only was Jack talking about leading a city, but to get there he had to first survive what was considered by several of our supporters to be a David and Goliath confrontation. At 5'6", Jack was half the size of the incumbent mayor, a former police officer. Plus, he had no experience either running for, or serving in office. Still, Jack and I felt confident that he couldn't pass up the opportunity to help a population desperate for good leadership.

That night, he dreamt he was brushing his teeth and they all fell out. He put them on the front seat of his car to drive to the dentist and picked up a hitchhiker who sat on them, breaking the teeth into tiny pieces.

I dreamt Jack's hair turned completely white in one day.

"Brockton is famous for its fighters and having watched Jack in action for years, there's no question he deserves mention with hometown heroes Rocky Marciano and Marvelous Marvin Hagler. He may have done his fighting in the political arena but Jack had the same toughness, skill and no surrender attitude that made Marciano and Hagler champions. Each and every day, he fought for the people of Brockton and would go toe-to-toe with anyone, me included, if he felt his community was being slighted in any way."

—U.S. Senator John Kerry

CHAPTER 4

*"We have enough people who tell it like it is—
Now we could use a few who tell it like it
can be."*

—Robert Orben

Within a week, Jack composed an outline of his vision for Brockton, which he called the "21-Point Plan." I set up an old typewriter in a room upstairs that was once a butler's room. Two small windows under the angled eaves make the room a bit snug. Maybe that's why there's no butler living there anymore. I have been waiting for him to return. But there's a built-in table and that's where I put the electric typewriter. Jack took our two youngest for an outing to Boston's new Computer Museum. I scooted a chair up to the table. The "21-points" included solving Brockton's age-old lack of water problem, investing in Brockton's children and uniting the Brockton community. The outline was prefaced by these words:

"In reshaping the future of Brockton, two priorities rise like mountains above the others: business and education. Everything else that we must confront finds its solution in those two areas, and in many ways the success of one depends on the other. Business leads to economic stability, and education leads to community stability."

Our campaign committee, which now had a professional manager, Chris Micklos, a witty graduate student from Emerson College, chose the slogan "Jack Yunits—Leading Brockton into the 21st Century." Jack dreamt that his campaign colors were red, white and black, so we ordered bumper stickers and lawn signs in those colors. The colors also happened to be the same ones that Brockton High School uses.

Jack's official announcement took place at the Brockton Boys and Girls Club on June 13, 1995, while a thunderstorm raged outside. Hundreds of enthusiastic supporters packed a large upstairs room where TV cameras and photographers were positioned. The smell of wet clothing hung in the air as people who'd been caught in the downpour scrunched together.

"Time will not wait for us," Jack said. "The 21st Century looms before the Brockton Community, and we must choose a path now. We can continue to look at our problems and ask 'Why?' Or we can embrace our tremendous potential and ask 'Why not?'"

The quick applause startled me so much I grabbed Casey's arm to keep from slipping on the damp floor. The raw exuberance magnified how hungry the area was for leadership.

Jack continued, his voice confident, serious, sincere. "Our future is just around the corner, and we have to begin to plan for that future. And that plan must revolve around the redevelopment of business, education, and the greater Brockton Community. Everything we hope for grows out of those objectives… and we can begin to realize those objectives through this 21-point plan."

A loud clap of thunder reverberated through the hall. Several people looked up, including Jack—he cracked some joke about the heavens, and proceeded:

"We cannot accept mediocrity. We cannot allow complacency and contentment to dominate us. And we cannot convince ourselves that our future is not worth the effort. I believe that it is worth the effort. Let's dream things that never were and say why not? Let's lead Brockton into the 21st Century!"

The crowd responded wildly and a sharp whistle from Mary Waldron pierced our ears. She does that without even using her fingers. The enthusiasm mixed with the cleansing rain outside suddenly felt like a new day for old Brockton.

Within two days, Jack's campaign committee rented space for its headquarters on Belmont Street across from our favorite Chinese restaurant, Chang Feng. The aroma from the fried rice and chicken fingers helped override the mildewed basement offices, which needed to be stocked with everything in order to be functional.

One afternoon while Jack was at his law office (he was working full-time while running for office full-time), a local college student volunteer and I drove to the home of William Gildea, a former city official. He lived in a magnificent home on Prospect Street, and had previously offered us everything he had in his garage—a collection of used desks, tables and chairs—to use for our headquarters, which we loaded into the pickup. Conor and Casey were putting up No Smoking signs and setting up computers—word processors, really. Once we filled the headquarters with furniture I scrubbed the toilets and drove to the store to buy coffee supplies. Several people said they'd help, but no one showed up. I had a nagging feeling that, other than the kids and me, there was no "team" to count on. Our close friends, while supportive of Jack's intentions and generous with their financial contributions, had gone off to their summer homes and weren't involved in the day-to-day campaign work.

"If it wasn't for me, you'd have no furniture, coffee or toilet paper!" I chided Jack when he arrived. "I'm a one-woman political machine!"

He laughed and picked up the newspaper from his campaign desk to read our horoscopes out loud. Mine—Gemini—was about needing preparation to climb a mountain. His—Aquarius—said, "Reach your goals, but maintain your sense of humor." Ha ha.

Thankfully, Kathy Shields and Tricia Cruise, both from our neighborhood, helped Casey and I prepare the headquarters for the grand opening party. We sweated in hundred-degree weather putting up volunteer lists and calendars. Casey worked non-stop, even though her dance recital was the following night and she had many other details to attend to. She's a lot like Jack—always thinking of others and trying to make their lives easier.

The party was a success—drawing a hundred or more citizens, several City Councilors and a terrific performance by our guitar-playing neighbor, Greg Buckley. As soon as the kickoff party was behind us, Jack had more energy than he knew what to do with. He barbecued on the grill, cleaned the house, made numerous fundraising phone calls and began door-to-door campaigning. To keep up with him, I drank more water and less alcohol—mostly—and adhered to a more disciplined yoga schedule.

One of the best escapes from the hectic pace was giving Mairi a bath. She liked to bathe in our old-fashioned tub playing a game where she pinched her nose and plunged facedown underwater to see how long she could hold her breath. Her dark hair would float on the surface, her little bum poking up through the water as I counted in the stillness, "One . . . two . . . three . . . four . . . five . . . six . . . seven . . . " Finally, she'd sputter up for air. "How many, Mom?" It was a game she could play forever, always trying to top her score.

Another escape, a bit trickier, was sneaking away once in a while for some "afternoon delight" with Jack. Things didn't always go as expected. One hot summer day, the kids were occupied downstairs, Casey was at the Cape, and Jack and I slipped upstairs. After a furtive session, we found that the skeleton key we used to lock out the kids was stuck in the keyhole. We couldn't get out of the bedroom. Our house has different skeleton keys for each of the thirty doors and I used the wrong one. We tried everything to jiggle it free. By now Mairi had caught whiff of our absence, though, and was banging on the door yelling, "Let me in! Let me in!"

"We will, sweetie, just as soon as we fix the broken door," I answered, my mouth pressed to the slit between the door and wall.

Jack yelled to Breck to find a flashlight. Breck clumped upstairs and aimed the beam through the keyhole so we could see how to dislodge the key. Several tries later, though, he got bored and left. "Breck! Come back!" I said. But he was off.

Mairi continued pounding, "Let me in!" Conor brought a ladder to our window, which didn't quite reach. Jack was on one knee, his hand working the key. After thirty minutes of getting nowhere I finally turned toward the phone and said, "Jack, maybe we should just call a locksmith."

"We can't do that!" he said, rather abruptly. "We're running for mayor. It would be bad publicity."

"Oh yeah, that's right," I said, grinning at the absurdity of the imagined headline: "Mayoral candidate trapped in bedroom with overzealous wife."

Finally, good-thinking Conor threw the flashlight up to us through the window and we were able to see the key from our side and waggle it loose. Jack pulled open the wooden door and Mairi ran into my arms. I carried her petite body downstairs wondering how little privacy our lives might soon afford us. My affection for the John F. Kennedy family increased tenfold.

"Line up the Brockton high school marching band tubas first. Mayor Yunits knew exactly what I was doing, why I was doing it and what it meant. A mayor who gets it. What a concept."

—*Bill Murray, actor*

CHAPTER 5

*"Cherishing children is the mark of a
civilized society."*

—Joan Ganz Cooney

Jack spent the entire summer meeting the citizenry by knocking on more than 6,000 doors. He wore out several pairs of his favorite shoes—wingtips —and dropped ten pounds. The kids and I held signs on street corners, often twice a day, during the hottest summer on record and eventually went on a two-week vacation to Cape Cod without Jack. He was far too committed to the campaign to risk taking time for a vacation, although he drove down for our final night—to help us pack up. Together the six of us returned to Brockton the night before the first mayoral debate.

Driving along the main road to Stonehill College in late August, I was amazed to see more than sixty men and women holding signs reading "Jack Yunits For Mayor." The campaign had picked up power in the two weeks we'd been away. Volunteers lined the roads and sidewalks, waving, as crowds of people entered the Martin Institute for the first public debate. The air was electrified with anticipation. Jack and I shook hands with streams of people as they cheered us into the building. It was a glorious moment—like we were heroes. There were rows and rows of folding chairs and I led the kids to a row near the front. Jack stepped behind the backdrop of the stage to prepare. My curiosity got the better of me, so I peeked through the dark curtain to witness him pacing. He was referring to his notes, his lips were moving, he was thinking, strategizing. The pressure on him to do well was staggering. Voters, volunteers and financial supporters had gotten a taste of hope for a better Brockton and this debate was everyone's first chance to see Jack in action. Everything he'd worked for this long hot summer was now on the line.

More than three hundred people were jammed into a room with no air conditioning. I was dressed up for the event, and though my hair was in a bun, the cotton, embroidered blouse I had on was sticking to me. A third candidate, an habitual one as it turned out, made people laugh (kind of at him), which broke the ice as Jack and the current mayor got down to discussing the serious issues. Jack was informed and sincere. The incumbent was a good sport, even jovial. The talk was intelligent and dramatic, in my opinion the best entertainment of the summer. Both men covered topics of major concern to voters, such as education, road conditions, and public safety. Jack received tremendous applause afterwards, although the next day, The Enterprise newspaper declared the incumbent the winner. I figured their opinion was similar to decisions sometimes made in the boxing world where a tie goes to the reigning champ—in this case, the incumbent mayor. Anyway, I felt tremendous pride that Jack had more than lived up to the crowd's expectations.

After the debate, he and I dropped a friend off at the Holiday Inn and stepped inside to glance at the newly redecorated dining room. What I saw was the mayor and more than a dozen of his supporters sitting down at a linen-covered table about to have an after-debate dinner. The group looked so qualified, so professional, that when Jack and I drove back to Owen O'Leary's Pub for a few cold beers I felt like the poor girl who'd just witnessed a feasting of the rich. How could we compete with this? Our volunteers were standing around the bar, yucking it up, excited by memories of the debate, horsing around. I feared we were lackeys, novices, not serious enough for politics. Jack, though, always made me see things in a positive light. He told me that the opposition had been termed "dull" by people he'd been talking with around town, while our side was "passionate." That helped me see things in a new perspective.

We were on a roll now. People started asking me how it felt to be the first lady. I said it felt like they were jumping the gun. But I had butterflies in my stomach thinking about the possibility. Every breathing moment was politics.

As a good example of how stretched our nerves were, one morning we were all asleep and our house alarm began screeching. Jack flew down the stairs so fast I thought someone was in the house.

"Call the police!" he yelled, loud enough to wake up the kids. I grabbed the receiver, but the phones were dead. I raced to the top of the stairs, bent over the wrought iron railing and listened for sounds of a confrontation—remembering his dad's sheathed sword lying under our bed. Jack eventually called up the stairs saying he found nothing. The disturbance turned out to be a simple wiring malfunction. But Jack's reaction indicated the pace and stress he was under as we barreled towards the primary.

Thankfully, I had the kids to focus on as school got underway. Mairi was so happy wearing a new dress for first grade that it was inconceivable how she could end up in the hospital by week's end. Lord help us. Three days before the primary election, when all our gears were on overload, poor Mairi appeared by the side of my bed in the wee hours, holding her stomach.

"What's the matter, puddin'?" I asked, allowing her to slide in next to me. She was writhing in pain. Alarmed, I woke up Jack. This could be serious because as an infant she survived a major tummy operation, a diaphragmatic hernia.

"We've got to call the doctor," he decided. I did, my hands shaking a bit dialing the number, and we were told to bring Mairi to the hospital immediately. When a nurse wheeled our precious Mairi away Jack and I barely spoke—hardly took a breath. He paced. I stared. Shortly, we learned from several surgeons that scar tissue was blocking her large intestine and another operation was necessary—right then. They disappeared down the corridor. In shock we held onto each other, picturing our little one so helpless, so vulnerable. Jack held his jaw in his hand as I rubbed his back, imagining the worst, praying for the best. An eternity later, the surgeon emerged from the operating room. As he walked toward us, we tried to read his expression. He was neither smiling nor grimacing. We balanced on our chair edges. We stood up and walked toward him. "I apologize for having to make a long incision around Mairi's bellybutton, but the operation was a lifesaver," he said, professionally. I felt giddy and did a little jump. Jack's eyes looked like he'd just won the lottery.

The following morning Mairi's room was inundated with flowers, balloons, cards, toys, Vermont Teddy Bears, and you name it. It was the wildest thing. The Boston Globe called, The Enterprise wanted to interview her. Local radio stations told of her plight. Beautiful notes offered to help in any way. Mairi received so many gifts we were embarrassed. There was even a teddy bear from the opposition! I was not supposed to like him.

Out in the political world the race was down to the wire. Jack visited the hospital in between knocking on doors and caring for our other kids. "There's not even a question about what's important here," he emphasized to me on one of his many stop-ins. Numerous visitors stopped by, including dozens of people who were employed at the hospital. I had no idea so many acquaintances worked there. Others, like inpatients, were simply curious; poking their heads in to see what all the excitement was about. The best thing was that the attention kept Mairi's mind off of food, which after the operation was the only thing she wanted but couldn't have.

"Foooood," she whimpered from her bed. She couldn't have anything until the nurses heard rumblings in her stomach. She begged me, saying she couldn't last another day. When anyone asked if they could get her something, she pleaded, "fooooooood." Her cries wrenched my heart. Being hungry made her so sad. We took a walk and she made a detour to the water fountain, like I wouldn't notice. She couldn't even have a sip. A friend brought me a tuna sandwich, which I ate behind a curtain because Mairi wouldn't let me leave the room. She kept asking for a taste until I dipped my finger in the tuna and put it in her mouth.

Conor, Casey and Breck, meanwhile, were getting little attention. Conor made the football team at B.C. High, but called me to say he didn't want to play anymore. Breck was upset because he heard on the radio that someone was stealing our lawn signs and throwing them in a truck. I suggested that the signs were probably being collected to hold at the polls on primary day. Casey continued cutting and pasting at headquarters, while fretting about her baby sister. She'd also been assuming a few of my roles—she's a better cook.

Primary day arrived and my friend, Ginny, came to stay at the hospital so I could vote with Jack. He and I drove to the polls, cast our votes and then met up with our kids. Together we walked in to thundering applause at Guido O'Shea's restaurant. Anticipating victory, our supporters were dizzy with joy. I blinked away tears thinking of how our family had pulled together to learn these new political ropes and how at the hour of Jack's imminent triumph little Mairi lay hungry in a hospital bed.

Once the celebration began to wind down, I slipped back to Mairi's room. The quiet was soothing. "Congratulations," Ginny whispered. Mairi was asleep, the plastic nose tube quivering slightly from her breath. "You should be very proud."

"Thank you, Ginny, I am," I said, straightening Mairi's blanket. "Sorry you missed a great party!"

"There'll be others," Ginny laughed. I walked her to the door as thoughts of the future raced through my brain. Jack mayor? Me first lady? Yikes. I called my mother to share the news and as a past President of the League of Women Voters in New Jersey she was thrilled. Later that night I walked Mairi into the bathroom rolling along her IV pole. Once she was settled on the commode, her little head cocked to one side. Her pigtails were sticking out and she looked so darn cute—even with a tube in her nose—that I could barely breathe for the swelling in my heart. In the sweetest voice she asked when she could eat again. Then she said for her first meal she wanted donuts, clam chowder, pasta, potato chips, macaroni and cheese, chicken tenders and noodle soup. The nurses removed the nasal tube the following morning, but her tummy remained quiet. "I can't last one more day," she moaned. "I'm going to faint this afternoon if I don't eat." She was six years old and had gone six days without a morsel of food or drink. Finally, the nurses heard some tiny bubble sounds and allowed her to begin ingesting simple foods, starting with ice cubes and lollipops. She had six.

The Enterprise wrote a story about her ordeal and we joked that the publicity probably helped put Jack over the top. When she was discharged, Jack took her by the hand and walked her down to the gift shop. Like she needed more toys. But the two of them looked absolutely adorable side by side in the hallway that I added that snapshot to my memory.

Back in the real world, there was frightful energy around the city as the incumbent pulled out what he had left. During the night, someone drove a car on the lawn by headquarters and smashed our big sign. Someone else tore up all the Yunits lawn signs in the neighborhood. Our wedding anniversary on October 8th was our worst ever. Jack and I didn't exchange presents or cards, and I was arguing with the kids while making supper. Tearfully I told Jack that this was the last time I'd ever spend our wedding anniversary cooking dinner, no matter what the circumstances. "I need to be romantically situated with you," I said, "in a candlelit restaurant and enjoying private adult conversation!" With the political tornado that had hit our lives, time for us was non-existent. "The only rule I have with regard to this political life is that one day a year be reserved for us," I concluded. As he slept, I felt guilty for my outburst. He was working two full-time jobs because he believed he could fix our broken city. I decided right then that my biggest contribution as his wife and support system would be to give him as much loving attention as possible, in order to smooth the hard edges of democracy.

CHAPTER 6

"What counts is not necessarily the size of the dog in the fight—it's the size of the fight in the dog."
—Dwight D. Eisenhower

With less than a week to go until Election Day, I had to remember to drink plenty of water to keep my stomach from knotting up. I was a nervous wreck.

Mairi told people that Jack was going to tear down the pond across the street and build a children's museum! The Enterprise wanted to take a picture of us doing what we usually do together as a family. Breck suggested we get takeout food and put it in nice dishes. Oh, what a sorry mother I was!

But I was proud to be part of Jack Yunits. He was going to be the next mayor, I was sure of it. He was in control and everyone wanted to be associated with him. The whole city was energized and the momentum was definitely swinging in our direction.

Election morning dawned cloudy, cold and threatening rain. Jack and I voted together at the Hancock School as Boston-based WBZ TV filmed the two of us walking into the building. The excitement was exhilarating, similar to how Christmas day feels—all the hard work was over and now it was time to reap the rewards. Jack and I drove to each of the twenty-eight voting places in Brockton, encouraging and thanking volunteers for their time. Jack's childhood buddies were helping out, including one friend, Mike Quinn, who stood through the sunroof of a car driving around the city yelling, "Vote for Jack Yunits!" Elderly friends who knew Jack's parents held signs in the chilling rain.

At noontime, Jack's running buddy, Mark O'Reilly, arrived at headquarters. He and Jack would do a six-mile run at D.W. Field Park. Before leaving, Jack told Tim Cruise, who had taken an active role in the campaign, to keep an eye on things.

"If I'm going to lose, I want to know about it," Jack said. Mark told me that was the one and only time he ever saw Jack voice doubts about his chances.

Later that evening I was driving to one of the polls with a volunteer. The Ford Explorer was in the middle of a busy intersection when my friend started to make a right-hand turn.

"No! Go left!" I yelled. She corrected the steering wheel in that direction and we heard the screeching of tires just before a vehicle slammed into us from behind, spinning the jeep around in a circle. The four young girls in the back seat, including my own, thrashed to the sides. Thankfully, the seatbelts kept them from catapulting forward. The car thudded to a halt, tossing everyone around again. When we stopped moving, the girls were teary-eyed but fortunately, unharmed. After a few tense moments, a police officer arrived. He began filling out a lengthy report.

"We don't have time for this!" I lamented through the open window. "We're running for mayor!" He kept writing.

Eventually we met up with Jack at a friend's house to await the results on TV. The tallies were slow coming in. Jack paced back and forth. Lasagna sat uneaten on the table. The TV commentators said some of the ballot boxes had disappeared. Campaign workers called from Guido O'Shea's telling us to "get down here, the place is packed, the crowd's waiting and everything is looking good!" We dashed into vehicles.

At the restaurant three of the precinct results came in quickly. "They're the defining ones," Tim told me. "If a city-wide candidate wins these three, they most likely win the city." Jack won all three. Then the counts stopped cold.

Sensing trouble, Tim said to Mark, "We're going to the high school!" As they drove, the rain was now a downpour. Jack's law partner, John McCluskey, had also joined the duo. At the high school, they saw the Police Chief standing near the voting machines.

"What is the chief of police doing here?" Tim hollered. "Something's going on! We want to see everything right now!" he said to the officials, stopping in place and putting his hands on his hips.

"Tim, now, calm down," the levelheaded Election Warden told him. Tim took a breath, paused, smiled, and cracked a joke to cover up his over-enthusiasm. "Something's wrong with the computers, that's all," the Warden said.

In due time all the votes were counted and Jack won in a landslide! He took every precinct, all twenty-eight—a feat unprecedented in city history.

The exuberant crowd at Guido's cheered one another as the music, toasts, and singing began. Casey and her dancing school friends swirled around the dance floor. I publicly thanked my new best friends—the sign-holders—and sang the Irish song "Wild Rover" with the band. Jack answered his cell phone a lot.

In the middle of the celebration, still floating behind the microphone I spotted the man who engineered the recording of my Christmas album coming through the entrance waving something in his hand. By the time he pushed through the boisterous mob, I realized he was holding the new cassette insert for my song titles. It was a perfectly timed sweet coincidence. Both Jack's and my projects of the past several months wrapped up on the same day. What a night to remember!

The next morning, Jack received calls from three Congressmen—Joe Moakley, Gerry Studds, and Joe Kennedy. U.S. Senator John Kerry phoned as well and Jack arranged several appointments to meet with them all in Washington, D.C. He knew that Brockton's financial future depended on the federal powers that be.

Mairi said the post-election day reminded her of her hospital time because an abundance of cards, flowers and fruit baskets arrived at the house. The phone rang non-stop. One call was for me. A voice asked, "Is this the first lady?" It was my cute friend, Suzanne.

"Yes, I guess it is," I said, doing a half-curtsy.

"Then this is the first friend!" she responded with glee. Suzanne's call made me smile.

An article in The Enterprise the following day read, "Yunits wins by the largest margin ever over a sitting mayor." In a picture, Jack was standing on the stage at Guido O'Shea's restaurant holding a microphone in one hand and giving a thumbs up with the other. I stood next to him with my hands in the pockets of my skirt wearing a goofy grin on my face. Above my head, on the wallpaper behind us, were two musical notes. Again, that feeling of synchronicity swept over me.

"The coffee is on," the article continued, "six-year-old Mairi is running around barefoot, fifteen-year-old Conor is flipping a football and in-laws are visiting from New Jersey. It is family life as usual . . . except that today Mairi is calling her father 'Mayor.'"

That afternoon, Jack and I gathered with several close friends, including Suzanne and "O.D.," Frank and Ginny, Tim, Mark, and Chris at Thorny Lea Golf Club for a victory brunch. Everyone was excited about Brockton's future. After several toasts, our Irish storyteller friend, Rob Creedon, admitted to me that the jingle I had written for the campaign really wasn't that good. Tim and I sang it together for the final time:

"This is the Nine-ties, we are U-ni-ted, we vote for Yu-nits, We get Ex-ci-ted! Hey!" Tim added the hey. Suzanne thought it was perfect.

The following day, Jack and I drove to the Cape to unwind for a few days at Frank and Ginny's summer home. Jack was up at six every morning and out the door driving to the beach, the stores, bringing home coffee and donuts. He read newspapers and made calls. I stayed cozy and managed to entice him back to bed once in a while.

During the night I had the strangest dreams. In one, my mother was lying on top of me and I had to push real hard to get her off. I did, but it was like my body had to press through a ghost or I'd die.

The anticipation of all Jack had to do was scaring me to death, judging by the dreams. Would I, as first lady, be able to give my own children the time and affection they needed? Before I had a chance to really think about this, all too quickly we were headed home.

Invitations covered the kitchen table for concerts, luncheons, inaugural events, dinners and every other imaginable thing. Suddenly I was the mayor's personal home secretary—without an added paycheck. Hmmm. The only good side to that was that handling them all helped me understand Jack's far-reaching involvement. And by RSVP'ing to everything I could redeem one of the past mayor's failings—that of not responding and rarely attending public events. Not to mention that all the events would necessitate buying outfits, lots of new outfits. And shoes. And hats for the parades. My new dress code meant our budget would take a beating, but somebody had to elevate the image around here.

There were also twenty-eight saved messages on the phone. Our lives had changed forever.

"While the City of Brockton that Jack Yunits governed as mayor was never in my congressional district, I did represent virtually all of the communities surrounding it, so we had a number of issues on which we worked together. I was always favorably impressed by Jack's commitment to the public interest in the most genuine sense, and his ability to employ his considerable political smarts in accomplishing this. Too often people try to make a distinction between pragmatism and idealism. But effective public service requires both. Jack Yunits demonstrated that very well."

——Massachusetts Congressman Barney Frank

CHAPTER 7

*"I am not a political figure, nor do I want to
be one; but I come with my heart."*
—*Princess Diana*

During the transition time from November to January, one of the most important actions Jack took was to attend "Mayor School" in Cambridge. (Who knew such a thing even existed?) The U.S. Conference of Mayors sponsored the meetings and Jack met new mayors from all over the country. In addition to the seminars, Jack also learned from the experts that he needed to start cutting the budget, because it could get disastrous.

When Jack returned to Brockton, transitional team meetings were held at our house. Tim and Chris participated in these, as did several others, including Mary Waldron—whom Jack hired to be his Chief of Staff.

Mary, or Wally, as Jack called her, hails from Chicopee, Massachusetts, where I was born (at Westover Air Force Base) and her grant-writing skills, as well as her master's degree in public administration were a good match for Jack. The two made for a double-barreled shotgun kicking off the race to shape Brockton's future.

On January 1, 1996, Jack was sworn in during a ceremony at City Hall. The golden brick structure, constructed in 1894, is cavernous with high ceilings and gold-leaf fixtures. In the grand hall of the building several war paintings adorn the walls and a clock tower outside can be seen from miles away.

Jack received a heartfelt standing ovation when he entered the City Council Chamber for his Inaugural Address. After he was sworn in he rose to the podium to read from his scripted speech:

"From what I've experienced in just these last six weeks," he began, a bit dry-mouthed, "from preliminary personnel decisions, to my examination and re-examination of today's issues—I can say with certainty that the campaign was the easy part. Now, all that was said over these last six months must be put to action."

Gaining in confidence, he packed the middle part of his talk with more specifics. Jack's mother was sitting next to me holding her pocketbook tight against her. The kids made me proud by not squirming. Jack concluded with: "I have been called a dreamer—and my 21-point plan a fantasy. Let me say to the doubters that without dreams there are no achievements—and without vision all achievements wither."

A hearty round of applause followed and after a final ovation the family made its way to Jack's new office. This was the first time any of us had seen the somewhat grimy space. The room was fairly large, but the furniture and drapes desperately needed updating. The desk and chairs were made of tacky yellow wood. The kids loved the small private bathroom and the dinky half-kitchen. Plus, the TV with a VCR, and a computer kept their interest. Hopefully they'd be able to teach Jack how to use the modern contraptions.

What was disturbing was that there wasn't a paperclip or a Rolodex. Everything on the computer had been deleted. City Hall workers told Jack that previous administrations shared at least some form of a transition—at the very least an inventory of department heads with phone numbers. This last mayor's parting gift to the city was to leave absolutely nothing, which severely handicapped the incoming administration.

But there was no time to think about that because the day Jack took office, the snow started falling. And didn't stop for five months. It was a record year. The phone calls we got at home were eye-openers.

"Is this the mayor? You suck!" a woman screamed in my ear at 5:30 one morning. She was angry because snowplows had blocked her driveway. Jack was long gone guiding the city through a snowstorm that eventually dumped 28 inches. He had to close schools for the entire week and parents were upset.

"Losing one child is too many," he told me in response. The dangerous snowdrifts towered over street corners in banks six feet and higher. There were few sidewalk plows and many of the 16,000 students in the city walked to school. Jack was interviewed on Boston TV, looking kind of cute, I might add, his dark hair emphasizing the rosy-color of his cheeks. He used my "Baptism by Snow" slogan to describe his first week in office.

The mayor's new staff was so overwhelmed with the flood of phone calls that Jack asked me if I would help out at City Hall. When I got there phones were screeching off the hook, people coming and going, the fire chief and police chief hurrying to and fro. Some callers exploded with fury, especially if they'd just finished shoveling and a plow blocked their driveway, or if the plows hadn't gotten to them yet. I empathized, but there were no easy answers. Jack himself was riding the plows, checking on salt and gravel supplies, helping people dig out their cars, and making sure the homebound elderly received their Meals on Wheels. One in a hundred calls was a considerate person saying thank you for plowing their street. The staff and I were downright cheery after those. But they were few and far between.

At one point, Conor called to tell me that Mairi was sitting behind a chair crying and crying, saying she missed me and wanted me home. But the city was in such crisis I couldn't leave. Even so, hearing about Mairi's emotions twisted me up. I was trying to help some of the most foul-mouthed people while my children were at home without their parents.

When I finally arrived, I steadied myself by drinking a Black Russian. Once the warm liquid of vodka and Kahlua filled my veins I began to unwind. I played a CD called "Chant," which brought my tattered soul to a level where I could finally practice yoga and find peace, trying to forget how awful people had been.

After a while, Mairi and Breck wanted me to play a "Mom loves me the most" game. So, they climbed onto my bed, ready for some attention. "Okay," I decided, patting the bed covers. "Whoever brushes their teeth first wins." The two of them jumped off the bed and ran out of the room. They returned quickly, but Breck hadn't brushed and lost for fibbing. I spun him around and pushed him back towards the door. Mairi's teeth were sparkly clean, so I told her I loved her the most and gave her a big hug. Just then the phone rang. It was Jack.

"How's everyone doing?" he asked, sounding wilted. He had been going nonstop since about five that morning.

"Hanging in there," I told him. "Kids are brushing and I'm getting lots of hugs."

"Sounds good," he responded. I heard him call out to someone in the mayor's office, probably Mary, then returned. "I don't know what time I'll be home," he remarked. "All hell's breaking loose here. There's a water main break on Pleasant Street." I empathized as Casey appeared in the door. Sensing the game we were in the middle of she insisted I loved her the most. "You're right!" I said. "Bye, Jack. Good luck. I love you," I said, returning the black receiver onto a phone that looks like a painter's pallet. Casey jumped on the bed. I hugged her, too. Hug-hug-hug. I told the kids it was my job to hug them. Breck finally returned with a fresh smile. How could I resist? I said I loved him the most, too, and squeezed the three together. They wriggled around like puppies. Our goofy game was all in fun and helped clear away some of the day's misery.

CHAPTER 8

"The bedfellows politics makes are never strange. It only seems that way to those who have not watched the courtship."
—Kirkpatrick Sale

Two weeks into his term, Jack phoned from City Hall to say he'd just accepted an invitation to attend a luncheon at the White House with President Bill Clinton. Jack's secretary, Lillian, my new scheduling pal, had taken care of the details and soon Jack and I were on a plane to D.C., to meet the President, and also to attend a 3-day U.S. Conference of Mayors. After we pushed our seats back to relax, Jack told me his sister, Amy, had a kindergarten student in Bridgewater who owned two goldfish. One was named George Washington and the other, Jack Yunits.

"How sweet," I said, stirring my tomato juice. "Your influence reaches all the way down to goldfish." I was just joking with him, but then suddenly got a premonition. "Jack, what if Brockton has a crisis and we have to leave D.C.?" By now I was so excited about meeting the President I didn't want anything to interfere. But with one snow emergency after another, I knew how dependent the city was on him when something crucial happened. Within minutes, in fact, he got a call from Mary that a tornado warning had been posted for Brockton. The city was expecting 75 mph winds and all the fire stations were in preparation. Fortunately, Mary's strengths lay in being organized and dependable, so we knew things were in good hands. After a few hours, the storm downgraded anyway, so Jack and I breathed easier. It was fair to say, however, that Jack was fast becoming known as the "Weather Mayor."

During the three-day conference in D.C., mayors around the country learned about an initiative started by President Clinton to revitalize the nation's cities. That made me feel that Jack was in the right place at the right time.

Additionally, one big-ticket item being talked about, or rather "buzzed" about, was a computer mechanism called the Internet. People were saying the Internet would become the way of the world, though most people at the conference didn't know much about the concept. Our son, Breck, however, was already savvy with computers at the tender age of 11, and called from home to ask if he could sign up for the new America-On-Line. Absolutely, I told him, not understanding what the service entailed.

On the last day of the conference, Jack and I, and hundreds of other mayors and spouses, rode in buses to the White House. After several layers of security checks, the mayors were corralled into a private meeting with Mr. Clinton while the spouses waited patiently in the "China Room." The pattern I liked best was the one Nancy Reagan had picked out—a handsome white with gold trim. Later, the mayors were reunited with their spouses. Jack, however, was nowhere to be found. When it came time to have our picture taken with the President, I was standing in line straining my body every which way trying to locate him. A waiter offered me a cold glass of white wine, which I gulped down.

What was I going to say to President Clinton? I'd been a mayor's wife for three weeks and here I was meeting the President of the United States! All by myself! A postcard with my name displayed passed over to a woman who announced my name into a microphone and suddenly I was walking across a shiny hardwood floor to greet the Commander-in-Chief.

The President turned my way and smiled. His graying hair contrasted with the dark blue suit he was wearing and I approached him with my hand extended.

"My relative is John Breckinridge, who was Vice President under James Buchanan," I said.

"Oh, really?" said Mr. Clinton. His hands were warm as they clutched mine and my composure began to falter. He was so tall and sexy. I started losing focus. I kept my hand in his. My knees were buckling. I felt compelled to add that I was a spouse, not a mayor—lest he thought I made important decisions and influenced people.

I stammered, "I'm May . . . may . . . mare . . . mare-eed to the Ma-yerrrr of Massachusetts!"

"Oh, okay," he laughed, "The Mayor of Massachusetts, huh?" and turned me toward the camera for our picture. Everyone was laughing. The tingles started at my ankles as I thanked him for allowing the spouses to be included. One more handshake and I floated out of the room a foot off the ground—an absolutely unique sensation. I had met the President of the United States!

When I alighted in the reception area, I requested a vodka and tonic from the bar. For a second I remembered reading a review about a book called "My Life and What I Wore." Mine, I thought, would be: "My Life and What I Drank." Jack had already been through the line—he couldn't find me either—and was standing with others sharing their Clinton experiences.

One woman said, "Just think how few people ever come to the White House, let alone get to meet the President of the United States!"

I agreed with her and said I couldn't wait to go on the radio talk shows back home to share the incident with the public. When Mayor Dan Malloy from Stamford, CT, and his wife, Kathy, heard that Jack and I had had separate pictures taken with the President, they insisted we go back through the line and get our picture taken together. Kathy removed the drinks from our hands as Dan gently shoved us through the double-doors.

"This is not my style," Jack argued. I agreed, but the doors closed behind us and we were handed another postcard.

The President smiled in recognition when we approached him. Hi, Bill, old buddy, old pal. Jack shook hands with him and with complete ease mentioned that we had a mutual friend in Boston.

Without missing a nanosecond, Clinton responded, "Oh, yes, Frank Keefe and I went to Oxford together, I know him very well." How could he do that after meeting thousands of people all the time? I was just floored. And gawking. But it was my turn to say something so I expressed how much we respected Hillary and wished her luck in her upcoming grand jury testimony regarding the Whitewater scandal. He looked down at the ground and closed his eyes. I admired the lines of age around them. I wanted to kiss him.

"I appreciate that," he said with a slight nod.

I moved over to the other side of the President for our picture, wrapped my arm around his torso and grinned at the camera. I was hugging the President of the United States! Biggest thrill of my life.

When I got home I called the radio talk shows to tell the Brockton residents about meeting President Clinton. That led to other callers sharing their stories. One woman said she met John F. Kennedy at the Walkover Club in Brockton during a time when he was running for President. Another saw Franklin Roosevelt in the nearby city of Taunton. She said she was close enough to tell Roosevelt that her father worshipped him.

Shortly after our return from D.C., in the wake of yet another snowstorm, the thrill of meeting the President came head to head with the grim realities that sometimes came with Jack's new job.

"Mrs. Yunits?" a male voice asked on the phone one morning, pulling me awake. I had overslept.

"Yes?" I said, sitting up and swinging my legs over the side of the bed. Jack had left for work already because my coffee sat on the nightstand next to me, cold. "This is the Chief of Police, Paul Studenski, calling."

"Hi, Paul," I said, switching the receiver to my other ear and bringing the cold coffee mug to my lips. "What's up?"

"I hate to tell you this, but your car was reported to be involved in a hit and run accident."

"What?" I exclaimed, the French Roast catching in my throat. "Which one?" "The Oldsmobile Cutlass," he said.

"Hold on a minute." I placed the receiver and coffee on the nightstand, and walked down the long upstairs hall to the small room with the eaves and the built-in desk. Peering out the window of the room I could see our car below, covered with snow.

When I got back, I picked up the phone and told him that our car was in the driveway. "In fact," I said, "it's snowed in."

"I'll be right there," Paul answered. I had time to pull my hair into a ponytail and throw on a silk robe before he arrived. Wrapping myself in a long wool coat and stepping into Jack's slush boots I walked out the backdoor to meet the chief outside. Paul could see that the icicles dripping from the fender had actually frozen our used car to the ground. Another officer brought the female accuser to see for herself. By then I was shivering, holding my elbows in tight to stay warm. The woman peered down at the icicles then apologized saying that someone had slipped her a paper after her vehicle was sideswiped earlier. The scribbled message noted our license plate number as the one who did the damage.

"What kind of person would do that?" I asked. The Chief shrugged his shoulders. My suspicions narrowed down to the past mayor's cohorts, believing they might still be sore about losing. But even so, how would someone know our license plate by heart, or think that fast when seeing a car get sideswiped? It was creepy.

Talk show radio host, Pat Barnes, called the house when he heard about the accusation, asking for Jack's comments. I called Jack and told him not to make a mountain out of a molehill, because there were so many other issues to contend with. He said, "Honey, when someone accuses the mayor of a hit and run, it is a mountain." We never did find out who made the accusation. Right after the car incident, the hairdresser/drug addict was murdered. Then the old woman was killed at the supermarket and my visions of meeting President Clinton became a distant memory.

To make matters worse, Boston Globe newspaper columnist, Mike Barnicle, visited the Brockton District Courthouse and penned a column about the high number of people being accused of drug trafficking, filing for restraining orders, and facing weapons violations. I read his words out loud one morning as Jack dropped whole-wheat bread into the toaster. "Jack, listen to this," I said: "Brockton is a small city, and—truth be told—a dying one, too. In Brockton, it appears that too many people wear an expectation of violence on their face. More than likely, government can do very little, and where it has tried the failure rate has been phenomenal."

Mike Barnicle had a large readership and I knew thousands of people would be reading his column. The thought of that happening made me shrink inside. Here was yet another atrocious slam on Brockton. Jack pulled a chair next to me.

I read, "Why, even the wind seems colder and crueler as it whistles through a graveyard called Brockton, an old shoe city with a heel at its throat."

"A graveyard called Brockton?" I asked Jack, frustrated. "What a description of our city!" Jack ate his toast and chuckled. He dismissed negative stories in this manner, preferring to stay focused on the positive. He also got a kick out of seeing me flustered.

When I arrived at the law office for work I found that an associate in Jack's law firm, Attorney John Buckley, had also read the article. He asked me, "What can you do? Keep defending Brockton, or let it pass? If you rebut Mike's words in a letter to the editor, more articles get published and we just keep on being defensive."

I couldn't help but think that Mike Barnicle had no idea Brockton had just elected a new mayor and that the people of Brockton were filled with renewed hope. "Give us a chance," I wanted to tell him.

As luck would have it, a week later Jack and I were invited to a black-tie affair at the John F. Kennedy Library in Dorchester and Mike Barnicle happened to be a guest. The event was celebrating the grand opening of a new oncology center in Quincy. Standing in a crowded reception area sipping a cold Black Russian, I was a bit awed to meet the locally famous writer. After our initial hellos and a tidbit of weather conversation, I conveyed to him, as politely as possible, how hurtful his recent article about Brockton had been.

"Do you know," I asked, "that hundreds of people wake up every day intent on stemming the negatives pouring into our city, and that we have little control over these gun-toting criminals? The majority of Brocktonians are well-mannered decent people."

"It's K through 6 you gotta' reach!" Mike yelled so suddenly I flinched. I ran my fingers through my hair, thinking about that for a second, and then added, "But Brockton is being swamped with Section 8/welfare recipients because of governmental relocation programs."

"K through 6!" he blurted again, a tiny spit landing on my bosom. My temperature started to rise. He didn't know anything about Brockton—only what he witnessed one day sitting outside a courthouse, which happened to handle matters from all over the county.

"The District Court, you know, is a regional one,"

I said, "and not all of the hoodlums you wrote about are from Brockton." Suddenly I was aware that others were listening. I swirled my drink and continued a bit quieter, "You should know that thousands of lifelong Brocktonians love their city and are working hard every day to stop these troublemakers from destroying everything."

That did it. He went off on some rant about how terrible it was to see unkempt people sitting on the curbs outside the courthouse. No kidding. And that Brockton was the pits because of what he saw taking place.

"But," I pointed out, "your observation describes only a tiny part of the population. And by emphasizing the negatives, you remain part of the problem. At least the majority of the people of Brockton have grit and determination and pride and they're not taking the fight sitting down! We are by no means 'a dying city.' The resolute citizens are going forward with a new leader against terrible odds, regardless of your bad press."

Mike wanted none of my rhetoric. "K through 6!" he repeated. Easy for him to say, but what was he ever going to do with that idea?

Finally his persona got to me and I lost my cool. "Fuck you, Mike," I said, casting my glance at the floor.

"Oh, now that's an intelligent response," he retorted, like I hadn't been trying all along.

"Fuck you," I said again, raising my face up to his, thinking what a jerk he was and sad that, moments earlier, I was actually excited to meet him. Jack tried to get me to stop, although it seemed he and our friend, Jack Shields, whose family's business we were there to celebrate, were highly amused by what was happening. They were drinking their Martinis and smiling at me. I was incredulous that they didn't come to my aid and looked from one to the other thinking, "Okay boys, anytime you want to just step in and help me out, feel free." But they didn't. I was alone in a verbal spat with a renowned writer, while beautifully coiffed women in long dresses swirled around us.

Finally a waitress asked us to take our seats for dinner. That's when I learned that Mike Barnicle was the keynote speaker for the night. I have no recollection of what he talked about.

The next day Jack told everyone he encountered in Brockton about my confrontation. Policemen, City Hall workers, and attorneys all gave me high fives when they saw me. The radio talk show host, Pat Barnes, called on the phone to say "good job." It wasn't something I was proud of because I lost my temper and used the "F" word too much. But everyone else was triumphant that I stood up to the patronizing Mike Barnicle. I just wondered how often I'd be defending the city or if one day that might not be necessary.

"Jack Yunits never once substituted politics for principle. His leadership is defined by his outstanding record of accomplishment. During tough economic times Mayor Yunits brought the Rox to Brockton for economic benefit as well as quality of life benefits. He rejuvenated Brockton public education with the construction of three new schools and was a driving force in motivating mayors across Massachusetts to become more innovative, compassionate and fiscally responsible.

I miss Jack's leadership. As mayor he was a good guy who loved his community and more importantly its residents. Jack set out to improve the quality of life in Brockton and unknowingly helped to improve it in Medford as well."

—*Medford Mayor Michael J. McGlynn*

CHAPTER 9

"It's easy to make a buck. It's a lot tougher to make a difference"
—Tom Brokaw

Somehow we survived the winter wonderland with the city breaking a record. More than one hundred snowy inches fell. Thankfully, though, Jack had purchased "snow insurance," which paid a majority of the plowing costs. That was the last year the insurance company offered it! Come spring, Jack was finally able to put the snow issues behind and was looking forward to moving ahead on his "21-Point Plan."

But there was a little delay, on my birthday, May 21. While driving home from the law office after what had been an idyllic afternoon weather-wise, the wind suddenly whipped up and the sky turned a deep, dirty green.

I parked my car in the driveway, struggled to push the door open against the wind, and, with difficulty, managed to hold my long hair back with one hand. I saw the giant oak tree in our front yard bend like a string mop, brushing the roof of our house. I turned around to see Breck, who had just finished his paper route, running towards me yelling, "A branch just came down!" He was a bit amused as we ran into the house together to avoid the sudden downpour.

Through the window we could see the pond across the street whipping itself into waves like it never had before. There were flashes of lightning, the wind was howling and rain cascaded down the street like a gushing fire hydrant.

Within fifteen minutes it was all over. Our phones were dead. The sun was beginning to poke out. The Weather Mayor was back on the job again.

Mairi and Casey arrived home with stories of their own, and before dark, the three of us walked around our neighborhood to witness nature's destruction. The air was fragrant with the scent of spring flowers and a pristine quality to the atmosphere felt as if even the ozone had been scrubbed clean. Tree branches littered everyone's lawns.

As the evening progressed, I learned through several phone calls that trees had fallen everywhere and live wires lay exposed on the ground. Jack arrived home at 12:30 a.m., exhausted and stressed from providing assistance and assessing needs. He was out again by 5:30 that same morning informing the public on the radio that schools were closed. He requested that people report live wires if any and to exercise caution around them.

I offered to go in and help with the phones but the calls were relatively few, so I only stayed until noon. The damage, however, was so severe that Governor Bill Weld came to Brockton to survey the destruction. The weathermen called the storm a "downburst," saying the 100 mph winds fell just short of a tornado rating. Jack rode with the Governor through Calvary cemetery on the east side of town where tree roots had been wrenched from the ground throwing up some buried coffin-liners from the earth. The iron fence surrounding the graveyard was mangled. It was the week before Memorial Day and a massive cleanup would be necessary for the upcoming Veteran's events.

Passing by old granite tombstones it was a bit quiet in the car. Jack cracked a joke saying: "These people can't vote anyway," hoping for a favorable response from Mr. Weld.

But the Governor stayed somber. Jack shifted in the back seat, then leaned forward a bit and added, "Except, of course, if you live in Southie," referring to South Boston's reputation for retaining the deceased on voter lists.

The Republican Governor turned his head this way and that, checking out the grave markers. "It's a good thing," he finally responded. "They're all Irish Democrats."

After Mr. Weld returned to Boston, Jack received a call from City Councilor Donna Daley, in distress. "You won't believe what's happened in Ward 6," she told him. Jack and I drove over to investigate and found towering pine trees resting on houses and cars. It felt like we were in Vermont instead of an urban industrial area. One path of destruction looked as if loggers had sawed down trees to sell for lumber. Some trunks resembled twisted corkscrews that had been yanked from the ground. One newlywed couple showed us where a tree had crashed down on the roof of their recently renovated kitchen. Another tree spiraled through a car's windshield, impaling the female driver. Horrific accidents the governor had no idea about. Shortly thereafter, though, Weld was brought up to snuff and declared Brockton a disaster area. Thankfully, he sent state work crews to help clear away the rubble in time for Memorial Day. I began thinking we should name a holiday after Jack, call it Weather Luther King Day.

The following Saturday morning, I took a call from City Councilor Vy Packard, who was hearing from her constituents that black water was sputtering out of their household faucets and that Droukas Tannery on the South Side was emitting a stench like rotten eggs. How delightful. Jack was standing at the sink shaving, while I was filling the tub for Mairi's bath, only to find the water brown.

"Well, there goes another half of Brockton, moving out!" I blurted, my hand swishing the brackish water.

"For God's sake, would you stop?" he said. He was really mad at me and I had to remember that I was fretting over only one tubful of brown water. He had to fix the city's entire water system—miles and miles of ancient pipes with so little water that a water ban had been in effect since before we moved to Brockton. For years no one had been allowed to water their lawns or wash their cars.

Still, I was getting a little tired of political life. His mayor's salary was so measly (on a scale of the one hundred highest paid employees in Brockton, Jack was so off the scale that The Enterprise ranked his salary as 307th), he was rarely home anymore, he twitched like crazy in his sleep from the stress, and now Mairi's bath water was the color of murk. As much as I marveled at Jack's energy and commitment to the public, this new lifestyle demanded way too many sacrifices of all of us.

One of the secretaries in Jack's office called the next day to tell me that Jack was scheduled for a big TV presentation and would I make sure he wore a blue shirt, because blue was best on camera. Jack didn't own a decent blue shirt, (I feel embarrassed revealing how lacking we were in some areas) and I couldn't afford to buy him one because our credit card balances were too high. So I found an old blue button-down shirt with an ink stain and rinsed it out with Rover Rust Remover. The blotch didn't disappear completely, but Jack assured me he wouldn't take off his jacket.

The next morning the kids and I said goodbye to our spring water bubbler because we couldn't afford to rent the five-gallon jugs anymore. We'd just have to drink murk. As the appliance man wheeled the rental container out the door I crossed my fingers that the City Councilors would vote Jack a pay raise. It had been more than ten years since the mayor's salary had had a boost.

Meanwhile, our family was involved in everything. The kids and I volunteered for a memorial golf tournament, I judged a poetry and a cooking contest, planned Casey's 8th grade graduation party, marched in the Memorial Day parade and promoted the spring House Tour. One night at a fundraising dinner I was caught off guard when Jack suggested to the M.C. that I sing the national anthem. When I finished singing, my clenched hands were numb.

A lighter moment came when I shopped at Macy's department store at the Westgate Mall and at the counter the saleswoman looked at my credit card.

"Mayor's wife?" she asked, tilting her head.

"Yes," I said, sheepishly. Pointing to my goods I whispered, "Mayor's underwear."

And just to keep things interesting, one afternoon, a woman who hotly pursued Jack during the campaign, slid into his office at City Hall, climbed like a wild cat onto the large conference table, hiked her skirt up, and pleaded with him to be with her. Right there, in the middle of the day! Just so we understand the rules, I am the only one who gets to crawl across Jack's table. And only after hours. Embarrassed, he declined and quickly ushered her out, telling his staff never to allow her back. The very next day she called me at home, wanting to know if she could give me a manicure and pedicure for a "good, first lady price." I believed she was trying to ease her guilty conscious.

"Um, I don't think so," I said slowly into the phone, thinking, "Are you kidding me?" She obviously didn't know that Jack had told me everything. "Thank you anyway," I muttered, and hung up.

As convoluted as our daily lives had become, though, the city was beginning to see progress. "Foot Joy To Stay In Brockton," one headline in The Enterprise read. Foot Joy was one of the last remaining, active shoe factories. Jack considered this feat his first real accomplishment as mayor because it meant keeping jobs in the city. Before he became mayor, he told me that the owners of Foot Joy had signed a Purchase and Sales agreement to move the factory to Taunton. But Jack met with them several times to get them to reconsider. While Jack was still working in his law office, in fact, before he was officially mayor, he received a call from the principal owner of Foot Joy. The owner was so impressed to find Jack still at work on Thanksgiving Eve that he decided to give him the benefit of the doubt and to keep Foot Joy in the city. It meant the world. Jack doubts that Brockton would have had an economic chance otherwise.

"I've often stated publicly and privately that Jack Yunits is the finest mayor the city of Brockton has seen since the days of the beloved Joe Downey. The only great difference between them is that Joe Downey was a confirmed bachelor. The city of Brockton had the extra benefit of Mayor Yunits having at his side his remarkable and beautiful wife, Lees. The two as a couple touched not only the lives, but in many cases the hearts, of Brocktonians from all walks of life. And politics seldom sees such a duo through the course of history. Brockton had ten bountiful years with these blessings, these gifts."

—Massachusetts State Senator Tom Kennedy

CHAPTER 10

A community is like a ship; everyone ought to be prepared to take the helm."
—Henrik Ibsen

Soon Jack flew to D.C. to be given an affordable-housing award from President Clinton. While he was gone I received a phone call at midnight. The caller was a woman nearly hysterical because the jackhammers on Belmont Street were preventing her from sleeping. She said the workers had been there for three nights and the noise and flashing lights were keeping her awake. I felt badly and tried to explain that roads were fixed at night when traffic was at a minimum. But she wouldn't let up. She wanted to bring the jackhammers to my house. Stifling a yawn I finally told her that we had a guest room if she wanted to come over. Suddenly she was speechless. Fortunately, the road crews moved on the next day and I didn't hear back from her. Years later we met by chance and shared a hearty laugh over the call.

A few mornings later a newscaster for WBET radio reported that a committee of three men had studied the raise situation and had recommended the mayor's salary be brought up to $73,000.00. Now, in 1996, that was not a lot of money for a family of six, especially for a full-time public official who was enticing millions and millions of business dollars into a city. But it was better than the $57,000.00 Jack started with. The reporter called our house for a few words from Jack, but he was out running. She told me she didn't think there'd be a problem with the recommendation passing.

We got a few calls at home, though, from some old-time Brocktonians who thought it looked bad for Jack to take a raise and that maybe he shouldn't. I think their frame of reference was set at a time when a loaf of bread still cost a nickel. He said I would kill him if he didn't take the raise. He was right.

The raise finally passed the City Council with a vote of 11-0. I was surprised and uplifted by the Council's decision. The story was on the front page and on the local news radio, but only a handful of people called City Hall, including one woman who said, "I didn't vote for Jack then and I won't now!" I could live with that. I mean it wasn't like we were suddenly rich and buying a house on the Cape.

The pay raise helped our financial condition somewhat so I booked a canoe trip in Maine for the entire family. We'd be meeting some friends and go canoeing down the Saco River. I couldn't wait for the adventure. We hadn't done anything fun with the kids for some time and we needed to.

But, two nights before the trip, Jack called me and let me know that Governor Weld was coming to Brockton to present money for roads. I had to cancel our trip.

"But our kids need to have fun!" I pleaded, squeezing my eyes shut, knowing I wouldn't win this argument. "Jack, life isn't just about discipline and work!" I said into the phone. He was still at the office, long past dinnertime. When I continued to express my bitter disappointment, he let me know that he wouldn't be taking vacations anymore anyway, since his raise went through. I tucked one hand under my armpit.

"Right," I said, pursing my lips and sucking in another sacrifice. I hung up the phone and could barely bring myself to walk into the living room and tell the kids the trip was off. They were disappointed, naturally, and I was left hoping there'd be time to create more fun memories before they were all grown up and leaving.

Sure enough, wouldn't you know it, the day that we would have left on our vacation, the Governor canceled his appointment.

Soon summer arrived with Conor cleaning office buildings and weeding gardens. He also played lots of baseball and I taught him how to drive a car in the Brockton High School parking lot. He was going along pretty well until I pretended that something ran in front of the car and yelled, "watch it!" whereby he slammed on the brakes. The car lurched and Breck's McDonald's lunch in the backseat went for a ride as well.

"Ma! Whadcha do that for?" Conor yelled, gripping the steering wheel.

"To prepare you for the unexpected on the roads, honey," I said, straightening out the rear view mirror. I congratulated myself on delivering a good learning experience.

Meanwhile, Breck's afternoons were being spent at a segment of Brockton's first website, BrocktonMass.com, called the "Kids Page." He used the code name "Brocktonboy," although he told me much later this was his email address, not his "code name."

For a while that summer, happily, it felt like the kids and I had a break from associated mayoral duties. It wasn't an election year, for one thing, and though we didn't get a family vacation, the kids made side trips with their friends. Casey remarked, after returning from a friend's house on the Cape, that she loved that no one knew she was the mayor's daughter.

But Jack's schedule stayed brisk. He accomplished so much I could hardly keep track—Steak and Burger Night at the Boys and Girls Club, the Puerto Rican flag raising ceremony, Spanish exchange students at City Hall, the Cape Verdean Festival, and kicking off the Thursday night free concerts in the park.

One morning, while still asleep, his foot was twitching like crazy and his teeth were grinding. When he woke up he told me he had to write a speech and craft a sewer agreement. Before 7 a.m., he received three calls from the media and learned that the supplemental Courthouse Bill failed to pass in legislation. The new Brockton District Courthouse, which had been in the works for nearly seventeen years, would be delayed once again. He was hopping mad. I finally convinced him to take two days off back to back and we arranged to spend a day on a boat with friends, who'd been asking us to do so for more than a year. By the time we finally got on the boat, nothing could hamper our enthusiasm—not even heavy, dense fog.

"It's clearing up! It's getting brighter!" we kept saying, as rolls of the white stuff obliterated the sun. We tried ignoring the fine mist that was making our hair damp while we pieced together ham sandwiches in the tiny galley. The boat was guided over to Martha's Vineyard, and from there we motored to Gay Head, now known as Aquinnah. But by now the fog was so thick it seemed we were sailing in a giant cocoon. Heading back to Cuttyhunk, it felt as if trouble was imminent because we couldn't see even a foot ahead of the boat. Suddenly the vessel listed. I lost my footing, and tumbled back, nearly spilling my drink—God forbid—and hit my elbow on the white leather captain's chair. The boat had hit ground or a large rock. Jack jumped into the water to push the boat, heaving it back and forth as our friend gunned the engines. We shifted weight on the boat as best we could, moving the ice-filled coolers from one side to another. Jack stayed in the water, shoving with all his might for more than an hour before the boat finally dislodged and was set afloat. Our friends were impressed by Jack's tenacity, and, of course, made fun of him all night. "Hey, he-man, do you have enough strength left to throw me a beer?" Still, though, because the boat was damaged and some other radar piece had stopped working, we signaled for help by blasting the horn.

After what felt like a long half hour, the "SEA TOW" appeared, a small emergency boat. The captain told us that he hadn't been able to hear our signals, let alone see the boat. He strongly suggested we anchor for the night and guided us to a safe haven.

After a few worried moments wondering what to do next, a small rowboat appeared heading towards us through the haze, loaded with men in yellow rain gear. Through the fog and their muted conversation, we somehow gathered that they were selling shrimp cocktails and oysters on the half shell. What? We wondered if we were seeing things. But the men were for real, and they reached out to grab the slippery sides of our bouncing boat as they snuggled up to our astonished faces. "Shrimp cocktail? Oysters on the half-shell? Is this heaven??" I asked. Scrambling below to get some cash I blurted, "I love Cuttyhunk!"

The remarkable thing is that all of our kids were in safe places and secure for the night. There weren't babysitters who needed to get home, we had cell phones to communicate what happened, and there were no emergencies in the city. We joked about our predicament appearing in the newspaper, hoping that it wouldn't, and when we could do nothing else and go nowhere Jack finally relaxed. Cheerfully, we ate our seafood tidbits and raised a toast to the Weather Mayor—whose long-awaited day off was spent hunkered down in a fog.

"Jack Yunits is a special breed of politician. Fiercely dedicated to his community yet able to see the need for progress and change. Despite a difference in party affiliation, I found him to be among the best of mayors to work with: fair, thoughtful, engaging and smart. Our shared passion for revitalizing aging blue collar cities where we grew up and pursuing innovative solutions to some of our nation's cities' most vexing problems resulted in some wonderful projects—my favorite being the Brockton Rox stadium."

—Former Massachusetts Governor Jane Swift

CHAPTER 11

"Every leader sells two fundamental things: solutions and a positive attitude."
—Roger Crawford

Even if it's a great attribute to have, my one pet peeve about Jack was that he consistently went the extra mile. I was often standing around waiting for him to conclude that night's activities.

For instance, after every free music concert in the lovely D.W. Field Park, Jack always stayed late to help put away the chairs. At those concerts, spectators enjoyed evenings of classical, jazz, rock or hip-hop music from the comfort of a tent. Afterwards, I longed to be home and felt that his being mayor should free him from those chores at least occasionally. At the same time, I recognized that it was this trait of his—of always giving more than expected—that made Jack an ideal public servant. There was nothing he wouldn't do for Brockton.

He even got Brockton's two enormous water towers to be painted a brilliant sky blue with the words "Brockton City of Champions" written in bold white letters. It was his way of beginning to establish Brockton's new "look," point number one of his 21-point plan.

Unfortunately, several drive-by shootings at the end of the summer took away from the overall feeling that Brockton was coming back. The publicity from those shootings sent more shock waves through the community.

To make matters worse, a police officer called me one morning to tell me that a man had been found dead at City Hall. Cripes. My girls and I had been at City Hall the night before and I shuddered to think the man might have been there then.

"It looks like another heroin death," the officer confided to me. "This guy was found in a bathroom stall in the basement."

"Oh, that's awful. Do you know his name?" I asked, trying to get at the coffee pot in my kitchen.

"Yeah, I'm afraid he's the son of a police officer," the caller told me. "Thirty-one years old."

"Oh, boy," I said, pulling a coffee mug out of the cabinet. I didn't know the family, but felt a profound sadness for their loss. Heroin is such a terrible drug.

"And by the way," the officer continued, "There was a note pinned to the man's shirt."

"What did it say?" I asked, holding my breath.

"It said 'waiting to see the mayor.'"

I laughed, in spite of the horror. "You're wicked," I remarked. Sometimes humor does indeed break the morbidity of a situation.

Shortly after that incident, I was awake from a morning dream and felt a finger touch my back, right in the middle of my spine. I twisted around in bed thinking maybe Jack or Mairi poked me, but no one was there. After a moment I decided it must have been the hand of God and wondered what message He was sending. Probably just "get up, you're late," but the sensation felt more mystical at the time.

During the autumn of 1996 the political excitement revolved around a heated race between U.S. Senator John Kerry and Governor Bill Weld. I loved being in the midst of people who were committed to making the world a better place. I was learning firsthand the sacrifices and effort involved, and to me, to be invited to an intelligent debate like the Kerry/Weld one at Stonehill College was more rewarding than a musical concert.

I was, in fact, so taken with the level of discourse that night, that the day after the televised debate, I called Jack's Chief of Staff, Mary, to talk about the thrill, only to find out that she was on the verge of quitting her job! I swallowed my words as I listened to her tell me how angry she was with Jack and with the complete lack of control she felt in the mayor's office. I remained speechless, knowing how incredible the amount of stress and tension they were all under.

All day, I mulled over the things she told me, and the first time I could speak with Jack was when we were crawling into bed late that night. He and I folded into our familiar embrace, and after a few tender hugs, we began to relax. I finally broached the subject. He listened attentively.

The next day—a Saturday—he called Mary and asked her to come over to our house. She and Jack sat together in the living room and Mary spent the first ten minutes crying. I was in the adjoining room and could only think of that movie, "A League of Our Own," where Tom Hanks yelled out "there's no crying in baseball!" "There's no crying in politics!" I wanted to say, but I knew the stresses she was under. She was a married woman, with a young daughter, and was as intent on "saving" Brockton as Jack was. The hours she kept at City Hall, the extra time she put in for the night events, and the extraordinary pressures she was feeling were finally getting to her. After a time, the two of them agreed that Jack needed to commit to a weekly meeting with her and his staff so that she knew what his schedule was. Mary left on good terms, feeling more relaxed from having vented, and I, too, was relieved. The last thing Jack needed was for her to quit.

But later he told me, "It's very hard to know what my schedule is. Things change so quickly. Politics is about people and crisis management—it's not like running a factory that makes widgets."

As if to prove this point, shortly after, we found ourselves driving to Arlington National Cemetery in Washington, D.C. for my Uncle Graham's funeral. The worst rainstorm in New England's history was upon us and the Weather Mayor was on the car phone constantly. In Brockton, the Salisbury River grew to such proportions that Belmont Avenue flooded and residents had to be evacuated in boats. Parts of the newly resurfaced Belmont Street (where jackhammers had kept that lady awake) caved in, and two schools closed due to flooding. Mary covered for Jack and people called her home at all hours of the day and night. The Waste Management facility flooded and she handled all of those concerns, as well. I think being in the hot seat helped her better understand what Jack went through every day.

The silver lining of Jack's trip to D.C. was that he arranged a meeting with a businessman from Maryland who was interested in buying a giant food-processing plant in Brockton. According to Jack, when he and the owner first met they were a "million dollars apart." Jack worked his magic, though, and convinced the man to invest in Brockton. Two weeks later they sealed the deal and Jack inched forward with point number twenty, recruiting new business.

But the political honeymoon was over for Jack and what worried me was the toll the job was taking on his health. Every night he kept us both awake with his coughing. I suspected he had contracted some bug after staying out all night on New Year's Eve helping close down Brockton's First Night gala. He drenched the bed in sweat several nights in a row. I started spreading out towels just to keep from changing the sheets.

I begged him to take it easy, and suggested he try leaving meetings earlier and maybe curtail his running. But every morning, regardless, he put in his six miles in the park before going to City Hall. His running partner, Mark O'Reilly, told me that Jack often stopped in the middle of their runs overcome with a debilitating cough.

I became obsessed wondering what would happen if he had a terminal illness during this resurgence of Brockton. I couldn't imagine how disastrous that would be, not only to our family, but also to the city that had pinned its hopes on him. Yet, he was resistant to the idea of seeing a doctor because he didn't have the time or patience to sit in a waiting room.

One of the many issues on his agenda involved a company that wanted to build a trash transfer center in Ward 4 next to the old dump. The tax revenues for the city would amount to half a million dollars a year, money Brockton desperately needed for more fire fighters and policemen. But the residents who lived near the dump feared an increase in truck traffic and odors and were quite vocal about their displeasure.

Before Jack had even had time to educate himself about the center's proposal, a group of citizens stormed City Hall yelling that all Jack cared about was money. Right. That's why he took a forty thousand dollar pay cut to become mayor, I thought to myself.

There was the recurring problem of flooding on Belmont Avenue. Some very angry people, who'd lived on that street for years, had suffered the effects of water and raw sewage pouring into their homes time and again. They couldn't sell their houses, nor could they stand living in them. The issue had been before several mayors in the past and none had found an answer. Jack attended a raucous meeting about the flooding and afterwards City Councilor Martha (Marty) Crowell called to tell me that Jack knew his facts and had convinced her there were real solutions down the road. She couldn't say enough good things about him. Her comments made my day because I rarely saw Jack anymore and he was usually too exhausted, or ill, to talk when he came home.

My health books were open all the time trying to diagnose Jack's recurring coughing fits and night sweats. He seemed better during the day, but my thoughts were downright morbid wondering what might be going on in his body. Around that time, former Massachusetts Congressman Paul Tsongas passed away from pneumonia after a thirteen-year battle with cancer and Boston's Mayor Tom Menino got hospitalized with kidney stones. I was certain Jack's ailments were stress-related.

One afternoon, I brought soup to him at City Hall and sat down in an armchair across from his desk. He was on the phone, scribbling something on a paper. I crossed my legs, leaned forward to hand him a spoon, and the chair started to teeter forward. Grabbing the front of his desk, I thought I'd caught the edge, but then lost my grip and before I knew it, the chair and I were sprawled on the floor and my skirt was up around my waist. Jack jumped up to peer over the big desk—still on the phone—to see if I was okay. Then he made fancy eyes at my bare legs, raised his eyebrows and sat back down. He'd survive this latest illness, he said, without my good intentions.

But I was trying to keep him going as we learned that there was a major public meeting that night about the Waste Transfer station going into Ward 4. He drove to an elementary school later to find hundreds of nasty, yelling residents there to berate him. One woman asked Jack if she could have a personal word with him. "Of, course," he said, reaching out his hand to shake hers and learn her name. Instead, she passed him a flyer saying "Dump Yunits."

Another man screamed from the back of the cafeteria, "The mayor's kids don't even go to Brockton schools!" He obviously was ignorant that three of them did.

Another yelled that the company should put the trash facility in our neighborhood. Jack told him we already had Route 24 nearby generating plenty of gasoline pollution.

One of Brockton's state legislators suddenly reversed her decision, which had been favorable, and commenced to yelling and screaming against the transfer center. She was chewing gum, smoking cigarettes and totally ignorant of state regulations.

A friend of ours, Paul Finn, an attorney who was one of Massachusetts premier mediators, volunteered to attend the meeting as a favor to Jack. He, like Jack, had had no previous briefing with the company, unfortunately, and before he could say a word, a man in the front row stood up and insulted him. The meeting went downhill from there.

Poor Jack. What he wanted was an intelligent discourse and a chance to hear the people's concerns. Instead, he was confronted by yelling creatures that had no intention of discussing anything.

By the time he finally got home around 11:30 pm, he was thoroughly agitated, completely dejected by the people's behavior. He made himself a stiff drink, but was too tense to eat any food. I offered him a backrub, but he didn't want that either. Our attorney friends called Jack around midnight to tell him it took three-quarters of a bottle of scotch to calm down once he got home.

"Please call me the next time there's another one," he said, sarcastically. "I don't want to miss the fun."

That night, Jack's body twitched and his coughing made him roll from side to side. In the morning our covers were mangled.

I took my beat-up hubby away to Newport, Rhode Island, for his forty-fifth birthday. He was supposed to see a doctor first, but skipped his appointment. The toll the episode had taken on him alarmed me. Few people can withstand the scrutiny, intensity, and demeaning accusations that sometimes go with being a mayor. Freedom of speech can be ugly. Americans get worked up without knowing all the facts and often assume politicians are out to "get them." What doubled Jack's load overall was that mayors before him had avoided the tougher issues and Jack inherited the responsibility of cleaning up years, sometimes decades, of poor decisions or lack of decisions. The flooding at Belmont Avenue, the lack of clean drinking water, and the deficiency of regular communication with the citizens, were just some of the inherited issues. I often found myself asking God to bless every ounce of Jack Yunits. He was willing to do the gritty work necessary to put the city back on track.

By the time we got to Newport, it was a sunny 48 degrees and Jack felt healthier. We walked up and down Thames Street and had onion soup at the White Horse Tavern. My "first" friend, Suzanne, always says that the "stinger" cocktail—a mix of brandy and crème de menthe—cures everything, so Jack downed a stinger at Christy's Restaurant to celebrate his birthday. We shared an

enjoyable evening and Jack spent the following day in the hotel room writing
his State of the City speech for delivery that Monday. For the first time in weeks,
I felt optimistic about his health. Until he woke up during the night with chills,
stomach pains and diarrhea. He was dying. I just knew it.

On the drive home to Brockton, against my advice, he insisted we stop at
a friend's Super Bowl party, where we watched the Patriots play, and lose, to
the Green Bay Packers. On Monday, Jack finally saw a doctor. That night he
addressed a live audience at City Hall for his State of the City speech. No one
knew how sick he was. With the help of Tylenol, he spoke about how the city had
turned the corner. He told us that crime was down and two new schools were
going up. City Hall couldn't keep pace with the building permits people were
applying for. Railroad tracks were being laid for the commuter rail and a design
had been chosen for the new District Courthouse to be built on Main Street.
Sustained applause greeted his speech.

The next day he went from meeting to meeting to meeting. He ended
his long day at East Junior High School. When he came home around 9:30,
he covered himself with a blanket and watched TV. His throat was so sore he
couldn't talk.

At my wit's end I sent a prayer up to Jack's father in heaven, hoping he could
pull some harp strings to help his son. Lying under my down quilt, I pretended
that "Grampy" could hear me. "Please work some magic and let him be okay," I
prayed. "So many people are depending on him."

When the results from Jack's blood work came back a few days later, the
doctor told him he was overworked, run-down, his blood pressure was too
high, and he should take it easy. He also put him on antibiotics for a bronchitis
infection. After a few days Jack felt better than he had in a month.

Granted the antibiotics had a lot to do with his recovery, but during the
course of the week I dreamt that I was in a basement room with Jack's brother,
Mike. Mike was sitting next to a window, pointing to "Grampy" outside playing
golf. He'd been on the same hole a long time and Mike and I laughed that he

must need the practice. Suddenly, Grampy came over to the window, stooped down and peered in through the glass. "Grampy! We love you! We love you!" I yelled. He smiled and a drip of sweat ran down his plump tan face, a vision so familiar it hurt. He then gave a wave, turned and walked away.

Within a few minutes of waking, I realized with a start that Jack's father had answered my prayer! He gave that wave as if to say, "Jack's all set." At the moment of my realization, Jack rolled over towards me on the bed and laughed in his sleep.

A week later, Jack nixed the Waste Transfer facility that no one wanted.

Several people called Jack to thank him for not supporting the project and a woman from the citizens' group, who'd vehemently opposed the plan, sent us flowers. Her kind gesture took away the sting of bad memories and I felt a renewed faith in people once again.

"My father's ten years as Mayor proved to young people in Brockton that strong, creative, committed leaders could make a real difference. He inspired a new generation of leadership for the city."

—Conor Yunits

CHAPTER 12

*"The way I see it, if you want the rainbow,
you gotta put up with the rain."*
—Dolly Parton

One morning Jack left for work and I jumped in the shower in preparation for
my own day at the law office. Some time later, after a refreshing yoga session,
I heard the beep of our security system, signaling that an outside door had
opened. We jokingly called those beeps the "Mairi alarm," because it was our
way of knowing if Mairi had bolted from the house. She was a quick youngster,
always trying to follow Breck over to the pond to go fishing.

"Jack?" I yelled, thinking maybe he'd returned. "Jack?" I said louder, going
to the top of the stairs. But no one answered and I got unusually nervous so
I hurried back into my room, grabbed the skeleton key and locked the door
shut. For the first and only time in my life, I called 911. The operator wanted
me to stay on the phone with her, which helped me feel less afraid. Within
minutes four police cars with flashing lights surrounded the house. What was I
thinking? I rarely received special treatment for being the mayor's wife, but now
it appeared that's what I was getting. One officer broke a lock and entered my
music room through the screened-in porch. He let others in through the kitchen
door. One hustled down to the cellar and another raced up the back stairs.
Geez. After awhile I began to realize that the beep I heard might have been
Jack leaving later than I thought, not some intruder coming in. Oops. I crept
down the stairs clutching my bathrobe around me as the officers merged into

the foyer of my house. One man, Lee McCabe, whom I recognized, suddenly pointed toward the living room. "Oh, my God!" he said. We all looked. "They've ransacked the place!" Scattered everywhere in our line of vision were toys, books, games, videos, pizza boxes, sneakers, football jerseys, dance costumes. My game was up—I was caught—a slob of a first lady, standing there in a scruffy bathrobe with no makeup on, hair looking like a ball of tumbleweed.

"Very funny, Lee," I said, pulling my hair behind one ear. "You try being the mayor's wife with four kids." Everyone laughed. He never lets me forget that one.

Then, on April Fool's Day, 1997, a snowstorm slammed into Brockton quite unexpectedly, dumping 24 inches of snow on the city. The Weather Mayor closed schools for four days and power was out in many neighborhoods, including ours. It was April for God's sake. When our oil burner didn't come on, I took the kids to Suzanne's for the night.

With the blizzard raging outside, Jack and a friend stopped at the Brockton Café, to get a bite to eat before heading home. The restaurant on the south side of Main Street was another spot for tasty pizza. The two of them got ready to dig into a steamy cheese with pepperoni when a very drunk patron confronted Jack about how the city was being plowed. His manner started to cause a disturbance. Jack rose from his seat and the two were nose to nose when our friend stepped between them. He was a good-sized man, with a substantial belly, so when he bumped the offender the guy flailed back a few steps.

The man yelled, "You're an elected official! You can't do that to me!"

"Hell no!" our friend yelled back. "I'm a fucking nobody! I can do anything I want to you!" Touché! That incident reminded us that Jack was finding it harder to be in a public place without being harassed.

Then there were the rumors. One man wasn't voting for Jack again because Jack was a "womanizer," he said. The gossipmonger saw Jack leaving City Hall after hours with a blond woman. Me, as it turned out. Not to add salt to your wound, mister, but Jack and I were possibly "doing it" on the conference table.

Then there was talk going around that I dressed too sexily. That annoyed Jack to no end. He loves the way I dress. In fact, he buys a lot of my clothes. He liked to tell me I was his "good-will ambassador" and not to worry about comments I couldn't control.

Near the end of Jack's first two-year term, when most of our friends were making summer vacation plans, Jack was about to enter into what turned out to be the worst phase of his administration. An alarming discrepancy in the city's budget was discovered, and could be traced back to the School Superintendent, whom Jack hired. First, it turned out that the Superintendent was not living in Brockton, which was a requirement. Second, with the former mayor's authorization, for the two years prior, he had been receiving a substantial raise every year. That was without approval from the school committee.

Jack had a genuine regard for the Superintendent, as did most people, but Jack's allegiance was to the city of Brockton. The man clearly was breaking the rules and Jack had to act. Unfortunately, the Superintendent happened to be African-American. That made the situation even stickier.

The City Solicitor, Tom Plouffe, summoned Jack to his office the next day. Closing the door, he turned to face Jack. Sticking his hands in his pockets and rocking on his heels he said, "Congratulations, Mr. Mayor. You appointed the first African-American Superintendent of Schools in the state and now you have to fire him."

Jack suspected that "doing the right thing" was going to be interpreted by some as racism. Sure enough, at a Jubilee Political Action Committee meeting, Jack was verbally assaulted for an hour and forty-five minutes. The media were there in full force. None of the more moderate black leaders were present—just the radicals. The minority community demanded to know more about the issue and why other administrators hadn't been investigated. Jack told them an audit was in the works.

They told Jack they wanted to be involved in the search for a new Superintendent. Jack said, "Fine, put it in writing, give me your agenda and we'll go from there."

They wanted to know why more minorities weren't on boards and commissions. Jack said he sent many applications to minorities and hadn't received any in return yet.

I honestly was astounded that these racial cards were still being played. It seemed far easier to cry racism, than to accept that the Superintendent had broken several rules. He wasn't being investigated because of his color, but for his financial indiscretions. However, the minority groups had been ignored by almost all previous administrations, and this incident fueled animosity. Jack faced the fire, though, and showed great courage by doing so.

Jack had the most diverse mayor's staff ever, including two African-Americans, one Puerto Rican, two Cape Verdeans, a Jewish man and a Polish-American. Of the fifty-five people who worked for the School Superintendent, not one was a minority! How does that make Jack a racist?

Ultimately, the School Committee cut a deal where the Superintendent could gracefully retire on full pay, instead of being fired or dragged through the courts at huge expense to the city. Jack said that was the right thing to do. He also wanted the city to keep moving forward.

As a result, though, callers to a local radio station berated Jack, saying he had no backbone. Some called him a wimp and demanded he be impeached. In the dark of night, somebody smeared the door handle of his official Crown Vic with peanut butter.

Days later, at the VFW hall for Jack's fundraiser, the room appeared too big and the crowd too small, and everyone knew it. My heart broke for him as he spoke at the microphone emphasizing the progress Brockton had made in the short time he'd been mayor. He looked vulnerable, trying to beef up his remarks by rising up on his toes to emphasize certain points.

And if that wasn't bad enough, a short while later, the Human Resources Department at City Hall made a devastating discovery. Jack's pay raise had gone into effect six months too early. I got the news at home while I was preparing dinner—chicken fingers and French fries—for the kids. The woman who called felt awful giving me the bad news and I felt terrible taking it. After I hung up the kitchen phone, I continued preparing dinner as the reality of what she'd just told me began to sink in. Because of the oversight, Jack owed the City of Brockton $8,500.00, plus interest. For the first time in a long time, all I wanted to do was cry.

It was not possible to feel any worse about political life. After what Jack had just been through regarding the Superintendent's indiscretion, my hands shook as I slid the tray of fries into the hot oven. All of the original fears I had about the newspapers writing bad things about my husband were about to come true.

Sure enough, the editors had a field day.

A giant picture of Jack appeared on the front page of The Enterprise with the headline "Payback Time." The article insinuated that the original vote for the mayor's raise had been done "quietly." That was incorrect. I kept notes of all the meetings about the raise. Any bill that was finally passed went the same way, with public hearings, discussions and debates that carried on for weeks or months before a decision was made. The mistake here was that no one in the payroll department had looked into the rules regarding the distribution of the raise.

Right away the payroll department began to deduct the necessary amount from Jack's paycheck every week.

When I withdrew money from the ATM machine and saw for the first time what our new weekly deposit was, the song "Take My Breath Away," from the movie Top Gun, swirled in my ears.

I didn't know how Jack, or our whole family for that matter, could work any harder and have any less money. "I Am Barely Breathing," a popular song that summer, accompanied me as I made my way to the van where my four hungry children were deciding which fast food they wanted for dinner. When I pulled into the driveway instead of swinging by Taco Bell or Wendy's, they were taken aback. "Mom, what's the matter?" they asked over the rock and roll blasting from the radio. "You okay, Mom?"

I wasn't okay. I was seething in contempt. Screw everybody, I thought. I hated Brockton. I didn't want to save it anymore. I opened the pantry cupboard and found a large can of tuna. I opened the refrigerator door and there was no mayonnaise.

We canceled The Boston Globe and cut our cable service back to the basics.

On July 4th, I didn't feel like celebrating. I was ashamed of us Americans. Ashamed of the way we handled our leaders. Jack was attracting millions and millions of dollars worth of business, i.e. jobs, to a city of one hundred thousand people and now I was withering from the invisible faces sneering at us for earning $73,000.00 a year.

Jack was nearly as despondent as me. "For four weeks I endured being called a racist. Now I'm being called a thief," he said morosely, shaking his head. He was standing by his dresser, and I walked over to put my arms around him. Jack's reputation and integrity are everything to him. I hated seeing him so blue.

The family got invited to a pre-party at the Brockton Fair—where the owners, the George Carney family, treated city officials and friends to lobsters, barbecued chicken and free amusement rides—but Jack stayed home. He didn't want to see or talk to anybody. I took the kids because the opportunity for a free meal was irresistible, especially in light of the circumstances. Everyone I spoke with felt badly about the turn of events.

The kids and I discussed selling the house and buying something smaller, less expensive to heat. But there weren't many places I'd trade for where we were on Fairview Avenue. Jack and I also spoke about transferring our two oldest to Brockton High, but I felt bad for them because they liked the schools they were in and the friends they'd made.

It became hard for Jack to go in to City Hall every day, knowing that I was hurting and questioning the whole thing.

What's worse, now there was a guy running against Jack for mayor and we had a campaign ahead. That man called the radio stations demanding Jack's resignation. Fortunately, U.S. Congressman Bill Delahunt phoned Jack when he heard he was getting bashed around and told him to "hang in there." "Politics needs good people like you," Bill added. "Get through it."

In another act of kindness, a friend gave me tickets to the Red Sox, and I brought along Breck and a few friends. The four of us were sitting in the front row of one of the upper sections, and halfway through the game, Breck dropped a dollar down to the tier below us, just to see what would happen. "Breck!" I admonished him, "that's your dinner!" Or, at best, a peanut. The bill landed in the aisle and the guy sitting there picked it up and put it in his pocket.

When I looked away Breck threw another dollar down which fell onto a woman's plastic seat, landing behind her back. She didn't see the bill, but we kept an eye on her throughout the game. She had to be the least mobile person in the whole park. Didn't stand for the homerun, didn't stand for the seventh inning stretch.

Finally after the ninth inning, the woman rose to leave, walked back and forth a few times, sat again, then moved over and sat in the seat next to hers. She did everything but spy the dollar on her chair. We were hugely entertained for just one buck. I figured we'd get through this latest financial crisis, too.

While we were at the game, Jack stayed home and vacuumed the entire house. With all the other stresses he was coping with, all the work he continued doing, he was still thinking of how he could make my life easier. That's the kind of thoughtfulness he has for others.

Another cartoon appeared about him where he was smiling and holding a paper ticket. The caption read, "After the 15th illegal payment, you get the next one free." I canceled my subscription to The Enterprise.

In the middle of July, Jack attended a school committee meeting and someone brought up the Superintendent's issue again. It was like beating a dead horse. The meeting lasted until 11 p.m. Jack crawled into bed well after midnight, hugged me and kept saying he loved me. At 2:30 a.m., the phone rang. The caller was very drunk or strung out on drugs. He insisted on speaking with the mayor.

"This better be a hell of an emergency," I said. No more missus nice girl. It wasn't. He wanted something done about his "bad neighbors," and was loud and obnoxious. I had visions of him driving to our house and blowing us all away.

"Take This Job and Shove It" rang in my ears as I rolled over. What a terrible position being mayor was. I covered my head with a pillow. How were we going to survive? God. So many of our friends were financially sound. Here was Jack, using his many gifts to offer hope to a sinking city, and the end result was—we had no money and kept getting terrible phone calls. In frustration I twisted back around and lay flat on my back. Soon, I started to calm down and another tune began to float through my head—The Star Spangled Banner. I mentally sang through the words and that helped me appreciate and understand the flip side of politics. Someone has to do the hard work—fight the battle. Democracy is hard work. That song, more than any other, helped pull me through the following days.

Jack lost a lot of respect for the reporters who trashed him. Until that point, he had been overly obliging, but now he stopped returning their calls, and decided to play hardball and let them have nothing for a while. Instead, he turned his attention to crafting a speech announcing his decision to run again.

CHAPTER 13

*"The harder you work, the harder it is
to surrender."*
—Vince Lombardi

Friends and supporters helped Jack set up his new campaign headquarters downtown in the old Shawmut Bank building at the intersection of Main and Center Streets. The kids loved playing teller in the drive-up window because it still had a live microphone. "Yes, may I help you?" they'd ask their friends who tapped on the outside glass. Inside were old large vaults with doors two feet thick. Giant floor-to-ceiling windows offered good visibility to drivers-by. Jack's new campaign manager, Kelly Therien, a young, energetic woman, scrubbed the toilets that year in preparation for our opening, and mopped the floors. I vacuumed.

Every campaign drew a few peculiar people who latched onto the hoopla because, I believe, no one else would have them. One of the earliest visitors to our new headquarters was one of these—a man with a baldhead and several long pointed teeth. He'd hung around during our first campaign and now I knew to avoid him, although, of course, the door wasn't locked. He came in to tell me that some people thought there was a fake Mrs. Yunits running around with Jack. He said that sometimes she appeared "tan and great looking" and other times "pale and not-so-together."

"Gee, thanks," I said, laughing. From then on, whenever he saw me he'd ask if I was the "real Mrs. Yunits."

"Oh, yes," I'd always answer, hoping he'd just disappear.

Conor was very helpful to Jack and I as we gathered our spirits to take on another campaign. One evening, while we were at a State Championship Baseball Tournament—which the Brockton team won—Conor had wiped the pollen off the outdoor furniture in the screened-in porch and iced down a six-pack of beer for us. He also put a Bob Dylan CD in the stereo, which was playing when we returned. Teenagers can sometimes be thoughtful.

Mairi, for her part, finally learned to do a headstand. She'd been practicing for months and months—often imitating my yoga postures—and talked me into joining her one afternoon in the backyard. She planted her head on the green grass and hoisted her legs up towards the sky. I was balanced upright, also, facing her, and wishing I had a camera to capture the moment. She then wanted to do headstands facing away from each other, as well as side-by-side. We timed ourselves, too, and the whole time I was hoping Jack would come home and see his darling daughter and wife having fun together.

In spite of the recent attacks on Jack's integrity, the Boys and Girls Club gymnasium was overflowing with TV cameras and hundreds of people when he announced that he'd be running for mayor again. It was hotter than heck that day as the kids and I stood with Jack on a wobbly stage. He told the crowd that he was ready to go again and that he needed everyone's help to get re-elected for another two years. The clapping hands helped move the humid air around the room.

Assuming he were re-elected I felt that Jack should probably get out of politics after two terms. There were many haters in Brockton regardless of how good a mayor he was. The citizens group, for instance, that succeeded in getting Jack to squelch the Waste Transfer facility, was now supporting another candidate in the mayor's race—a bus driver. That candidate made fun of Jack on the radio saying that his many trips to Boston just weren't important. He had no idea that Jack met with state and federal legislators regularly to bring money to the city for roads, garages and/or hospitals, or that he conferred with businesspeople about building affordable housing and creating jobs.

In fact, on a dry beautiful day in August, I accompanied Jack to the Statehouse in Boston. He and seven members of the Emergency Finance Board were ushered into State Auditor Joseph DeNucci's office. I was allowed to sit nearby. Mr. DeNucci's secretary took notes as the Board talked about qualified bonds, or the borrowing power of a city. Jay Condon, Brockton's brilliant Chief Financial Officer, spoke to the group about Brockton's financial status, which was stable at the time. Jack talked next about the exciting things happening including the upcoming District Courthouse, the pending commuter rail, two new schools, a lower crime rate, and the property values, which were increasing steadily.

The board listened. The members asked a few questions and after a serious discussion the State Auditor addressed Jack:

"I just want to know one thing—how are those Boxers doing?" he asked, grinning. DeNucci himself was once an amateur boxer. He was referring, however, to Brockton's high school football team.

"They won the State Championship this year," Jack told him proudly. "Just like the baseball team did."

DeNucci then turned to the men and asked that they suspend the rules and vote in favor of the bonds right then and there. They did. All in favor! The process was very exciting to witness. Especially when the Massachusetts State Auditor say to Jack, "Congratulations on doing a great job in Brockton!"

On August 19, 1997, our campaign headquarters grand opening occurred the same day as the groundbreaking for the new Brockton District Courthouse.

What a day for the recovering city. The new governor, Paul Cellucci—who replaced Governor Weld when Weld resumed his law practice after losing to Senator Kerry—addressed the hundreds of people standing outdoors near the new Courthouse site. Jack spoke also, acknowledging the Honorable Judge George Covett, who initiated the process to build the new courthouse for Plymouth County seventeen years earlier. Jack had worked as Judge Covett's law clerk at that time. Now, years later, the Judge was retired and Jack was the mayor welcoming the citizenry to the groundbreaking. The words "inspirational" and "historical moment" went around in my head.

The tide had turned, I believed. Brockton was coming back. The Courthouse was a joint effort, but Jack's leadership had propelled a change in attitude around the city. Brocktonians were beginning to believe in themselves again and people were hopeful that Main Street had started a long awaited rebirth.

At the end of September, Jack and I, along with several elected officials, including our friends, State Representatives Geri Creedon and Tom Kennedy, rode the new commuter train from Brockton to Boston for the first time.

The delightful day began with a sunny, catered breakfast on the platform served by a local chef, Terrie Stone. Always dressed up and smiling, Terrie arranged fresh fruit, croissants and coffee on a white lace tablecloth. There were a few speeches, a ribbon cutting, and a ride to Boston so smooth no one's coffee spilled. An exhilarating feeling came over me again that history was in the making.

Jack's involvement with the commuter train began before he became mayor when he was a member of the 21st Century Corp. His expertise focused on where the stations should be located. He and a previous City Councilor, Joe Kelly, had arranged a bus trip to show Governor Weld and other officials where to put the stations, arguing that locating the platforms near reusable old buildings and factories would be beneficial once those places were rehabilitated. Indeed, several years later two such buildings became condominium complexes now perfect locations for commuters.

That fall, Jack's new radio commercials were recorded with train sounds in the background. Kids' voices (including Mairi's) shouted: "Brockton's coming Back, Jack! Brockton's Coming Back!"

One night, while waiting for Jack to come downstairs so we could drive to one of his political debates, I attempted to clean out my purse. What I found was a reflection of the life we were living.

In the outer pocket were two tickets to the annual Plymouth County Democratic breakfast, three bank deposit receipts from my law office, a podiatry appointment card, a pay stub, some "Re-elect Mayor Yunits" flyers, Mother Theresa prayer cards, half-stubs from a pancake breakfast, foot care instructions for Breck's sore toe, keys, a reminder to take my car for a check-up, dentist appointment cards, a song list with "Crazy" highlighted, a postcard about the Teresa Heinz conference on Women, Health and the Environment, a Charlie Horse Restaurant card entitling us to 8 free tokens, a Board of Bar Overseers membership card, a mortgage payment receipt, 3 free Whopper tickets to Burger King, a postcard telling of an upcoming artist's exhibit, a stub for a Domestic Violence Action Program dinner, a thank you note addressed to a girl who babysat for us, a note with a name and phone number of a woman author in Caffrey Towers, a schedule of play rehearsals at Massasoit College, yellow Post-It notes, a pink note with instructions for poison ivy medication, free bagel coupons, a gift card for flowers for Casey, a grocery list for her cast party, phone numbers of friends from a Canadian Mayor's conference, a flyer from the same, a business card for a candidate for state representative, a business card from the "Industrial Development Commission" of Taunton, names and phone numbers of volunteers for our campaign, gasoline receipts, a school shoes receipt, three crayons, 2 unsharpened pencils, 2 pens, a used band aid, 3 paper clips, one hair elastic, 2 dimes and a guitar pick.

Inside the purse itself was one bottle of expired fluoride tablets, a liquor purchase receipt, a Supercuts punch card, a Filene's basement receipt, two checkbooks, one date book, a calculator, a receipt for Chinese food, a disintegrating library card, more bank deposits and withdrawal receipts, a calendar for sign holding, a pack of our kids' pictures, social security cards, a bagel club punch card, bank books, a sneakers receipt, a pack of business cards held together with a rubber band, the back-up disc of my office files, a beautiful watch in need of repair, two lipsticks, some matches, a mint wrapped in an

American flag foil, a Supreme coffee and donuts punch card, a pack of credit cards, my driver's license, and $2.38 in change.

Before I could do anything besides toss out the fluoride tablets, we were in the car rushing to the debate.

For the next two months, Jack and I attended coffee hours, tree plantings, fundraisers, celebrations, Cape Verdean dinners, Mairi's soccer games, Casey's concerts and the boys' football games. One morning the Temple Beth Emunah held a mayoral forum. The Jewish men who organized the event guided Jack into the kitchen to give him a shot of Schliver, a brandy from Yugoslavia, before he took to the stage. I got a kick out of that. When I mentioned it to my friend, Ellie, she exclaimed, "Oh, sure. The breakfast of champions!"

Closer to the election, I enjoyed a day being home alone changing everyone's bed sheets, straightening the kids' rooms, vacuuming and scrubbing the bathrooms. I felt an overwhelming joy. Call it maternal instinct, motherly devotion, or just plain contentment I loved being home alone with my thoughts, caring for the most important people in my life. Puttering around my children's rooms inspired quiet reflection. I remembered in particular an episode with Breck, whom I'd just taken over to Macy's department store to buy him some clothes.

He was in the middle of a major growth spurt, with sneakers a size 9½ and the top of his head reaching my eyebrows. He walked through the main door ahead of me into the store and let the door close in my face. I stopped him in the vestibule.

"Breck," I said, "it's polite to hold the door for the person behind you."

"Oh, okay," he responded, and then let the second door shut in my face. I stood there waiting for him to realize his mistake, but he didn't. He kept walking. His thirteen-year-old mind was elsewhere. As I watched him saunter away I could tell my little boy wasn't yet used to his growing body. He fiddled with the bottom of his shirt, clumped forward in his too-big sneakers, and bobbed his head as he ducked around shoppers. I cherished the vision of part-boy, part-man—so lovable.

Jack won his second election in a landslide with seventy-nine percent of the vote. We were ecstatic at our victory party at Sidelines restaurant where everyone from the different camps gathered once the polls closed.

The crowd joined me in singing "16 Tons," "On Vacation For A Week," and the Pat Barnes Hearing Aid Commercial I had written and recorded months earlier. All the candidates for City Council and School Committee, winners and losers, poured in to the party. I kept looking around thinking, "What a team! The Brockton Team!" There were so many people that the bartenders served warm beer in bottles when they ran out of cold ones.

The biggest news coming out of the election was that Wayne Carter became the first African-American in the history of Brockton to be elected to public office as a member of the School Committee. Wayne was a kind, gentle man with big saucer eyes who was full of hugs when he saw me. His supporters came to our party, too, and the crowd was overjoyed as everyone mingled together. The next day, The Enterprise adorned the front-page with an impressive picture of Wayne and his campaign people noting the historical moment. Below that was a smaller picture of Jack, who mentioned in an article that he'd definitely be running again in two years. It seemed the more he accomplished the more he wanted to accomplish. I suggested we talk about his decision during our getaway to Martha's Vineyard.

"If there is one thing that will always stand out in my mind, it's Jack's deep love and affection for the city of Brockton. The job was really never about him—it was always about helping a city reconnect with its great heritage and character. That is the way I will always remember his tenure as mayor."

—Massachusetts Congressman William Delahunt

CHAPTER 14

*"The future belongs to those who believe in
the beauty of their dreams."*
—Eleanor Roosevelt

On the island of Martha's Vineyard, specifically Chappaquiddick, where Jack
and I ferried to after the election, it was easy to imagine what life would be like
one day when politics was behind us. Jack would stay industrious, that's for
sure, as evidenced by his current motion. He brought a tape player out to the
deck where I was sitting with my glass of merlot and popped in a Frank Sinatra
cassette. He then started gathering kindling from the scrub pines in preparation
for a Nor-easter', collecting enough wood to keep the woodstove burning
through a New England rainstorm. But Jack's idea of staying put as the rain
thrashed outside meant that he started the next day with a six-mile run on the
beach. I stayed warm and cozy, indoors.

Once back in Brockton, we marched in the Veteran's Day parade and
afterwards met up with friends at The Pub. "The feeling is great out there, real
up—real strong," our good friend, Mark, said afterwards, in reference to the
city's cheerful atmosphere. Indeed, there were more people at that parade,
lining the streets, than I'd yet seen, definitely a sense that Brockton was getting
back on track.

Soon the busy winter holidays were upon us and weekends gave Jack no
time to rest and rejuvenate. By Monday morning he started that awful choking
sound again. I grimaced.

"What's the matter? Why are you making that noise?" I asked from across the bed.

"I can't breathe," he told me, rolling off his side, placing his feet on the floor and standing up.

"Why not?"

"My nose is stuffed up," he said, limping out from the bedroom.

"Then breathe through your mouth!" I called out. I've been doing yoga for years—even before we met each other. You'd think he'd take a cue, and a deep breath once in a while. But, his nervousness, or energy, whatever that spark is inside his frame, rules him—makes him who he is.

Soon Breck and Conor were helping Jack empty his campaign headquarters and bringing the copy machine home where it stood on the floor of our kitchen for weeks. Among other uses, Breck found it especially entertaining to copy pictures of dollar bills and paste Mairi's face on them.

It was this machine I made my way around, as I left to attend Brockton's first "Red, White and Black Ball," wearing a tantalizing black dress and coat I'd bought on the Vineyard. With my long red satin gloves I felt especially sexy and elegant, because that event was like no other. City Hall had been transformed! The high ceilings, the sculpted rotunda, the Revolutionary War paintings now were mere backdrops to the intimate couches and cocktail tables that were set out on the basement level. At the event, a quartet played classical music to entertain the guests. On the first floor, sounds from the high school orchestra filled the air, and on the second, thousands of tiny white lights hung between statues of Greek gods and goddesses, making the setting more intimate and romantic. Men and women in exquisite attire lingered on the wide marble staircases. Caterers passed around trays of hot hors d'oeuvres. We could hear squeals of laughter as friends were reunited for the first time since high school.

Jack initiated the idea behind the ball, and his committee ran with the concept, choosing to model the event after San Francisco's Black and White Ball. The event was simply magical. Jack, however, dressed in a handsome tux, ended up standing in the mayor's office for hours as people took pictures with him or asked for his autograph. He didn't have as much fun as I did.

Later in the evening, the pulsating crowd was rocking to the sounds of a local band, "Dale and the Duds," when Dale spied me on the dance floor and encouraged me to get up on stage and sing my song "On Vacation For A Week." Before I knew it, I was propelled up and so began pulling my long red gloves off my hands in order to play the guitar. The band broke into a striptease song. Ah, what the heck. I slowed down, peeled each glove off seductively—while whistles and hoots filled the hall—and tossed the gloves into the audience. There was a hilarious uproar, and when I finally started playing the guitar and singing, everyone sang along. People were so energized by the new Brockton energy that those who weren't at the Ball could hardly believe what they missed.

The next day, Jack told me that a very attractive woman tried to seduce him in the elevator. Oh, sure. Another one, I thought. Being mayor was definitely a chick magnet. And Jack's openness about them all could sometimes try my patience. But because he shared these incidents with me, it defused any jealousies I might have otherwise harbored. I believe, also, that his honesty kept him faithful, and that was good enough for me.

"Jack and Lees Yunits, as a young couple and family, gave the city of Brockton hope and promise that the city could become a better place for middle class families to live and raise their children. Both Lees and Jack brought a cultural presence and an educational presence to the city and Brockton is a better place for it."

—State Representative Geraldine Creedon

CHAPTER 15

"Never let the fear of striking out get in your way"
—Babe Ruth

I was used to being the city's doormat by then so when I picked up the phone one day and heard a woman complaining about the roads in Brockton, I figured I'd just let her vent. But she went on and on and on. I empathized and tried explaining nicely that streets take time and money to fix. But she didn't like that answer. I told her Brockton had more than 300 miles of pavement. "No!" she screamed, working herself up. "Something has to be done today!" I told her the highway department had repair schedules. But she wanted them fixed right now!

"If I could wave a magic wand I would," I pleaded, twirling the phone cord around my neck.

"We don't even fix potholes!" she screeched, going over the edge. "Politicians should take a year and do nothing else but replace roads!" I actually agreed with her, but she was beyond listening. Finally I asked where she lived.

"Whitman," she told me—the next town over.

Great, I'd just wasted time over a loony tune who didn't even live in Brockton! "Thanks for calling," I said meekly, untwisting the cord and replacing the receiver.

Perhaps it was particularly stressful at that time because our whole family was being pulled in every direction. Mairi had started ice skating lessons, Casey was in rehearsals for "The King and I," Conor was coaching Little League and had begun a new job at Hoyt's Movie Theatre, and Breck was designing a website for Brockton's first Jazz Festival. My schedule at the law office consumed four days a week, and, of course, every night I accompanied Jack to one function after another.

Citywide, construction continued for the Courthouse, the new Transportation Terminal, and two elementary schools. A Dunkin' Donuts set up shop near the Courthouse site, and I counted our lucky stars that Brockton had finally entered the twentieth century, never mind facing the 21st!

At Christo's restaurant on the east side of town, one day some customers were talking about Brockton. "You know why so much building is going on?" one fella said, with a mouthful of Greek salad. "Because the mayor gets one percent of everything that comes in!"

"Yep, that's right," I wanted to tell him, "and that check must be in Charlie's pocket on the MTA! ("Did he ever return? No, he never returned!") Now, wipe your chin!"

Jack called me from his car phone one afternoon to say he had just heard the song, "Wind Beneath My Wings," and was thinking of me. Funny, that's how I felt about him, too, I said. We were each other's support through all that was going on, and yet we'd been so busy there hadn't been much time for romance, or even to share our worlds. I had yet to tell him about my dream where ex-Beatle Paul McCartney and I felt a sexual attraction toward one another!

Oh, I had so much to share with Jack. But our time would have to wait because Jack flew off to Washington, D.C. again to meet with some Massachusetts Congressmen. The excursion was a productive one, especially because he had a chance meeting with a man from Chicago who was interested in building a minor-league baseball stadium in Brockton. Jack had been thinking about bringing professional baseball to our city ever since he met with Mayor Mike Albano from Springfield, MA. Mike's city was getting a team, so Jack wanted one, too.

Jack took off the following weekend to attend Mark's son's wedding in New Jersey, and I stayed home to enjoy some quiet time with the kids. Casey helped me make chocolate chip cookies and the kids and I played the board game "Life." I got a call from a constituent who requested that I throw the first pitch for the Brookville Little League on opening day, since Jack was away. It was a touching request and I was giddy about the idea. The organizer called me the day before the game with instructions to be at the field by 10. Gotcha.

During the night, however, Casey came down with a fever and sore throat and I was placing cool cloths on her head and giving her Tylenol. The next day Conor had baseball practice and Breck needed a ride to his job at the golf course. By the time I remembered the first pitch I was two hours late!

"Shit!" I yelled, throwing down a dishtowel. I grabbed the phone to call the man and tell him how sorry I was. I asked what else I could do to make good on my word—sing for the kids, read to them, poke myself in the eye with a box cutter, anything.

Two weeks later, while performing for a crowd at the Special Olympics opening ceremony, I forgot the words to the Star Spangled Banner. There is nothing worse.

I was standing outside in the cold, shivering, and couldn't stop my jaw from shaking while waiting to sing. The special athletes were spread out behind me in a long row. The second I started singing, I realized that the microphone had a significant delay, so I slowed the song down to compensate. But the echo from the speakers was throwing my words back at me and suddenly I had flubbed the lyrics. I froze. There was a short second's pause and behind me a young man yelled, "Hey, those aren't the right words!"

"You're right!" I said, looking for help. "Would you sing it with me?" (Please, please, please). And they did! All the athletes joined in! They sang with complete abandon and the result was gorgeous. I wanted to hug each and every one of them.

"Good save," someone said later, but it was little solace. No one flubs the National Anthem. My musical days were numbered.

Jack called from the road later that afternoon and after hearing my tale of woe, he crooned, "You know, honey, I love you more than anything in the whole world?"

Where did I find him? "Thanks hubby," I responded. "Does this mean you'll visit me at the funny farm?"

The next day I sang the National Anthem again at South Little League's opening day. Fortunately I got the words right and regained a shred of my dignity.

During the night, however, I dreamt about a man playing a guitar. He looked like George Clooney, the actor, and played the instrument with his fingers flying everywhere. When the man finished, he indicated he had performed his masterpiece and was putting his guitar down forever. I interpreted the dream to mean that my musical goals were now officially on the back burner. Jack's ambitions for the city had won over.

CHAPTER 16

"A woman's life can really be a succession of lives, each revolving around some emotionally compelling situation or challenge, and each marked off by some intense experience."
—Wallis Simpson, Duchess of Windsor

Warmer weather began to brighten our days as Mairi, who was on a synchronized ice-skating team at Asiaf rink, practiced her "spins" while waiting at the bus stop. I found myself staring at her, overcome with feelings of deep love. She twirled and jumped and I wanted to freeze time—I prayed she would always be adorable and entertaining. My other kids had passed that stage of life and I could barely remember their younger selves. I think that must have been God's plan to keep mothers from missing their babies too much.

It was especially trying with Casey then because in her "terrible teens" she often shrugged off my hugs and kisses. The best time to express my love was when I woke her up for school. I'd stroke her satin-soft cheeks and kiss her forehead. She didn't push me away then. Maybe it was a coincidence, but we both acted more kindly to one another when I did that.

Looking around her bedroom one morning I absorbed the essence of my 16-year-old daughter's life. The long room was divided between her and Mairi's sides by a low, white wicker table. The table held an array of colorful candles. Casey was fascinated by candles and spent hours sitting on the floor lighting them and playing with the wax. I reminded her to be extremely careful. The walls of their room were covered with paper—mostly poems and proverbs illustrated by Casey's friend, Shannon. Mairi was "allowed," by her sister, to display one poster—of the ice skater, Tara Lipinski. Another large poster of Leonardo DeCaprio, the star of "Titanic," the new blockbuster movie, took up most of the space on a fourth wall.

Conor, who worked at the movie theater, gave me two tickets to see "Titanic," and throughout the tense movie I had a strong urge to be with my kids, to love and protect them. When Jack and I drove our car out of the theater parking lot, I spied Conor atop a movie marquee structure twelve feet high in the air putting up the letters for the premier of "Godzilla." Not exactly the best way to relieve my parental anxiety.

That night, Jack yelled out in his sleep and jumped out of bed. He said he had a leg cramp. I felt it was more indicative of a stress nightmare caused by his unrelenting duties, and couldn't wait to take him to Canada in August for an annual mayors' conference. Flying over Prince Edward Island, we could see the gorgeous red sand beaches sparkling in the sun. I knew Jack would get some down time finally, free from city worries and family obligations. When we got to our room, he began unpacking his suitcase and putting his clothes into the drawers. "Jack, it's a beautiful summer day. Let's go for a walk," I said, pulling his arm. He obliged. When we returned from the walk to change our clothes for dinner, the message light was blinking on our room phone.

"Uh, oh," I said, dropping my purse on the bed, praying there hadn't been a murder in Brockton.

A voice urged one of us to call the front desk ASAP. Jack learned that there was a serious matter at home and was given our neighbor's phone number. He placed the call.

Casey got on the phone quickly, but she was crying so hard Jack couldn't understand her. "It's okay, honey, it's okay," he kept repeating, but wouldn't tell me anything. Suddenly I knew. I was sure of it. Mairi had drowned! She had drowned in our neighbor's swimming pool! Why else would Casey be calling from there and be so hysterical? I tried to grab the phone but Jack stopped me.

"Jack! Where's Mairi?" I asked, holding my breath, my heart pounding. Lots of different people were talking to him by then. In bits and drabs the story was unfolding.

Fire, candles . . .

"Jack! Tell me!" I shouted, feeling panic rising from my knees.

"Okay, Chief. Thank you," he said to the Chief of Police. Finally he said, "Mairi's okay, she's been found, everyone's okay." I stared at him, and plunked down on the bed.

"There's been a fire," he managed, although now he was talking with Bob Finnegan, the Building Superintendent. Turns out that nearly half the city was at the fire scene. Everyone, that is, except my parents, who were still in route from New Jersey to babysit our kids! They had had car trouble and hadn't yet arrived.

When I was finally allowed to speak with Casey she was inconsolable. In pieces, I learned that a fire had started from the candles on her wicker table. "Casey, how could you let that happen?" I asked, incredulous.

"Mom, it wasn't me! It was my friend," she said.

"What do you mean? Which friend?" Casey sniffled and said she'd called a friend to babysit Mairi because she got asked to work unexpectedly at the movie theater. It was the babysitter who lit some candles on the wicker table and forgot to blow them out. In a sick way, I felt better about that. Not my kid's fault.

Mairi got on the phone then, and in a tiny voice asked if I knew where her favorite stuffed animal, "Zulu," was—the pink and green striped critter she took everywhere. I told her I'd thrown him on her bed before we left. Now both Zulu and her bed were gone. It was heart-breaking to be so far away from our kids at a time like that.

There was no plane home until the next morning. Thankfully, my sister, Cynthia, who worked in Boston, had heard the news on the radio and drove swiftly to Brockton. She rounded up the kids and they'd spent the night at the nearby Holiday Inn. Mary Waldron drove our girls to the airport the next day and when Jack and I arrived we simply clung to one another. When we arrived at the house, news people followed Jack and me inside. I asked if that was necessary and the photographer said other people might benefit from seeing what happened as the result of candles left unattended.

The kitchen looked normal to me when we entered and I started to question what all the fuss was about until I passed through the den and reached the main staircase. The unmistakable smell hit my nostrils. I paused halfway up the stairs as the calamity began to sink in. The white rounded walls of the turret were scorched with black inky lines dripping to the floor. The upstairs hall looked like a cave. The girls' room was charred so severely the plaster had broken up into discolored splotches. Burned mattresses, toys, lamps, night tables, and two closet doors lay in a gross, wet heap in the backyard. Several of us walked cautiously around upstairs, as the photographer took pictures and a reporter from The Enterprise scribbled notes. Smoke residue permeated every medicine cabinet, light fixture, and toilet in all three bathrooms upstairs. Streaks of a tar-like substance ran into the tubs. Every square inch of Breck's room—which was closest to the girls'—had smoke damage. The girls' clothes were piled high on Breck's bed. There was nothing worth saving—not even their First Communion dresses. Our bedroom was hideous—the dresser and bed were layered with filth, all the windows were broken. I guessed the firemen had tried to get the smoke out of the room by smashing the glass. The closet contents all had soot damage. Conor's room at the end of the long hall survived the best, although there too, the smoke had made its way into and around the exposed beams and built-in window seat.

Several people told us the firemen had been dealing with a truly dangerous situation. That between the slate roof and the cement walls, the girls' room had been an inferno. Luckily the fire was contained there.

But we now faced a grueling uphill climb to put our home back together.

The panic-stricken babysitter couldn't talk through her tears when we called her. As upsetting as it was, I told her that her error could have happened to anyone. I emphasized that she'd been hired to watch Mairi and that Mairi was safe and we were grateful. She calmed down a little, but never said a word, just sniffed. The newspaper printed her picture the next day and included her name, a grossly insensitive mistake. The poor girl, the tone implied, not only caused a fire, but she destroyed the mayor's house. My prayers went out to her and her parents. I believe they must have thought we would sue them, though, because we never heard from them again.

Friends started showing up. Andrea Bates, the Executive Director of the Brockton Symphony, gave me folders and pens so I could keep track of all the details that would follow. An attorney from my office, Kim DeVeau, brought us homemade lasagna, and Ginny and Frank, our neighbors, insisted we stay in their home across the street while we figured out our next step. Jack was deeply glum but got right to work. He sprayed the bees in the attic so he could re-cover the vents and the next day he and Breck paid a visit to the fire stations to thank the firemen.

Our first night at Ginny's, Casey crawled into my bed during the wee hours. "I want to go home," she sobbed. I wrapped her in my arms. "Mom, sixteen years of my life was in that room! Everything I had—the notes from my friends, my pictures from childhood, my scripts, playbills, programs, all my awards are gone!" I pulled her closer as tears streamed from her eyes to her mouth. "All I want is to be lying in my own bed talking to my friends on the phone and I can't!" Her sorrow devastated me.

She also kept reliving the episode when Breck suddenly appeared at the cinema where she was working yelling, "Casey, our house is on fire! Where's Mairi?" During the ride from the cinema to the house, she learned the awful details from Breck—how he walked into the house thinking everything was all right and that Mairi was upstairs, playing in her room, until he smelled the smoke. He had realized the bedroom was on fire. All Casey could think was that her sister had escaped into a closet or crawled under a bed. She couldn't shake the awful image the worst of her imagination had whipped up: of firemen bringing Mairi out in a body bag. The most terrible day in her life had occurred and I hadn't been there with her, for her.

"When Dad called, everyone wanted to talk to him, and I was getting so mad," she recalled. "I wanted my mother!" I hugged her tighter, crying myself by then. We talked about how the babysitter forgot to blow the candles out before she took Mairi for a walk. It wasn't until the two were headed home and saw the fire engines racing by them that the young teen realized her mistake.

Casey said that Mairi was a different person until Jack and I got home. She wouldn't eat or drink, and barely spoke. Breck was traumatized too, imagining his baby sister upstairs and being unable to save her. He'd been forced to flee when he heard the bedroom window explode. Conor, bless him, had wanted to spend the night at the house to keep the contents safe from would be robbers, but the home was uninhabitable because of the smoke residue.

Days later the insurance adjustors finished recording the contents of our home and Jack ordered a 40-yard dumpster for the backyard. For three hours he loaded the burned debris. He was covered with soot and sweat when he returned to Ginny's, but slept better than he had in days.

Cars drove by constantly after The Enterprise wrote "Memories Go Up in Smoke." They also printed a map showing the location of our house. Over the next few days, Jack and I guided a steady stream of people through. The smoke destruction was something to see. Of course, I let people know that underneath the rubble the home was immaculate. All the beds were made, and the laundry was put away, I swear.

On the "Metro News," we watched a rerun of a TV clip showing a fireman in the girls' room battling a blaze and striking the ceiling with an ax as smoke billowed from the window. That was a scary sight.

Still the beat of the city pulsed on. That was early August 1998, and without warning, the high school principal resigned. Then Jack's Cultural Affairs Director quit.

Mary labeled City Hall as "absolutely crazy." To heighten his staff's anxiety, the new Republican Governor Paul Cellucci vetoed a library bill and denied a request to replace a generator at a senior high-rise apartment building. The public rallied against the Governor when he came to Brockton.

When Jack threw out his back trying to push a sleeper-couch through the window of the girls' room (the couch I was saving for my Cape house) I wondered how much more he could take. I was having post-traumatic stress disorder myself imagining spiders coming down from the ceiling and crawling on me. Mairi was sleeping with us often, too, and I got so frustrated one night I bit her on the nose—lightly, of course.

Thank God for Frank and Ginny's peaceful home. We had the place to ourselves because the two of them lived at the Cape during the summer. So for the month of August, every morning before the kids awoke, I'd sit on the blue sectional couch in Ginny's den overlooking the pond, enjoying my coffee and watching the ducks and geese swimming in circles. Every other hour was spent making decisions about the house, or preparing the kids for school, which was soon about to resume.

Mairi, bless her heart, was battling some inner demons. One day, while swimming in the neighbor's pool, she heard sirens, flew out of the pool and ran across the street to be with me at Ginny's. I was in the tub and she got right in. Then jumped out. Then she motioned for us to be together on the couch. When Jack and I tried to talk with her, she wanted to be back at the pool—outside immediately—and with music playing. She was having a difficult time and couldn't express herself verbally.

But she revealed to me that she loved ice-skating because she didn't have to stand still when the teacher was helping someone else and she was free to glide around. She loved to glide, she said. I encouraged Mairi to keep skating.

Jack continued his 6-mile runs, helping to maintain the stamina he needed to lead the city. One Saturday morning I was at the house sorting through some stuff that had been marginally damaged by the fire when he called unexpectedly.

I picked up the receiver gingerly so as not to get black fingerprints all over it. I could tell he was enraged because he asked me to find City Solicitor Tom Plouffe's phone number right away. Of course there was no phone book in the house so I couldn't help him.

He'd had a confrontation with a contractor at D.W. Field Park. A bulldozer was knocking down trees and Jack went ballistic. He yelled at the driver to stop and when he wouldn't Jack threw rocks at the tractor.

"This isn't how a mayor should act!" the guy shouted at Jack, adding, "I gave to your first campaign!"

Jack didn't care. He had met with the guy previously about his plans to build four new homes near the park and they had verbally agreed that nothing would be done until Jack had researched the legal issues. Now the contractor had gone back on his word and the demolition was affecting Brockton's beautiful public land.

"Good for you, Jack," I told him. "Finally someone is standing up for Brockton. What guts you have."

Jack was able to summon the police there to enforce the failed "gentleman's agreement" and then drove to the City Solicitor's house. The attorney chuckled when he heard the story, but advised Jack not to get in any more fights, that he was "wound too tight."

The apartment we rented at the beginning of September took up the entire second floor of our friends, Michael and Barbara Palladino's, enormous old stucco house at the corner of West Elm Street and Moraine, about a mile from our home. The rambling space with light maple wood floors and large windows was unfurnished, so by the time we moved in, I'd bought towels, sheets, blankets, lamps, clothes, school books, school supplies, shoes, cleats, an iron and ironing board, a toaster, a coffee maker, a round dining table, a card table with four chairs, pillows, CD's, an electric piano, a CD player, a sofa table, a fan, a mop, five mattresses, and a toilet bowl brush.

During the first week of Casey's junior year at Cardinal Spellman, the school had a fire drill. Casey was suddenly grabbed from her line and taken to the office. As part of the drill, a teacher had to pull a student from the lines and then the other teachers had to figure out who was missing and where they were. But that action was too close a reminder of what Casey had just been through causing her to get emotional. When the teacher realized what she'd done she felt terrible and brought Casey into a quiet room to sit down. All the school officials surrounded her apologizing profusely. The nuns said they'd picked Casey because they knew she'd be someone they could chat with while the rest of the teachers figured out who was missing! We laughed about it later, but at the time the incident was traumatic.

I was determined to get the family back home by Thanksgiving, but on any given day, more action went on in the mayor's life than could be imagined. That month alone, three major companies agreed to build in Brockton—a Marriott Residence hotel, a medical office building near Route 24, and a petroleum recycling company.

To top if off, New England Development finally signed a Purchase and Sales Agreement for the nearly vacant Westgate Mall. The corporation had been reluctant to buy the mall due to the area's deterioration, but Jack and other professionals met with them steadily for more than two years, until they convinced the principals that the city was on the rebound and politically stable. The contract signing was another important step on the road to Brockton's recovery.

One morning I awoke from a dream so suddenly that when I jumped out of bed my arms were asleep. In the dream someone else had had a fire, too, and their insurance adjustor gave them a hundred and twenty thousand dollars, although there wasn't any damage to their home—it was clean as a whistle. The same adjustor told me we might not get anything because I "took an advance." The dream so closely portrayed our pay raise fiasco it was unnerving.

And, lest we were to get too comfortable living out of boxes away from home, rumors started that City Councilor Martha (Marty) Crowell was seriously thinking of running for mayor against Jack. I wanted to pull her hair out because of the mental stress those rumors added to our current agony. Instead, I messed up my own hair by choosing the wrong highlights. I didn't have the money or time to fix the problem before showing up at the elegant 100th anniversary party for a popular office supply store, W.B. Mason's. I felt self-conscious with two wide strips of artificially blond hair framing my face.

On our 21st wedding anniversary in October, Jack had another run-in with his former Cultural Affairs Director, who technically resigned in August, but who continued to go in to City Hall. The squabble had something to do with the Rocky Marciano homestead, though Jack wasn't forthcoming with details. He only said, "She quit the day of our house fire and now she's screwed up our anniversary." He was madder than I'd ever seen him and vowed never to hire another friend.

Fortunately, he agreed to celebrate our wedding anniversary by going to the Monet exhibit at the Museum of Fine Arts in Boston. Jack loves Impressionism and I felt it would be good for both of us to get away, which it was. We even bought a colorful print to hang in our bedroom once we got back in our own home.

I couldn't wait to have our normal lives back again. I knew Mairi would be all right, once she saw how the house was being restored. The girls' room walls and ceiling were replaced and painted a cheerful white. There was also light blue wall-to-wall carpeting installed. Except in Conor's room.

Conor, Breck and I were laughing one night at the rented apartment as Conor recreated our conversation about the rug he wanted for his room.

"Hey, Conor, what color rug do you want?" he said, mimicking me in a high voice.

"Blue, I'd like a blue rug. I think blue. Yep, blue's my choice. Love blue," he said. "But I got beige!"

Well, the way I figured it, there was too much blue and besides, he'd be going off to college soon. If I wanted to turn his room into a guest room, beige seemed more neutral. But he never let me forget his disappointment.

During our stay in the apartment, the song "Broke Into the Old Apartment," by the Barenaked Ladies, was on the radio a lot and reminded the kids and me of our situation. Mairi also sang another song by the Barenaked Ladies called "She's On Time." I told her the words were inappropriate for her to be singing because of what the song meant. She wanted an explanation and was very eager to learn, so I pulled her onto my lap facing me and told her about menstruation. After a minute she had a question.

"If you have a baby every month, would you not get your period?" she wondered, playing with the buttons on my top.

"That's right, you wouldn't," I said, "but the chance of having a baby every month is zero." That seemed to relieve her.

We didn't talk about intercourse, by any means, but after a minute she whispered in my ear that she knew how babies were made. Standing up, she wiggled her butt and spelled out with a big smiling face "S-E-X."

Later that night, a few of us were watching the video "Look Who's Talking, Too," which had lots of sexual references and nine-year-old Mairi kept giving me big, knowing smiles.

One night after a meeting, Jack stopped at The Pub still believing he could have a relaxing drink there until several regulars peppered him with questions. Joe, the bartender, asked them to stop, but they wouldn't. One man in particular kept harping on about downtown. Jack told him the downtown business owners needed to invest some money to keep their buildings in pace with the times in order to attract better tenants. The conversation turned sour and finally in frustration Jack left his drink on the bar and walked out.

He got to the apartment completely drained. "I just want to go home," he groaned.

Jack's running bud, Mark, was there and the three of us sat side-by-side on our new king-size bed. There aren't many people I can say I've done that with, but there was no place else to sit. Jack was at the end of his rope.

I worked as fast as I could and the day before we moved home, I was at our house guiding deliveries and unpacking bags of sheets and towels enjoying their clean fragrance when suddenly I heard Conor's voice coming from the kitchen.

"Breck, keep going, don't let Mom see us," he said. The boys were huffing up the back stairs with a mattress hoisted over their heads. They'd already emptied their apartment bedroom and were moving home a day before the rest of us. I loved their spunk.

CHAPTER 17

"I'm a home girl. I like to stay home."
—Faith Hill

In the four months since the fire, our house had been painted, sanded, scrubbed, planed, papered, stained, polished, carpeted, tiled, and rewired. The walls had been plastered and spackled; grout had been applied and everything had been touched up. I'd had my fill of making decisions and was utterly sick of defining myself by what items I could buy in stores.

Yet, my time had paid off nicely and being under our own roof again was priceless. We were home! And we had about thirty delicious minutes to enjoy our space before getting ready to attend the 2nd annual "Red, White and Black Ball." Most of the attendees knew from reading the paper that we were back in our house, which was a good conversation opener. Funny how I got so aggravated when the newspaper printed mistruths, and then when they printed something uplifting, all was forgiven—at least temporarily. It was a shame that the paper didn't have a more consistent positive outlook.

The following morning I awoke and stretched my arms, feeling a bit like Cinderella who'd just been to a ball (oh wait, I had). Rolling a yoga mat out at the foot of the bed I marveled at our newly refinished furniture and the light yellow and blue wallpaper. The messy gunk was finally gone, leaving but the barest whiff of smoke in the upstairs hallway. That, too, would soon be just a memory.

As much as we wanted to spend time in our new home, Jack and I had multiple obligations that kept us out night after night.

That same Sunday, for instance, St. Casimir's church celebrated their 100th Jubilee. Jack and I sat on hard, metal chairs and were treated to several speeches, and finally to the singing of a beautiful Lithuanian song while children danced in traditional costumes.

We left there for a ribbon cutting at the new Salvation Army building. A full brass band played while the congregation sang hymns. We were so exhausted that we were on the verge of nodding off. Finally we excused ourselves to pick up Mairi from the skating rink.

That week we also attended a Brockton Hospital fundraising Gala at Stonehill College, Attorney Paul Finn's Christmas party, the Brockton Symphony's Christmas Pops (I helped lead the sing-along with Andrea Bates), Mairi's piano recital, The Charity Guild's annual luncheon, another sing-along at The Little Red Schoolhouse, the Fuller Museum's Gala, our neighborhood's Christmas party, the first ever "Jingle Bell Run Road Race," a fundraiser at Christo's Restaurant, and our friend, Mary Buchanan's, holiday party.

Brockton's first snowfall of the season fell the day before Christmas Eve. I braced for the usual onslaught of belligerent phone calls, but not one citizen called our house. It was a miracle! I was so grateful. My six-member family was peacefully together and the holiday was without incident—truly my favorite one. I knew the following year Conor would be off to college and from then on, little by little our family togetherness would begin to fragment. I took extra care to enjoy every fleeting moment.

Jack continued running in the park through the winter, regardless of ice and snow, and was determined to keep all the projects in the city on track. The Brockton District Courthouse was looking more magnificent every day and the new BAT Bus Terminal was about to open. I greeted City Councilor Peter Asiaf at the dry cleaners who said to me: "It's not like Brockton was 30 years ago, but it's getting there!" Grabbing my hand he added, "People say it's all because of Jack, and they're right!"

Yet, try as he might, Jack couldn't win every argument.

One issue he lost was a judge's ruling that the mayor couldn't prevent adult entertainment from coming to the city. A local restaurant, "Frank's," wanted to add a nude dancing club, "The Foxy Lady," to its establishment, and some who live in the vicinity were vehemently opposed. Jack submitted a zoning ordinance requiring such places be relegated to an industrial zone—namely down by the Waste Water Treatment Plant—but to no avail. As a compromise he was able to work a deal with the owner of the Foxy Lady who agreed to contribute tens of thousands of dollars to the Brockton Public Library, the Senior Center, and the High School Bandboosters Club—quite a nice concession, if you ask me.

Shortly after that, Jack gave a speech at the Thorny Lea Golf Club, whose members were trying to decide whether to tear down the existing clubhouse and replace it with a more deluxe one. He convinced the "hold-outs" to build something valuable for "those who will follow," as he put it, like the men and women who "did it for us a hundred years ago." His commentary seemed to have worked because construction plans began shortly thereafter.

The following week, The Enterprise published a good article about Jack's desire to bring a baseball stadium to Brockton—his "Field of Dreams" the paper said. The mayor from Springfield, Mike Albano, was quoted as saying that it had taken him eight years to lure a stadium to his city and that construction still hadn't started. Knowing that Jack had already begun meeting with league officials, he suspected that the Brockton project would get done faster.

In Jack's State of the City speech in early January 1999, he told the audience: "Together we've made the city turn around." He emphasized that there were many challenges ahead, especially for the school system, and that teachers and administrators seemed up to the task.

"It is with great pride that I come before you tonight with the confidence that if ever Brockton has lived up to its legacy as the City of Champions, it is now," Jack said.

He spoke about the upcoming Rocky Marciano tributes to be held during the month of May and concluded: "Join me in this ongoing quest to restore greatness in our community."

He and I flew to D.C. again for the U.S. Conference of Mayors, and while he met with President Clinton I walked over to the Capitol Building hoping to catch a glimpse of the president's impeachment trial. The President was still in office, although he was impeached on December 19, 1998, for lying to the grand jury about his tryst with Monica Lewinsky. Even so, his popularity rating had soared to 70%. On the way I stopped on the sidewalk to have my picture taken with two giant cardboard likenesses of Bill and Hillary—my new imaginary friends.

Fortunately, the January day was balmy and standing for an hour in a line outside the Capitol Building was rather pleasant. Finally I was able to get into the visitor's gallery of the Senate Chamber. The Senators were in recess—dang it—but I watched four pages quietly pour water into a dozen drinking glasses. The people next to me were yawning. Minutes later the pages returned to the vacant room and emptied the water back into the pitchers. At least I saw something for my tax dollars.

The only other sign of life was when Senator John Kerry walked in one door and out another. I happily pointed out to my fellow visitors on the balcony that he was my home state Senator.

Back outside, my parents called to tell me that my great aunt, the late Mary Breckinridge, had been honored with her picture on a postage stamp. Kind of a funny coincidence, knowing that Rocky Marciano's stamp was due to be unveiled in May. My aunt's claim to fame was that she founded the Frontier Nursing Service in Kentucky—an organization of horseback-riding midwives who delivered health care to the mountain people. The FNS is still alive and growing, although jeeps replaced the horses years ago. I stopped by the Old Post

Office Pavilion, and sure enough, the small, blue and white stamps for my great aunt Mary were on sale for seventy cents a piece so I bought several and stuck them in my purse.

By February of 1999, it became common knowledge among local political activists that six-year City Council veteran Martha "Marty" Crowell wanted to be the first woman to run for mayor of the city of Brockton. At that point, however, I was convinced that Jack's leadership was working and had pledged to support him fully.

For some unexplained reason, at the next City Council meeting, Marty wore a hat on her head throughout the meeting. "Is this the Easter Parade?" someone asked. After that, she was fair game. Politics can be, um, childish, at times. A few of our supporters began referring to her as the "Cat in the Hat."

"Jack deserved to not have an opponent," Tim told me, knowing the strain our family faced. The thought of being involved in another embattled campaign, even though I was supportive, was disconcerting, knowing that Marty would be a worthy opponent. Casey was planning to live at the Cape most of the summer working as a nanny, and would then be flying to Ecuador for three weeks in August to volunteer in an outreach program. My time with her was limited enough. Conor would be heading for George Washington University in D.C. in the fall, which was already giving me separation anxiety. Also, I worried that Jack's job was either going to kill him from over-exertion or that he was going to be shot to death. I'd just learned that the police had removed guns from the home of the bulldozer guy in the park because he threatened to shoot Jack. Now, Jack would have to add to his already full plate the task of setting up headquarters, raising money, buying advertising, preparing for debates, buying a bullet-proof vest, and so on to his lengthy list.

At a packed campaign meeting for volunteers at the Polish White Eagles club, Jack said that his third campaign in four years was going to be a challenging one, but added, "I've worked too goddamn hard not to be able to finish the job!" Everyone gasped when he said that, but then broke into lasting applause because his words were so true. Jack had shown over and over how deeply he felt about the city, and how hard he was willing to work to improve Brockton's quality of life. Brockton's overall optimistic atmosphere and the many buildings under construction were proof that his leadership was working.

Jack's pace never slowed, and he didn't once feel sorry for himself at the thought of having to run against a qualified candidate. After his talk at the Polish White Eagles, one supporter, our friend Popeye Monahan, happily distributed tickets to sell for our May 13th campaign kick-off party.

Shortly after the speech though, Jack came down with the flu, and for four nights his feverish body drenched the bed. Again. Still, he showed up for a charity Easter egg hunt, a campaign meeting, and an interview on the radio.

On Wednesday, April 7th, 1999, Marty Crowell announced her candidacy for mayor. The wind was whipping across City Hall Plaza as she held on to her hat and a copy of her speech. The "Rocky" theme music played on a boom box nearby. Mark said there were about forty people in attendance. The next day, The Enterprise placed the story on the front page.

Since Marty was running for mayor, her Ward One City Council seat opened up. My singing friend, Tim, who I love to sing with at parties because he knows all the words, contemplated entering the race, and so did Peter Marciano, Jr.—a nephew of Rocky's. Jack and I were in a quandary over whom to support because both men were our friends and, likewise, had ties to lots of our other friends.

Within a few weeks, however, Tim decided not to run after all, telling Jack he spent a leisurely day at home with his family and loved every minute. We hated him.

In contrast, Jack had one of his busiest weeks ever. He attended the Kids Road Races, a blood drive, Dick Johnson's jazz concert, Mairi's skating show, a Catholic confirmation meeting for Breck, a City Councilor's fundraiser, an Eagle Scout Court, a screening of a film about Rocky Marciano, a walk-a-thon to raise money for battered women, and watched Breck participate in the City Hall Corporate Olympics.

I attended most of those functions with him, in addition to Mairi's rehearsal for "The Wizard of Oz," Casey's prom dress fitting, and Conor's Seniors/Mother's night at B. C. High. I sang at both the Duxbury Storytelling Festival and the Boston Flower Show. Everywhere Jack and I went, citizens commented that Brockton was looking so much better. The new pear trees that were planted by Ron Bethoney on Main Street were in bloom—their white blossoms fluttering in the spring wind. Preparations were in full swing at the Historical Society for the upcoming Marciano tribute, and it seemed to me that—happy with the city's new direction—people were leaning heavily toward reelecting Jack.

"Jack supported education and recognized that a strong school system was essential to having a thriving city. Without strong schools and an investment in them, the city could not flourish. Placing the new schools on main thoroughfares sent a strong message; champions are nurtured in the classrooms and Brockton supports them.

Jack supported my efforts to dramatically change Brockton Public Schools. He championed: full-day kindergartens, creation of the Gilmore Academy, Chinese language classes, global education, and middle schools.

He recognized the competition for jobs in the future was not going to come from Bridgewater or Holbrook!"

—Brockton School Superintendent Basan (Buzz) Nembirkow

CHAPTER 18

*"What could be better than walking down
any street in any city and knowing you're the
heavyweight champion of the world?"*
—Rocky Marciano

Born Rocco Francis Marchegiano, but best known as "Rocky Marciano, The Brockton Blockbuster," Rocky remains the only undefeated world heavyweight champion in history, with a record 49-0. He is Brockton's claim to fame—the heart of our city—the pride of its citizens. More businesses are named "Champion" something, or use it in their slogans. Rocky is the man, and his legacy continues to dominate.

The private unveiling of the Rocky Marciano 33-cent postage stamp kicked off the month-long tributes to Rocky and was held at the elegant Brockton Historical Society Homestead. The colonial home, with slanting wood floors and the fragrance of an old house, hosted tea parties at Christmas time where members of the Historical Society ceremoniously poured hot brown tea from silver teapots. Attached to the home is the more modern addition that houses Brockton's shoe museum, and that was where the Rocky Marciano kickoff event happened. As I was waiting for the speeches, I strolled around the museum checking out celebrity shoes. In a glass case was a pair of Rocky's leather "ring" shoes. On a shelf sat a set of high heels that once belonged to Mamie Eisenhower. A pair of sneakers once belonging to former President Jimmy Carter was placed next to some old shoe "lasts," the wooden implements used to mold shoes. I was told that President Carter phoned the museum a year or so after donating the sneakers to find out if he could get them back! The museum's curator, John Learnard, loved telling that story. Over the course of Jack's administration, I was able to secure shoes from Red Sox Baseball player, Moe Vaughn, and from the actor, Bill Murray, for the museum.

When Jack got up to speak, he reiterated his appreciation for all that Rocky had meant to the city of Brockton. He said that Rocky died so young (at the age of forty-six Rocky died in a plane crash) that he didn't get the chance to give back to the city. But with his bravery and amazing career, he gave Brockton its identity as the "City of Champions."

Congressmen Joseph Moakley and William Delahunt each took turns speaking and were abundant in their praise, of not only Rocky, but of Jack. They compared the city and its mayor to the undefeated champ, saying that he was knocked down but never knocked out.

That event was the first of many honoring Rocky. In between them, the Louis F. Angelo Elementary School opened on the north side—a state of the art building constructed in honor of the late State Representative Louie Angelo. The school brought much needed promise to a failing neighborhood. Jack hosted a campaign fundraiser the same night, drawing more than five hundred Brocktonians of every color and faith—Greek-African-Jewish-Hispanic-Lebanese-Portuguese-Italian-Irish-Haitian and Cape Verdean-Americans. The ebullient atmosphere was proof that everyone in the city was willing to work together under Jack's leadership.

Jack took the microphone and emphasized that his goals were still to focus on educational progress, to build a baseball stadium, and to stay on the path of encouraging private industry to locate in Brockton. Thirty-five million dollars in new business had come into the city already and property values were up by twenty-five percent. The bond rating had risen again and he reiterated that teamwork was how progress sustained itself.

The next morning, Jack had to be at the police station at 8:30 a.m., then pay a visit to the Hazardous Waste Day at the fairgrounds, make a quick stop at a blood drive, and go back to a memorial. Finally we met for our godchild's First Communion ceremony. By four o'clock, he and I collapsed on the couch unable to move. The movie "You've Got Mail," with Meg Ryan and Tom Hanks was on TV and was a welcome diversion. When that ended we willed ourselves to climb upstairs and get ready for the evening's activities.

I was so drained when the phone rang early Monday morning that I didn't want to answer. It was too soon to start the week. After Jack left for work, I retrieved the messages. One was from his chief of staff, Mary.

"I am burned out! Lillian is burned out! You're losing the two of us!" she said. "Come November…"

I hung up not wanting to listen anymore. Her tone of voice made my heart freeze in my chest. I took several deep breaths before calling her back. "No one on the planet is more burned out than Jack," I said, feeling so impatient I was fluttering my hands in the wind.

Pressing commitments day after day besieged the whole group—from staffers and volunteers, to our families. No one could keep up with Jack, or with the progress he had initiated. The Jazz Festival, the Special Olympics, the NAACP, spelling bees, Rocky Marciano month, the Haitian flag raising, the Agudas Achim black-tie event. The multitude of obligations was mind-boggling. Jack missed a graduation at South Junior High and a school committeewoman said to me, "It's an election year, Jack should have been there!" I wanted to tell her she had no idea what we were all going through.

I phoned Lillian, Jack's secretary, in her calm telephone voice, I heard the words I needed—"everything will be okay," and that Lillian was "with Jack all the way." What a dear.

Later, at the law office, Jack's former law partner, John McCluskey, asked if Jack's job was as stressful as our law office.

"Are you crazy? It's a zillion times more stressful," I said. I was surprised he asked that, but realized how little people knew of what went on in a mayor's office, especially with a proactive mayor like Jack. The cool thing was that Jack kidded around with everyone, making us all feel like we were an important part of the maelstrom. In that way, he was trying to soften the stress.

Later that week, I seized a moment to take Casey driving for the first time. She'd been hesitant about learning and at seventeen years old still hadn't gotten her license. We drove to the Melrose cemetery and at first everything about driving scared her. But after a few spins around the narrow roads, she started to see that driving was just a matter of practice. We endured some grinding stops and did wheelies over one or more graves, but other than that she did well. At one point, we parked the car and walked over the grass to look at Rocky Marciano's parents' tombstones. It was kind of sobering, thinking about the couple that produced the world famous boxer. Rocky's remains are in Florida, but on his parent's stones is an engraved pair of boxing gloves and a reference to Rocky's famous career.

At the end of the longest May in memory, the final event, the public unveiling of the Rocky Marciano stamp, took place on a bright, sunny day at City Hall Plaza. I'd never before seen so many people in the plaza. It was a tribute to the hard work put in by Mary Waldron and others.

One of the guests of honor was Max Kennedy, son of the late Senator Robert Kennedy, and nephew of President John Kennedy. He stood at a decorated podium reading a letter from his uncle, U.S. Senator Ted Kennedy.

He spoke with such eloquence that I found myself daydreaming about marrying him. Call it spring fever, but Max was just oozing seductive Kennedy pheromones. I imagined how we'd honeymoon in Fiji, maybe, or Monte Carlo. We could be so happy if only we weren't both, whatdoyoucallit? Married! I tried focusing on Jack when he walked up to the stand. My cutie. He loved that Rocky was finally getting his due. His words captured the essence of the American dream that Rocky fulfilled—that of prospering in the land his immigrant parents adopted. He also told the crowd that the fighter had been an inspiration to many people.

Grey clouds rolled in overhead as Rocky's adopted son, Rocky, Jr.—who was just one when his father died—and Jack, lifted the silk cloth from the large wooden replica of the Marciano stamp. The famous boxer looked exuberant dressed in a black robe with a white towel around his neck—bare fists posed high over his head in victory, while a referee lifted up one of his arms.

Rocky, Jr., then thirty-one, expressed to the crowd that he'd waited a long time to see his father honored in a big way, and was proud to be visiting in Brockton.

Of the fifteen stamps issued by the U.S. Postal Service to represent the 1950s, Rocky was the only individual person honored. Some of the other selections were for the "I Love Lucy" show, the polio vaccine, Rock and Roll, the Korean War, drive-in movies and, "The Cat in the Hat."

Jack was the last to leave City Hall after the day's numerous events, shutting off the lights before heading home.

He was still energized when he asked me to join him out on the porch. Smoking a cigar, drinking a vodka/amaretto—a/k/a a Godmother—he wanted to talk about the future. (I hoped it included Fiji.) The midnight moon was shining through a patch in the trees. I scooted my chair over by the screen to get a better view. It was the first moment of solitude we had shared in our house in a long time.

"Assuming I get re-elected," Jack said, striking a match to relight his cigar, "I can lay claim to having guided the building of three new schools, a courthouse, a Senior Center, a bus terminal, an improved shopping mall, hopefully a baseball stadium, and other stuff like new windows in all the schools and a larger police force."

I was stifling a yawn as I pushed the ashtray closer to his match. He continued after puffing on his cigar and taking a long pause, "If I could do anything, I'd like to go to an African country that's in serious trouble and turn it around."

"What?" I asked. "Jack, be serious."

He was serious, that's the thing. The more good he could do for people, the better he operated. It was exasperating. What about Fiji? Monaco? Finally I said, "Uh, do you think we could wait a week, honey? Because I'm pretty sure we're too busy to fly to Africa right now."

CHAPTER 19

"You'll be in my heart, yes, you'll be in my heart. From this day on, now and forever more."
—Phil Collins

On Mairi's 10th birthday, August 2nd, 1999, Jack opened his third campaign headquarters. Actually it was two small offices side by side on Main Street, where traffic drove by constantly. The night air was hot, but a cool wind refreshed us. As several people stood outside, the exhaust was less than appealing. At one point, Jack was talking with Chris Tsaganis, owner of Christo's Restaurant, about whether to make the traffic on Main Street flow both ways again. Years earlier, a previous administration had made the busy route one-way. Now a reversal of the traffic pattern might be better for downtown businesses, but would involve mega-funding, strategy and years of planning. Chris had a better idea. "Jack, I can fix this in no time. I'll just switch the traffic lights around. Done! That's it! Simple!" If only it were that easy.

The next morning, the mayoral candidate, Marty Crowell, was talking on the radio and hearing her say that "listening to others" was the most important thing for a mayor to do I knew that being a good mayor, especially in a city like Brockton, required so much more. It meant managing hundreds of personnel problems, being open-minded and intelligent and visionary and creative; having an educated business sense, municipal sense; and improving the quality of life for the destitute while keeping the more comfortable taxpayer happy. It entailed being out all night during a storm, and up early to keep people informed; negotiating with countless unions to make things right for the city;

supervising the running of a large school system from the top administrators to the janitors to the students and their parents; withstanding criticism from people who had no clue how anything worked and answering questions from the press who printed whatever they wanted anyway. It also meant giving speeches at the drop of a hat, finding solutions to the eternal problem of lack of funding, and watching your back constantly. Sometimes the radio shows depressed me. "Don't listen," Jack said. I listened anyway.

The next week, one local man told me Marty knocked on his door and he asked her what she could do that Jack wasn't already doing. She didn't have an answer.

Meanwhile, Conor was packing a trunk for college and every moment with him seemed weighted and precious. I found my eyes welling up all the time. I would miss everything about him, especially our late-night conversations. That was the time when I'd really gotten to know him. We shared conversations about music, movies, politics and sports. His humor lightened many situations. "Gee, gosh, sorry I won't be around for the sign-holding and literature-dropping during campaign season," he wisecracked one evening as I was preparing dinner. "Oh, yeah, too bad," I responded, stirring a vegetable dish. "Maybe we'll just fly you home to help." Ha.

Casey was planning to leave for Ecuador soon and I'd set the large oval table in the dining room for a special family dinner. The mahogany table—the one that belonged to Jack's Italian grandparents—now seated my beautiful family and during the meal I choked up with emotion. "This is our last meal as an intact family," I managed to blub, pressing a corner of a linen napkin against my eye. All the kids gave each other looks. "Okay, mom, whatever," Conor said, although Casey was sensitive and put her hand on mine. The rest laughed as Jack stood up to gather the plates. Once he finished eating he was done, no chitchat, time to do the dishes.

The surprise was that he cooked breakfast the next morning and I was overjoyed when all four kids showed up at the table again for another last meal together. "See?" I said. "You guys love our family, too!"

"Nah, we just love Dad's cooking," they said.

Afterwards, in my bedroom, Casey climbed onto my bed for a long satisfying hug break. Hug breaks are our answer to most of life's troubles. It's usually obvious when a hug is needed—about the time we can't take any more stress. Hug breaks work better to calm the soul than any doctor's visit or drug. Casey loves them as much as Jack and I do.

The six of us drove to Logan airport to see Casey off to Ecuador and I knew she was going to be okay when I saw how excited she and her classmates from Cardinal Spellman High School were. "I wish our family was going on a trip together," I lamented. After that, my throat was constricted and I couldn't talk so I took pictures instead.

In a sense I got my wish the following week when the rest of us drove south to take Conor to George Washington University. He kept the music playing the whole way—Billy Joel, Guster, movie themes, Counting Crows, Pearl Jam—I love his taste in music.

The caravan was packed to the rafters with Mairi squished in the backseat beside the boxes holding Conor's computer monitor and hard drive.

"You don't know what it's like! I can't feel my legs!" she whined, twisting this way and that. She was relieved for a spell when we accidentally drove by the exit for the New Jersey Turnpike and ended up in Cape May, New Jersey, and had to ferry across to Delaware. She and Breck ran around the boat while Conor read "If Men Were Angels," a novel about a man with a dark secret who runs for President. Even if he couldn't put his book down, to me, the boat ride with Conor was a blessing because it meant more time spent with him. Jack and I thought that was one of those times when we were really glad to have missed a highway exit.

After settling Conor into his dormitory, father and son shook hands when it was time to go. My eyes teared up, but I didn't sob out loud. On the drive home, though, Phil Collins' new song "You'll Be In My Heart," from the animated feature "Tarzan," came on the radio and the real tears started. I turned my head toward the window so no one would make fun of me. The tune became my song for Conor and to this day I think of him when I hear the song.

The house seemed so quiet when we returned. Jack went right to work in Conor's room, clearing away any mess. I saw Conor's empty green leather chair, the chair with the wooden arms that we tied his car seat into to bring him home from the hospital. (We had an old van then without any seats in it.) It was the chair he read hundreds of books in, the one we reupholstered after the fire. I had to sit down.

"Well, we've done it," I said to Jack. "We've raised one kid to 18. It's been long, wonderful, difficult, and all of that, but we did it! Three more to go!"

He tossed a pair of dirty socks into the laundry basket and gave me a stern look. "Done it? We've just begun to pay for it!" he anguished. Conor's tuition bill was rather daunting. I'll give him that.

Later, Breck asked Mairi and me if we wanted to go to breakfast at the Stonebridge Cafe. "Sure!" I said, comforted that that was how life went on. Besides, they cook the best veggie skillet there.

Mark and Jack went running the next day and saw that Marty Crowell had put up her lawn signs. There were dozens of them on well-traveled streets. Jack said that the signs didn't bother him, but they tortured me. He'd helped several of those residents over the years. How did people forget? Where was their loyalty? My friend, Geri, calmed my anxiety by pointing out that signs don't vote. I appreciated her wisdom and have since learned that people will put a sign on their lawn simply because they're asked. And that doesn't necessarily mean they will vote for the candidate.

When I got to work, one of my employees, Lynn Miller, at the law office told me her son, Johnny, became angered by Marty's signs and proclaimed, "Webster's should just change the dictionary so that next to 'mayor' it says 'Jack Yunits!'" I called Jack to cheer him up with that tidbit.

My personal challenge was trying to get through Shaw's Supermarket without crying because everywhere I looked I saw the foods Conor loved—Fenway Franks, Tony's Pizza, Pepperidge Farm hot dog rolls. But the time for such nostalgia was short-lived because at 4:45 pm on the last day to submit signature papers to run for mayor, the travel agent candidate who ran for mayor every two years, even if he got only 4% of the vote, handed in his qualifying papers. Until that point, with only Jack and Marty in contention, a primary election had been unnecessary. The eleventh hour submission obligated the city to hold a primary that would cost $65,000.00. It was especially ironic since the candidate's platform was about saving the city money.

Driving home from the law office, the familiar roller coaster of emotions that was a part of politics hit me again. I drove along Belmont Street past George's Café, where I'd be attending a fundraiser later; by the long customer line overflowing the sidewalk at Dairy Queen; to our first campaign headquarters, which was now a Yoga studio. Further along I saw two new banks—another welcome indication that businesses were returning to Brockton. Something caught my eye. A brightly lettered sign on the property of Donahue Real Estate was hammered onto a wooden base and read "Yunited We Stand." My heart did a little waltz: "Thank you, Donahue Real Estate!"

"I've known Jack since he was a young man working for the late Judge George Covett. I spent many years running in the park with Jack, including the New York City marathon. He continually encouraged me to run for mayor of Brockton. I declined and he ran.

"When I think of Jack as mayor, I always think of Jack and Lees as mayor. They both brought a youthful enthusiasm to our body politic, which translated into new schools, a rebuilt library, and a professional ball park and convention center—all of which enhanced the city's image. I can't thank the two of them enough for what they've done."

—State Senator Robert S. Creedon

CHAPTER 20

"I'm a great believer in luck, and I feel the harder I work the more I have of it."
—Thomas Jefferson

Casey came back from Ecuador with a life-changing attitude toward the less-privileged, and eased back into our busy political life. Perhaps because she was on her own and had come face to face with severe poverty, she felt better about public service and her dad being mayor. She was also more comfortable talking to adults, and presenting herself in public. I was proud of those qualities in her and pointed out that someday she'd see the benefits of what we, as a family, were doing for the betterment of our community.

That said, however, several days before the primary several events reminded us that the city still had a long way to go.

Jack heard about a new rise in street violence near the Sacred Heart Church near the city's center. The nuns and priest felt terrorized by gang members who lived nearby. One City Councilor begged Jack to accompany him to a house to speak with several bikers who resided there, and who might be willing to help with surveillance. The nervous City Councilor stayed on the sidewalk pretending to pick paint chips off the fence while Jack walked up alone to pound on the weathered front door. A burly man opened it abruptly, stood a minute, and then turned back to someone inside.

"Hey, it's okay! He's my lawyer!" he yelled. It took a moment for Jack to remember that he represented the man, years earlier, and the two exchanged a hearty handshake and did some catching up. Eventually, Jack told him he needed the guy and his buddies to keep an eye on the neighborhood, that the police had enough on their hands with the excess violence plaguing the area. In exchange, Jack said, he'd erect a Jersey barrier—a cement roadblock—at the end of the street to keep out unwanted and troublesome traffic. The guy agreed to help, the two shook hands again, and Jack turned to step down the stairs. He joined the City Councilor who seemed satisfied that maybe that trade off would initiate the end of the troubles.

But that supervision wasn't enough, and a few days later, Jack stormed over to another street in the same neighborhood and told the tenants who were known to be gang members that it was time to get out. Two hoodlums hanging out on the porch said, "Hey, man, we're only protecting our turf!"

"So am I!" Jack hollered, and had them evicted the next day.

It was hard for me to imagine Marty having that kind of strength.

As if those little episodes weren't enough during an election season, another City Councilor, Donna Daley, and her husband, Paul, rang the doorbell at our house unexpectedly one evening.

"What a nice surprise!" I said, opening the door. They entered my kitchen and Paul hit his head on the flying wooden duck that hangs from the ceiling. I love that ornament and showed them how when you pull the string, the duck's wings flap. But the light-hearted banter wasn't well received.

"Something terrible has happened," Donna said.

"What?" I asked, bracing myself.

"Jack hit a girl with his car." Jack appeared behind her in the doorway.

"Jack! What happened?" I said, going to him. His green eyes were vacant, his mouth tight. I helped him take off his jacket as he lowered himself down onto a kitchen chair. For a few minutes he said nothing. Donna started to explain that Jack showed up at her house to drop off a contribution he collected for her upcoming charity bike ride.

Jack took over then, his voice barely audible. "I was driving through a dense section of North Montello Street when a girl suddenly darted in front of my car. I wasn't going fast and my car barely touched her, but the impact was enough to knock her down and seriously injure her leg."

"Oh, baby," I said, patting his shoulder.

"Some witnesses helped me make her comfortable until the ambulance came, and after she was taken away I drove to Donna's house to deliver the money. But then I couldn't drive home." The room was quiet as the reality sank in. There was one week left before the election. I brought him a water tumbler. Our friends talked with us another few moments, and then said their goodbyes.

Jack and I drove to the Good Samaritan Hospital where we met the girl's mother. She told us her daughter tried to outrun the car. Several witnesses apparently agreed.

"I can't take any more stress," Jack confided to me on the way home, adding that hitting the poor girl was the worst thing he'd ever done. "I can still hear her screams," he said, closing his eyes. "If I could trade places with her, I would in a minute."

The story hit the airwaves the next day and The Enterprise printed an article on the front page. The wrap up said a doctor had set the young woman's leg with a rod and that the prognosis looked good.

Jack drove to the store and bought a "Millennium Bear" beanie baby and the book "Chicken Soup for the Teenage Soul" for our next visit. The teenager was still in recovery. We later heard that the gifts made her happy.

The next morning, Jack was on the radio answering several questions about Hurricane Floyd, which was bearing down on Brockton. As Jack prepped the citizens in case of an emergency, another call came through from a man saying that Brockton was just going "down, down, down," and that if the mayor had been a regular citizen, he'd be in jail for hitting a pedestrian. My jaw tightened. One lady blessed our family for sharing Jack with the city. I relaxed again.

It was amazing how many people approached us over the next few days with stories about hitting kids with their cars or being hit themselves. One vehicle struck Mark when he was fifteen. "Just nicked me," Mark said, "but the impact broke my leg!" Another friend struck and killed an eight-year old boy who, like Jack's victim, darted from nowhere. It saddened me to know my friend lives with that memory every day.

Notwithstanding the accident, our supporters felt confident Jack would win the primary election. Still, he and I were fraught with nerves. On Election Day Jack forgot that the house alarm was set, went downstairs for his coffee and activated the motion detector. The sirens blared, making his heart race and scaring us all to death.

The night of the election, I dropped Mairi off at CCD—her Catholic education class—and watched her hurry up the sidewalk alongside Our Lady of Lourdes church. Some girls joined her and they all disappeared down the stairway and into the church hall. It struck me anew that Mairi was the only girl out of eighteen thousand public school students who was related to the mayor. That put her in somewhat of a spotlight, which she seemed to handle well. Except, of course, when there were snowstorms. If school wasn't cancelled she took a lot of grief from classmates.

By 9 pm, Jack and I were together on the couch in front of the TV. I offered him cashews, but he said no. The primary results were slow coming in—as usual. With all the technological advances, you'd think Brockton would have results by 8:10. According to Jack, the station had the money for coverage.

But he wasn't big on micro managing and the cable TV group functioned independently. There was no radio coverage either. I popped a few cashews into my mouth, crossed my legs and shook my foot nervously.

Jack barely took a breath. It was like a report card of all he'd been doing the last four years. Finally we learned that Marty won her own precinct, Ward 1-A, by thirteen votes. Her comment to the press was: "I guess the voters see that my six years as City Councilor are more important than Jack's four as mayor." As it turned out, her comment was a bit presumptuous.

At 9:03, Jack had won every precinct in the city but two. By the time we drove to Sidelines, the sports bar near the Lithuanian village, the crowd was ecstatic and clapped for a long time. The final tally was 61% for Jack, 33% for Marty, 4% for the travel agent, and 2% undecided. Jack's committee was satisfied and we trained our sights on the November election.

The following night, as tired as Jack was, I begged him to go to Thorny Lea Golf Club with me for a final dinner in the soon-to-be-torn-down clubhouse. Our good friends and neighbors were there, sitting at a large banquet table covered with a white tablecloth. Someone brought out a portable microphone, which got passed around as the crowd came alive, telling jokes and singing songs—like the good old days. Our friend, George Walsh, sang a splendid "Danny Boy" in his rich Irish tenor, and O.D. crooned "Galway Bay". Everyone joined me singing "On Vacation For A Week" and Suzanne warbled a jazz standard, "True Love." The camaraderie and celebration lasted for three hours. Sometime after midnight the party finally broke up. We were crazy to have stayed out so late again, but the evening was the kind that made us all feel great about living in Brockton.

Three days after the primary, Jack called to see if I would swing by the football game to talk with our sign holders. He sounded so tired. My heart ached a little bit, knowing how driven he was to fix everything wrong with the city. He told me he was heading to a Hospice meeting, then to the Boys and

Girls Club, back to the football stadium and finally to the Holiday Inn for the National Night Out Against Crime dinner. He was assuming more and more responsibility and covering the events by himself. Even his die-hard supporters found that keeping pace with this mayor was nearly impossible.

CHAPTER 21

"I think that people want peace so much that one of these days government had better get out of their way and let them have it."
—Dwight D. Eisenhower

One thing that bothered me was that Marty kept pointing out to Jack that Brockton was a blue-collar town, as if to say, "we're lower class, we'll stay lower class, I'm lower class and know what the people want."

From my point of view, Brockton was a mixed bag. There were plenty of working class people as evidenced by the social clubs, including the VFW, the Conte Club, the Enterprise Club, the Club National and the Polish White Eagles. But there was also Thorny Lea Golf Club, which was about to build a multi-million dollar facility and whose members were doctors, lawyers, and bank presidents. Hundreds of citizens often attended black-tie events at the Fuller Museum and the Massasoit Conference Center. The formal gatherings were so numerous, in fact, that long gowns took up half my closet. In comparison, my parents lived in an upper middle class, all-white neighborhood in New Jersey, and never went to a black-tie affair. Goes to show how varied city life can be.

What I appreciate is that in general, people in Brockton accept one another—residents do what they do, earn what they earn and that's that. There are some very wealthy people, who, along with their parents before them, have lived in Brockton all their lives. Everyone is fairly comfortable mixing together at fundraisers, football games, concerts, wakes, retirement parties—you name it.

Some wear minks, most don't. No big deal.

Jack closed his portion of the final debate, being held at the nearby Jewish temple, saying that it was the mayor's job to promote the city and its people in the best light. He emphasized that education was Brockton's new industry and that we must get behind it to survive. "The road to hell is paved with leaders who are afraid to act," he said, meaning he would battle for new schools. Marty agreed that she was all for education, as long as we didn't have to spend any money or build schools.

On the way home from the temple, Jack pulled the car into the lot at Cleverly's convenience store and lots of people recognized Jack and wished him good luck on Tuesday. I was returning to the car with bags of Halloween candy when a lady ran over.

"You're the mayor?" she asked Jack through his window. "I moved here two years ago from Taunton and I think you're doing an excellent job!" Her comments were uplifting for us both.

The Enterprise endorsed Jack (thank the Lord!), with an article: "Yunits Deserves Third Term." It said that Jack was a consensus builder, a responsible caretaker of our restored fiscal health, and had shepherded the brick and mortar initiatives through to completion. In short, Yunits had shifted Brockton's prospects in a positive direction.

The night before the election, Jack and I stayed home to watch Teen Jeopardy with Breck. We were relaxed and talking casually when Breck informed us that he had a project due the next day and needed a picture of himself in front of the Underground Railroad tree, or Liberty Tree, as it was known. The large tree was famous for being a Civil War meeting place for slaves escaping from the south.

"Breck! Couldn't you have told us about your project beforehand?" I asked, incredulous. There was just no such thing as truly relaxing. Jack and he were out of the house by 6 a.m. to take the picture. I heard Marty's voice on the radio and pulled the pillow over my head, hoping that would be the last time I did.

As usual, my stomach was full of anticipation. The day flew by and in the evening, while Mairi was at Girl Scouts, Breck and Casey joined Jack and me at home to await the results. Election coverage, naturally, was scant on radio and Cable TV. Breck scribbled down a few poll numbers as people called them in. Finally, Tim phoned. Trustworthy Tim. Those calls on Election Day were becoming a family tradition. "Better get down to the Polo Club," he said. "I think Jack's done it again." As soon as Mairi got home from Scouts we raced over.

To this day I give kudos to Marty for putting her name on the ballot and enduring the political tribulations. That takes guts. She ran a strong campaign, and came closer to winning than we expected. But Jack defeated her, garnering 64.4% of the vote, a solid win.

Hours later, after another walloping victory party, Jack and I crawled into bed as a downpour rattled the windows. I pulled the blankets up to my cheeks and swore I heard weather mayor rumble from a thunderclap.

There was hardly time to rest, however, because New Year's Eve was fast approaching and Y2K, or the "millennium bug," was on the world's collective mind. The worry was that computers might interpret the year 2000 as 00, or 1900, and cause a misreading of essential data, thereby crippling airports, banks, and who knew what else.

Jack had been meeting with his Civil Defense team for months. One night I told him I was sorry he was so stressed, but he reassured me that the challenges he faced, like getting new schools built and surviving Y2K, were goals to achieve, not problems. He said he hadn't been sleeping well because of the over-abundance of information in his head, not stress.

The good news was that three friends of ours had recently bought homes in Brockton. People were at last moving into Brockton, not out. Also the new clubhouse at Thorny Lea was well under construction and a Residence Inn by Marriott was going up near Route 24.

Right after Christmas, Breck mentioned he had a desire to go to New York City for New Year's Eve. "Not on your life," Jack told him. Breck was only fifteen for one thing, but we never would have allowed him to be in so vulnerable a place on Y2K night. Nothing much was going on with his friends for New Year's Eve, though, so he stayed with Jack and me at home. Mairi invited two friends to sleep over and the three of them ran around the house wearing headbands that had "2000" scribbled across the front.

Jack's biggest concern was that if the cable lines were tampered with people's house phones might not work, which could cause panic. The Emergency Management Director, Al Doyle, was in constant contact with Jack. The city's computers had been checked and rechecked for months and fire and police forces were working overtime to insure a peaceful evening.

On TV, Pope John Paul II blessed the massive flock of people in St. Petersburg Square. The Eiffel Tower was illuminated with more than 20,000 lights, and in Athens, ceremonial fires burned in a circle around choirs singing hymns. The smoke got so thick I could practically feel the soot burning the singers' throats.

Times Square had the most people ever, two million they said, and we watched the Waterford crystal ball drop while the little girls blew horns and threw confetti. I kissed Jack and the girls, but Breck wouldn't let me kiss him. Teenagers could be trying.

Casey called to say Happy New Year from a friend's house, and Conor told me later he had a real good time, from what he remembered.

CHAPTER 22

*"A leader has to lead, or otherwise he has no
business in politics."*
—Harry S. Truman

On Inauguration Day, Monday, January 3, 2000, Jack's address focused at length on why education was Brockton's most important objective. He hammered home the point that the city's future depended on investing in new buildings and state-of-the-art technology in order for our youth to compete in an increasingly global economy.

Mairi was seated to my right on the wooden bench and after about ten minutes of listening to her father leaned over to me and whispered: "Whatever happened to short and sweet?" I rested my hand on her leg to keep her from kicking.

At the Martin Luther King, Jr. breakfast, Jack spoke again about the importance of funding new school buildings. I was pleasantly surprised by the audience's attentiveness. The following day at the Temple Beth Emunah's annual MLK luncheon, the diverse crowd from the area's churches and synagogues quietly nibbled egg salad sandwiches as Jack repeated the need to focus on children and education. School Committeeman Moe Hancock, sitting next to me at the table touched my arm. "By God, he's taken the gauntlet and he's running with it," he exclaimed.

A ballot question asking whether the voters would support a small increase in their tax bills to pay for new educational facilities was brought up. At the next City Council meeting, the vote was 6-5 against even putting the question on the ballot. The city's CFO, Jay Condon, kept his cool in the face of such a letdown. Jack, however, was seething and couldn't understand the Council's shortsighted decision.

I could sympathize with the fact that some of the Councilors feared their constituents' wrath. Haters, as we called the negative people, could make Councilors' (and mayors') lives miserable. But if the officials could just think beyond those few spoilers, they would have seen that if you ignore the haters long enough they went away—and positive things would happen. Jack's guiding principle was always "govern for the next generation, not the next election." But few politicians abided that wisdom.

A letter to the editor appeared in The Enterprise criticizing Jack for "even thinking of building new schools." The woman said teachers were "already being paid twenty-eight thousand for only working 180 days and that the hidden costs of the new schools will kill us all in the long run." She continued by saying we'd "pay and pay and pay for years to come."

I wondered what we'd pay in the long run if we didn't put education first. As a perfect example, I received a call from a man who was enraged because he'd heard gunfire in the Court Street area. There had been three murders there recently. "We can't even watch TV without ducking bullets!" the caller told me. He went on that his girlfriend's kids were scared to death. I asked if he'd called the police, suggesting maybe he could help them.

"No!" he roared, "But I'm going to call channels 2, 4, 5, 7 and all the papers!" Duh. That would really help. That was the standard line whenever a citizen got worked up. They were always going to call "channels 2, 4, 5, 7 and all the papers."

Jack and I attended a birthday party at The Pub for a member of the School Committee who, believe it or not, was against fortifying the school system. His wife, however, grabbed Jack's arm on our way out, telling him, "Jack, you are the only one with vision, and this is what makes you so vital. No one else has ideas and optimism like you do and this is your strength," she added.

Her words rejuvenated Jack. "I love that woman. She's a saint," he said to me driving home.

On Saturday, I cleaned house all day wondering if it was time for Jack to move on. I sponged down counter tops and threw dollhouse furniture into the toy box, growing aggravated about a population that only wanted to grow so far. The defeat of the education initiative emphasized our country's addiction to mediocrity. Our neighbors, Frank and Ginny, told me that the City Council had always been nonchalant about education. That's why, years ago, the residents demanded the formation of a separate School Committee. Sadly, though, today, most Brockton School Committee members aren't even college graduates. I'm sure it's the fear of the press that keeps most educated people from running for local government. Or maybe it's the fear of the vulgar and pathetic, whose voices we hear most often. I read once that saying the word "no" makes people feel stronger, thereby empowering them to shoot down new ideas.

On Sunday, when I would have preferred to see Jack take a break, he attended two meetings about schools and one meeting about The Foxy Lady. I was home baking a birthday cake for him. When he arrived, he continued several discussions by phone.

Frank and Ginny walked over to our house to help us celebrate Jack's birthday. A fire was glowing in the fireplace and a football playoff game was on TV. Breck and Mairi had been skating on the pond across the street most of the day and were tuckered out, although apparently still rambunctious enough to fight over which one got to sit on the Patriots beanbag chair. After sharing a lasagna dinner the group sat at the dining room table for the longest time. Our upright piano was in that room and Mairi tinkered out "What A Wonderful World." I was thinking, "It doesn't get much better than this," when the phone rang. Casey answered it in the kitchen and told the caller that Jack was busy (he was blowing out his candles) and would have to call back.

"Oh? He's busy? Well, don't have him call back! I'm going out!" the man shrieked, shaking Casey up. The phone rang again. The caller was a news reporter from WBZ radio. Two teens from Brockton had been killed during a police chase in Taunton and they wanted to know if Jack had a comment. He hadn't heard about the accident until then.

The next day Jack turned 48. Right after he stepped out of the shower Casey came hobbling up the stairs. A minute earlier, she had left for school in the Dodge Caravan. She was crying and shaking when I saw her at the top of the stairs. "Honey! What happened?" I asked. Jack was wrapped in a towel, his wet feet hurrying behind me.

"Mama, the car skidded on the ice and slammed into a telephone pole!" was all she could muster before breaking into more sobs.

"Are you okay?" I asked, checking for blood.

"Yes, but the car was crushed," she told me.

"It's okay, it's okay," I said, fingering a strand of her hair. "As long as you're not hurt, everything will be fine." Jack hurriedly got dressed, called a tow truck company and headed out the door.

"Happy birthday honey!" I called meekly as he left the house, knowing he was ready to implode.

In D.C. later that week for the annual mayors' conference, the school superintendent from Arlington, MA, Charlie Lyons, raised his glass in a toast to Jack. "To the mayor with enough courage to build schools for the kids and to push for the debt-exclusion bill!" the man called out. I blew him a kiss.

The next day, I returned to the Capitol Hilton hotel after spending the afternoon with Conor, to find the cocktail lounge full of professionally dressed men and women. People were shaking hands, talking to each other and on cell phones. Jack had been speaking with the Assistant Secretary of Labor, Ray Bramucci, for about ten minutes by the time I showed up. At issue were several youth grants available for the asking and Mr. Bramucci's office was in charge of distributing them. After our greeting, Jack walked off and I was talking with the Secretary. He was a good-looking man and wearing seductive cologne. I felt a tad intimidated by his title, however, even though he was easy to talk to. He bent close to my ear and made a joke about Jack being Italian and how that was a "good thing."

"Well, he's also half Irish you know," I answered back, flirtatiously. Ray smiled.

"That was the perfect thing to say!" Jane Oates whispered behind me. Jane worked for Senator Ted Kennedy at the time and was thrilled to have had Jack speak with Mr. Bramucci.

The Assistant Secretary seemed charmed to also have made my acquaintance and afterwards made his way back into the crowd.

"Honey!" Jack said later, brightening up. "You might have just nailed us the grant!"

Sure enough, several weeks later, Brockton was notified that the city would receive a Youth Opportunity Grant worth eighteen million dollars over a five-year period! The prize was so acclaimed that President Clinton announced the awards on CNN. To this day, Jack honestly believes I cemented that deal.

While we were gone, Breck wrote a letter to the editor in defense of his father's education initiative saying, "Nobody has done more for Brockton in the last four years than the mayor. He works day and night, seven days a week. You see the courthouse, the revitalization of the mall, the two new schools, a declining unemployment rate, a declining crime rate, millions of dollars in new revenue from new businesses, the new transportation center, skyrocketing home values. The community and business groups of Brockton, the School Department, and yes, even the mayor are moving this city forward regardless of the pessimistic remarks of you and a few others. And the school plan is just another step forward." Way to go, Breck!

People around town made comments about the letter for weeks. Teachers pinned it to bulletin boards.

At a friend's party back home, Jack worked his way across the living room to speak with a friend, Sue Costigan—a history teacher and secretary of the teacher's union—about pushing for a more substantial education agenda.

"Where are the teachers in this quest to shore up the education system?" Jack asked her. "Where are their letters to the editor? Why aren't they helping me?"

"Point taken," Sue responded, averting her eyes to the floor.

Meanwhile, our good friend, O.D., walked across the floor with his hand out. "Thank you, thank you, thank you for all you've done for Brockton!" he said, shaking Jack's hand aggressively. Our children are coming back!" His three kids had all just bought homes in Brockton and O.D. was thankful that the next generation would find Brockton an equally wonderful place to live.

The people at the party were also excited because the long awaited Thorny Lea Clubhouse was about to open. The next day, Jack and I stopped by to see the place, as Mairi and her friend, Angela, ran off to explore the new facility. Several people were admiring the handsome building when the club president, Steve Roan, hurried in. Someone jokingly asked whether the liquor license had been delayed. "Not a problem! In fact, drinks are on me!" Steve proclaimed. He motioned for me to help him, so I ducked under the bar gate and sized up the new bottles and glassware. We added ice to virgin glasses, poured vodka and scotch and toasted to the newest rendition of Brockton's prestigious golf club.

Suddenly the warning lights, which were tucked in the corners, started flashing and a recorded voice urged us to leave the building. No one moved for a moment. Then it crossed my mind that the Titanic went down on its maiden voyage and my pulse quickened. "Mairi! Where are you?" I called. She and Angela came flying around the corner of the bar. In a rush, they blurted that the mist from the ladies steam room might have set off the alarm.

Within minutes, fire engines arrived, their sirens wailing, and half a dozen firefighters in black and yellow battle gear poured into the building. We were still standing near the bar when one firefighter walked by whom I recognized. He happened to have been on duty during our house fire. "Hi Lees. Hi Mairi," Tom Goodale said, with a smile, causing me to feel embarrassed. Jack tried fading into the background, but the firemen—once they realized there was no emergency—were as excited as anyone to see the new clubhouse and Jack ended up giving them all a tour.

The Canadian artisan who was hired to do the finish work in the new clubhouse wanted Thorny Lea to be his crowning achievement and he more than succeeded. The polished cherry wood glamorizes every fixture with its reddish tones, including the main bar, the sidebars, window casings, and the banister leading downstairs to the locker rooms. Even the lockers themselves bear his rich, handcrafted excellence. Brown leather dining chairs and hooded lamps hang from clusters in the ceiling, adding to the charm. The beautiful new building finally matches the quality of the links.

At a fundraiser for Jack, the new owners of the Westgate Mall were in attendance and I struck up a conversation with them. They told me that a Bath & Body Works store was coming soon and over the next few months, Victoria's Secret, Gap, Gap Kids, Children's Place, American Eagle and Old Navy would be opening. That was big stuff for the once down-and-out mall.

One friend startled me when his two hands grabbed my waist from behind. "Jack will go down in history for changing Brockton," Yiannis Davos said. He was one of many successful Greek businessmen in the city. Yiannis loved to make me jump and I admonished him for scaring me. "I'm so-ree," he said. "But let me tell you something. Brockton is explosive right now," he said, gesturing with his thick arms. He was in the process of renovating the Thomas Edison building on Main Street into condominiums, taking great care to ensure each condo was high quality.

In addition, the new Senior Center was on its way toward completion. In late June 2000, more than fifty senior citizens marched from their temporary accommodations at 36 Main St. to the new site at the corner of Father Kenney Way. The President of the Council on Aging, Ralph Tamalonis, stood on the sidewalk, praising Jack, saying he was "a man of his word." He told the crowd that two days after Jack's first election, Jack had promised he'd help the seniors get their own place and within two weeks, he'd found a temporary place and set his sights on building a brand new facility.

Ralph also told the press he and several board members voted to name the center the "John T. Yunits Center," but Jack declined, feeling that the naming should honor "an ordinary citizen who has done extraordinary things in the service of mankind." Jack's choice was Mary Cruise Kennedy, a nurse supervisor at the Brockton Hospital, who, as of this writing, is a strong 97 years old (and still enjoying an occasional Manhattan).

To top off the summer, on the very warm day of August 7th, 2000, the long-awaited Brockton District Courthouse opened, three years after the groundbreaking. It was another enormous achievement for the downtown area. Jack and I strolled through the beautiful building in awe. Like Thorny Lea, fine attention had been paid to design and architecture. Conference rooms, libraries and balconies decorated the interior and the judge's lobbies were large sunny rooms with teak bookshelves. We recognized several employees from Jack's days as a lawyer, which made me nostalgic for our former legal life.

The work behind the scenes, which helped bring new city landmarks such as the Clubhouse, the Senior Center and the Courthouse, were taxing on Jack and his staff. It was hardly a surprise when, at the end of the summer, Mary Waldron decided to step down from her position as Chief of Staff. Mary had been invaluable to Jack for five years, as loyal a worker as you'd ever find. She was teary-eyed at her going away party at The Pub, thanking Jack for his guidance and friendship and for making her more professional. As friends craned their necks to see around the corners of the narrow room, she also thanked her husband, John, and young daughter, Casey, for putting up with her absences during many long days and nights.

The following week, Joe Angelo's Café, opened, and to add to the excitement, the Brockton Transit Authority introduced three shiny red trolley cars to the city bus fleet. I should say re-introduced the trolleys to Brockton because there was once a trolley system plying Main Street.

Jack's former Civil Defense Director, Al Doyle, said that back "in the old days" in Brockton, he and his friend, Rocky Marciano, sometimes took the trolley. But they preferred to save the nickel fare and spend it on an ice cream soda at "Nick's—The Milkshake King." He remembered always paying for his friend because Rocky was very poor.

"The one thing that comes to mind about Jack's time as mayor was the tremendous amount of sacrificing regarding his family. We should be forever grateful for what he did.

"When I was a City Councilor and Jack was mayor, our dealings were always business, never personal, which allowed us to accomplish a lot. We didn't always agree, but we found a way to get things done. We're still doing that now. He wants to hit me over the head sometimes, but we remain friends."

—Brockton Mayor James Harrington

CHAPTER 23

"My plan after office is to get up and spend that entire first day helping my wife move into her new senatorial office."

—*William J. Clinton*

In the fall of 2000, George W. Bush won the presidential election. No wait—Al Gore won, no, George—no Al, no, geez—who was our newest President? Conor and Casey both called home on election night to find out what was happening locally. Casey had joined Conor in D.C. when she enrolled at Catholic University. As the results swung back and forth between Bush and Gore Conor predicted that whoever won Florida would win the Presidency. Breck watched TV with us at home and bet on Al Gore because he had met the Vice President when he accompanied Jack to Boston the previous month. Breck was the only kid at the fundraising event. He said when Gore walked in the room everyone fell silent and the man's presence was somewhat awe-inspiring. When the two were introduced, Gore asked Breck if he liked golf.

"Yes, I do," Breck replied, looking up at the tall man. "I work at a golf course near my house."

"My son likes golf, too," the Vice President said, patting Breck on the back.

He and Breck turned toward the camera for a quick photo, shook hands, and Breck walked away—not quite floating like me after meeting Clinton, but equally impressed.

At the time, little did anyone know that the election process would take six weeks for Bush to be declared President of the United States. And Florida was the deciding factor—with dimpled and hanging chads becoming part of the nation's vocabulary as the recount dragged on. In the end, Gore won the popular vote by more than 300,000. But in America, one more electoral vote wins the presidency. Enter George "dubya" Bush.

Jack and I arrived in Washington, on January 16, 2001, for the annual U.S. Conference of Mayors, which coincided with the inauguration of President Bush. One of the first things I did was purchase a bag of souvenir "chadfetti" for Breck.

It was a sunny 45 degrees, and D.C. was preparing for the historic event. Red, white and blue buntings hung from office windows and a big grandstand was set up for the parade.

A definite change was in the air from past conferences. One cab driver told me that in comparison to when Clinton was inaugurated, D.C. was quiet. The cab drivers, he said, weren't in favor of Bush. On the other hand, the Capitol Hilton had been taken over by loud, boot-wearing Texans. It seemed Cowboy America had replaced the more communal feeling between mayors that past conferences shared. Yippee-kie-yo!

Nonetheless, the conference continued as usual with panels and seminars, and one bonus, for me, was hearing the first Mayor (ever) of London speak. Jack and I were sitting at a table in a banquet room and as interested as I was in the speaker, the dessert that day was unbelievable. An edible picture of Big Ben adorned the top of a chocolate box that contained the best tasting whipped cream with fresh berries. Next to the box a chocolate cake dusted with confectioners sugar sat side by side next to a tiny fruitcake muffin. The whole presentation had lines of chocolate syrup drizzled back and forth across the plate. It was so beautiful I had to take a picture of it. But for some reason, my camera wouldn't work. No matter how far away I pushed the dessert, or how close, I couldn't get the camera's button to click. It was maddening. I tried and tried. Jack thought I was nuts. Finally I stuck a fork into the creation, and simply enjoyed every taste sensation on my tongue.

The following day, Conor stopped by our hotel room. Speaking a mile a minute, he relayed that he had just been at the Mayflower Hotel dropping off some client's luggage. (He worked for a lobbyist, whose clients were in town for the inauguration.) While standing in the elevator, minding his own business, he told us, someone punched him in the back.

"What the heck?" Conor had said, turning around.

"Surprise!" It was Muhammad Ali, former three-time World Heavyweight Champion. He and Conor shook hands, bumped shoulders together and everyone in the elevator laughed.

About an hour after Conor's news the hotel phone rang. The caller happened to have two extra tickets to the Inaugural Ball at Union Station that night if Jack and I wanted them. "Sure!" I answered. "Love to!" I'd brought along a fancy dress just in case. Jack wasn't as enthusiastic. Not that I had a special interest in a Republican Ball, either, but it was still America, and Bush was my President, too.

Security was tight as we hung up our coats and slowly passed through the metal detectors at Union Station. Inside the huge, dimly lit area pictures of the Presidential Seal were being projected onto the vaulted ceilings. Jack and I stood in line to have a formal picture taken, but he got restless, started walking around and never came back! I played with my program a bit, and then finally had my picture taken in front of the Presidential Seal by myself.

Afterwards, I noticed that the jazz band was taking a break so I walked over to talk to the saxophone player. I found out he once played in Brockton at Westgate Lanes. Someone always seems to have a connection to Brockton. I suppose Brockton just could be the center of the universe.

Finally Jack reappeared. We picked a few appetizers from trays before taking the escalator to the floor below to retrieve our complimentary wine glasses. He guided me over to a bench and suggested sitting for a while. Great, I thought, the marble floor was killing me in high heels. I put my evening bag down and sunk back. Jack, however, abruptly got up and walked over to speak with a jolly crowd. After a few minutes, they waved me over. I learned that the two couples hailed from California. I shared that my son worked for a firm in D.C. that represented California pistachio growers.

"That's our lobbyist!" they said in unison. "Who's your son?"

When I ever said "Conor," they nearly fell out of their chairs. They were the clients Conor picked up at the airport before he met Muhammad Ali! Fifty thousand ball attendees at eight different balls around Washington and Jack picked Conor's "clients" to talk to. Unbelievable.

Jack and I headed back upstairs and the roar of the crowd was deafening when President and Mrs. Bush came in. I couldn't get close to the stage, but took an overhead picture with my throwaway camera. Later, Vice President Dick Cheney and his wife appeared. She seemed comfortable speaking at the podium because she went on for a bit.

There was a sense of wholesomeness surrounding the otherwise tame evening. The Bush family represented a return of the moral dignity our country desperately needed. But I was reserving judgment because President Bush had yet to be tested.

And I found satisfaction in knowing that, regardless of his tainted legacy, Clinton left office with the highest popularity rating of any president ever—sixty-eight percent.

Back home, during the spring and summer, Jack's "spirit" was thrusting him forward with his plans to build a baseball stadium. He and I did the college circuit with Breck, who decided to apply to Duke University in North Carolina. While there, we visited some minor league stadiums—most notably, the Durham Bulls stadium where the film "Bull Durham" was made. Jack met with the president of the Northern League—the league he was interested in. I began to see what Jack had in mind: good, old-fashioned fun for the Brockton community. Still there was a long way to go in the process and I knew the burden of high college tuitions was causing Jack deep anguish over whether to stay in politics or go back to his private law practice.

One night I left him to run to the store and when I returned he didn't look so good. "Are you okay?" I asked. He was sitting in the darkened living room, his hand around an icy old-fashioned glass.

"No. I'm depressed!" he said. He was in tears. Finally he confided how hard it was on him that his mother was beginning to show signs of Alzheimer's disease and that he had so little time for her. It was also hard that he had to rely on his sisters, Amy and Patty, for their mother's care.

"I can't believe you talked me into running again!" he suddenly blurted out.

"Me-e?" I was aghast. "I'm the one who wanted a Cape house, remember?"

He apologized immediately saying that the day had been a bad one for him and that he just wanted to get drunk. He was so overwhelmed he couldn't even tell me what the issues were. I had to guess. It could have been the stadium financing, the Brockton Hospital nurses strike, the Main Street Mile road race, International Day, a proposed natural gas power plant, the Desalinization plant, new traffic lights, and/or the third new school being a wee bit behind schedule. What was the big whoop?

"No one has any idea how much goes on," he said wearily, placing his glass on the coffee table.

"I know," I responded, patting his thigh. "I know."

Jack finally convinced Mark O'Reilly, his long time friend and running partner, to leave his job at the YMCA and join him as Chief of Staff. It had been eight months since Mary resigned. Jack had had no helper. Mark, who was a former Marine and winner of two Purple Hearts and a Bronze Star for his Vietnam service, eventually became a hard-working, devoted assistant to Jack. But Mark was used to working in the private sector and didn't understand that vacation time wasn't as plentiful in the political world. Shortly after being hired, Mark flew off to Montana and our family was left to organize volunteers and run a phone bank for our friend, Stephen Lynch, who was running for Congress. Jack was a bit perturbed.

When I returned home from locking my office after winding up the phone bank, he was stressed yet again, eating cheese and crackers for dinner and wondering where the hell I'd been. "I can't believe it's just us again!" he said, referring to how our family was making the phone calls for Lynch. Jack was more agitated than before. "I'm getting tired of this." I heard him rattling around by the liquor cabinet when Casey called from D.C. to say she was agonizing over whether to stay at Catholic University or to transfer. She'd just started her sophomore year at that point and was "miserable." Jack appeared with his drink in hand, and wanted to know "the facts."

"Jack, this isn't a good time to talk about it," I said, jotting down some notes for Casey. "You're volatile and emotional. Let's talk tomorrow." I poured myself a glass of wine and said, "Follow me," waving my hand. I walked through the swinging door of the dining room, through the music room and out onto the porch hoping he'd do the same. A cool late summer breeze was blowing and the fresh air would do us good. He got as far as the porch doorway.

"Being mayor has prevented me from being a better father and that's why Breck quit football!" he stated. "Now Casey wants to quit college, come home and marry an electrician!"

"This is not a good time to talk about it," I repeated, turning on a table lamp.

"When is a good time? After we've paid $10,000 more in tuition?" he yelled. A few more heated words were exchanged and finally he grabbed the handle to the glass door and slammed it on his way back into the house.

"See?" I said, acutely aware of how still and quiet the neighborhood was. Not even a cricket. Our words had traveled loud and clear through the dark, including the ones where I called him a fucking asshole. I closed my eyes and prayed that everyone within earshot was either asleep, on vacation, or not quite voting age. Then I finished my glass of Hacienda Merlot, adjusted the gooseneck lamp and picked up the book, "Widow for One Year."

CHAPTER 24

"Great tragedy has come to us, and we are
meeting it with the best that is in our country,
with courage and concern for others because
this is America. This is who we are."
—*George W. Bush*

I finally convinced Jack to take a break from his responsibilities before the school year commenced. He and I drove Breck, Mairi, and her friend, Angela, down to New Jersey to visit my parents for Labor Day. While there we took a day trip to New York City to visit Ellis Island and the Statue of Liberty. It was an exquisite day, blue skies, crisp white clouds. I snapped several pictures of the kids at the Ferry landing using the two tall World Trade Center buildings as the backdrop.

When we returned to Brockton, the election season was heating up and I volunteered to be a "checker" at the polls. That meant that when voters came in I'd check their names off a long address list. Jack wasn't on the ballot for the primary—the only one running against him that year was the (snore) travel agent, who ran for mayor every two years, simply, I believe, to promote his business. Anyway, it would be a slow day at the Hancock School polling place so I brought my summer pictures to put into a photo album.

Shortly after the polls opened, however, the world learned the terrifying news that a Jet airliner had flown into one of the Twin Towers of the World Trade Center in New York City. Within eight minutes, the second airline hit. A TV set was wheeled into the gymnasium where the voting booths were, and from then on everyone's attention was riveted. The Pentagon in Washington had also been struck. I couldn't get through to Conor or Casey who were in D.C., and chills ran through my legs thinking that the invasion might be the start of World War III. The TV kept replaying the second plane flying into the tower with the giant flames erupting and the smoke billowing. A giant cloud further horrified us as evidence that the first tower had imploded. The second tower followed quickly, and to escalate the nation's fears, another jet airliner crashed near Pittsburgh.

Finally, Conor called me. He was safe, he said, but his neighborhood had been evacuated and Washington, D.C.'s subway system—the Metro—had been shut down. Before he could say more my cell phone went silent. Talking to my fellow poll workers, I had a difficult time breathing. I hadn't yet reached Casey, although Jack phoned in shortly afterwards and relayed that he spoke with Casey and she was nervous, but coping, and would call me later.

"Okay, what about Breck?" I asked, crossing my legs under the table.

"I'm betting he's still at B.C. High," Jack said, although we weren't entirely sure. There was no way to reach him.

"Mairi?" I asked, uncrossing my legs and sliding them under my chair.

"She's staying at West Junior High," he said. "I'm keeping the schools open because I don't want kids going home alone and learning of the tragedy."

I calmed down a bit. Meanwhile, in spite of the calamity, school bells rang, kids yelled in the hall and people continued to vote.

"Is this where we put the ballots?" asked one familiar woman.

"Isn't it awful?" said her friend, touching her fingers to her mouth.

The TV replayed the utter destruction—the ghastly smoke, people running. One woman being interviewed was crying hysterically seeing people jumping from skyscraper windows.

"I bet you wish you weren't here right now," a middle-aged man said to me, diverting my attention from the screen.

"I can't think of a better place to be," I answered. I mean, if I couldn't be home in bed with my four children and husband in a pig pile on top of me, then I might as well be at the polls where the action was.

The man continued that his son was supposed to have been on the Boston plane, but overslept and missed the flight. "There but for the grace of God," he murmured.

The volume of voters kept the activity brisk. "No chads, that's a good thing," said a woman dressed in a running suit.

"Aren't your kids in D.C.?" a neighbor asked.

"It's another Pearl Harbor!" a Korean War vet announced.

With a touch of disbelief, I showed people my Kodak pictures taken a week earlier—a portrait of Mairi and Angela posing on a pier—the Twin Towers dominating the background.

Governor Jane Swift addressed the Commonwealth on TV saying, "We must keep the polls open. We must not stop our democratic process." I applauded her.

Soon after, Jack appeared and told me he'd begun organizing to send Brockton's Canine Police Officers down to New York, as well as teams of firemen.

Mairi eventually called from a friend's house. She asked me if there would be cheerleading practice.

"No, honey, not today," I responded, wanting to wrap my arms around her and pull her to me through the phone.

"The world's gone mad," said City Councilor Peter Asiaf walking by my table.

"All band students please come to the cafeteria," a loud overhead speaker announced.

"20 Greenbriar Road, Mary Svirsky, check."

An Enterprise photographer approached my table and told me the Westgate Mall had closed and locked its doors.

At 4 p.m., Casey finally got through to my phone. Catholic University had cancelled all classes and the staff members were delivering pizzas to the dorms and encouraging everyone to stay on campus. The clergy would be holding an emergency Mass with all their Bishops. Casey was on her way to give blood.

After leaving the polls, I met up with Jack and Mairi at home. "I have never heard New York City this quiet. Graveyard quiet," said a TV newsman.

Conor phoned again to say that he and friends were cooking dinner and watching President Bush on TV.

"Make no mistake," the President said. "We will hunt down and punish . . . will do whatever is necessary. I ask the American people to join me in thanking all the people helping the victims. We will show the world that we will pass this test."

As news continued pouring in, Jack and I were dismayed to see that the Emergency Operations Center, also known as Building No. 7, had collapsed.

Earlier that summer, as guests of New York's Mayor Rudolf Giuliani, Jack and I were given a grand tour of the Emergency Operations Center. The spacious taupe-colored area looked and felt like a command center from "Mission Impossible." The darkly lit indoor concourse was full of state-of-the-art computers, big screens and telephones with dozens of separate stations labeled with signs like NYPD, Bronx South, and Staten Island. The place was the brainchild of Mayor Giuliani. We were told it was impregnable, and though it had yet to be tried during a catastrophe, could handle any emergency. There was also an efficiency apartment where the mayor could live for up to three weeks if necessary.

Giuliani gave a presentation during which he told us that New York had been dubbed the largest and safest city in the world. I was impressed by his speaking abilities, lacing facts with a touch of humor. He also introduced a cutting-edge technology known as E-government, which would soon make government accessible to everyone. He explained in depth how computer websites would improve the quality of life in cities. "New York," he said, "is about to launch a website called NYC.gov which will allow municipal services to be dealt with online. People will be able to reserve baseball fields, pay parking tickets, register for yard sales or check on the latest restaurant inspections." The audience was in awe, the technology nearly unimaginable. Mayor Giuliani checked one restaurant for us and there were no violations listed. Everyone clapped.

On 9/11, Mayor Giuliani barely escaped from the Emergency Operations Center before the building caved in. I lamented the loss of all those computers and data banks, all that superior equipment. Within minutes, the Hotel Marriott, where we stayed that same week, crumbled to the ground.

Jack, Mairi and I drove to Brockton City Hall for the election results and continued to watch TV in Jack's office. Mairi commented that the World Trade Center now looked like the coliseum from the award-winning movie "The Gladiator."

The one piece of good news was that candidate Stephen Lynch from South Boston became Brockton's newest federal representative, winning the late Congressman Joe Moakley's former seat. We learned later that Stephen humbly thanked the crowd at his victory party while acknowledging the nation's tragedies. No alcohol was served and the band didn't play.

That night, Breck dreamt that all our living Presidents were assassinated.

Casey called the next day to say she wanted to come home. She needed to hug Mairi.

Two days later, Jack had to attend a meeting regarding the new trash company he'd hired for the city and to help explain the system to the public.

I knew the meeting might be combative and thought that if I went with him the citizens might soften their blows. No such luck.

We entered the dim auditorium and lowered ourselves into two folding seats in the front row. The smell of "school" bothers me to this day, and that night, it was accentuated by the tension that permeated the air. Jack had worked on changing trash companies for years, submitting to people's complaints about the old company, and agonizing over what the higher rates charged by the new company would mean to constituents. In addition, dumps had started closing down around the state and recycling was absolutely necessary.

The people there that night were yelling, screaming and blaming the government for making them recycle. I squirmed in my seat as men and women took turns standing up and yelling at the Waste Company officials who hovered by the podium waiting for a chance to educate the attendees. One tall man yelled out that Jack lost all his values when he moved from West Elm Terrace to Fairview Avenue ten years earlier. A woman with scraggly, shoulder-length hair said the raise Jack received (a few years prior) should be returned because she didn't make that much money. She added that she couldn't possibly get by if households were only allotted one barrel for their trash—she needed at least two. Jack stood and tried to tell the protesters that more barrels would make the rates go up even higher, but they weren't there to listen, just to vent. They loved each other for their crass ways, too, and clapped for every dig at politicians.

One fat-bellied man said the issue had been "stuffed down our throats while we were sleeping." I guess he didn't read the paper or listen to the radio. After all, the city had been giving out free recycle bins for six years.

"You've insulted my intelligence," said another man, dressed in a T-shirt and jeans. What intelligence? I wondered. They dished out every excuse explaining why they couldn't recycle.

"It'll blow around!"

"People will throw their garbage in our yards!"

"We don't have room!"

"Everyone in surrounding towns has it better!"

"The other system was the best!"

Jack and I sat there for two hours listening. Finally he walked over to the front of the stage and faced the crowd. Using his hands to emphasize certain points, he explained how long a process it'd been and that he'd kept people informed all along the way with radio shows and public hearings.

City Councilor Peter Marciano, Jr. came into the auditorium at that point. Walking halfway across the front he paused, and then grabbed the lapels on his handsome suit. His dark Italian eyes surveyed the crowd. In a firm voice he told the audience he voted against the new company. They applauded wildly. He took a step forward and, transferring his hands to his pockets, added that he gave Jack credit, however, for implementing the novel service, saying the majority of Councilors voted in favor. The audience inhaled abruptly. I loved the Councilor at that moment. Then again, I've always loved the guy. He's a character. When he was first elected it bothered him that the City Council meetings were the same night as his card game.

"You guys have to get behind this now and deal with the change," he said dismissively, strolling to a front row seat. The people shut up for a wisp of a minute, and then continued squawking.

I honestly wondered if anyone in the audience remembered there had been an attack on America two days ago! Thousands of innocent people were dead and the world was in flux. And these folks were unruly over recycling? How would they react if, God forbid, chemical warfare happened in Brockton? Or if citizens had to cooperate with one another, say, in an evacuation or a massive inoculation drive? I trembled to think.

Jack and I stayed until nine o'clock, and before we could make it to our car a man stopped Jack in the parking lot to complain some more. After twenty minutes, he wasn't impolite, but he wasn't listening either.

"Jack we have to go," I finally said pulling his arm.

The ironic thing was that two short years later, Brockton won an award for its recycling efforts. Another example of why we, as Americans—or Jack, as a politician—have to get past the negative thinkers—those who seem to wield so much power initially—but really don't have much.

Casey, God bless her, in the aftermath of 9/11, began making hundreds of red, white and blue ribbons to sell in order to raise money for the Red Cross. She collected two hundred and forty dollars the first day and eventually raised so much money that she received an appreciation letter from the charity.

At the first Red Sox game following the tragedy, the fans in Boston hooked arms, swayed back and forth and sang "New York, New York." Gotta love Boston fans. That was probably the most affection ever demonstrated between the two teams that had had a historic rivalry for a long time.

"If you really want to help New York, come to the city and buy things," Mayor Giuliani reported. From his mouth to my ears. Jack decided that for Christmas, all six of us would drive to Ground Zero. He rented a van with a video player and television to make everyone really comfortable because he felt guilty taking us away on Christmas day. He bought several videos, like "Spy Kids" and "Bring It On" to keep Mairi amused. Finally we arrived in the Big Apple.

Our family walked around the entire two-mile border, even though there wasn't much to see. Thousands of onlookers like us climbed on anything they could to peer over the barricades. Every now and then we'd catch a glimpse of the cavernous void where the Twin Towers once stood. In the chilly air people were quiet and respectful. The lingering stench I'd heard about had dissipated by then, or maybe you couldn't smell it in the cold.

Afterwards Jack maneuvered the enormous van uptown to meet friends of ours from Brockton. They traditionally spent every Christmas morning in New

York City enjoying a Christmas drink at the Plaza Hotel. That was a wonderful experience with many hearty New Yorkers chattering, rubbing their chilled hands together and generally exuding bright holiday spirit. Four hot chocolates and four cocktails later, however, the bill came to $120.00. I swallowed some air on that one and tried not to wince as Jack picked up the tab. I let the kids know that our stop at the famous hotel was a special holiday treat, and that they should be happy to know we were helping New York City, even if it meant we must return all their Christmas presents once we got home.

"Mayor Yunits is a man of great integrity. He has not forgotten where he came from, where he is going and those who have and will continue to help shape his place in the history of Brockton.

O Prefeito Yunits é um homém de grande integridade. Ele não se esqueceu ded onde veio, onde ele quer ir e de aqueles que o ajudou e continuarão a ajudá-lo no seu acento na história de Brockton."

—Moises Rodrigues Brockton Cape Verde Business Association

CHAPTER 25

"Success seems to be largely a matter of hanging on after others have let go."
—William Feather

I wasn't able to say this too many times, but I learned that Brockton had officially been awarded the six million dollar grant for the baseball stadium before Jack did. But I couldn't tell him. I was seated in Governor Swift's reception area at the State House in Boston waiting for Jack while he had meetings elsewhere in the building regarding an unrelated matter. While I waited, a reporter from The Enterprise, Jocelyn Meek, appeared. She walked across the carpet and told me she'd been called by the Governor's office to be present when the good news was announced.

"What good news?" I asked, standing up.

"The stadium," she said, matter-of-factly, drumming her pen on a notebook.

"What about the stadium?" I asked, feeling a growing sense of excitement.

"We got the stadium!" she explained, grinning when she realized I didn't know. Jack was hoping his pending meeting with the Governor would lead to that conclusion, but it had been such a long haul of ups and downs he wasn't sure what to expect. Former Governor Cellucci once promised Jack the stadium money, but the bill failed to pass the legislature. Cellucci subsequently was

appointed Ambassador to Canada. Lt. Governor Jane Swift took over as
Governor in April 2001, and with that change came more uncertainty about
the future of the ballpark. When Jack showed up in the lobby to await Governor
Swift's private conference, I struggled to keep the surprise.

"Hey, sweetie. What's going on?" I said, pretending to search for something
in my jacket pocket. I found an "I love Brockton" pin.

Jack was preoccupied, however. When he had a lot on his mind he couldn't
identify with small talk. "What did you say, sweetheart?" he asked, immediately
turning to a colleague and starting another conversation. I slipped the pin back
in my pocket.

After a few minutes, the Governor appeared to shepherd Jack into the
corner office. Our state's first female Governor looked fantastic for someone
who'd recently given birth to twin daughters. Her jet-black hair and youthful
face didn't even look tired. I wondered how she managed. I also marveled
at people who built skyscrapers or bridges. I was lucky to get three loads of
laundry washed and put dinner on the table. Now that was a productive day!

After about ten minutes, Jack emerged from the Governor's office. He
winked at me while a dozen people in the lobby shook his hand and slapped
him on the back. What a great day for Brockton. Finally, we were making
wholesome progress! The news reporter took notes furiously.

Afterwards, on the sidewalk in front of the Statehouse, as Jack and I were
heading to our car, he abruptly stopped in his tracks. "This sets things up nicely
for a new performance center!" he said. It was another dream of his to establish
a performing arts center in the heart of downtown Brockton, preferably in the
War Memorial Building. Still, I had to interject, "Jack, people can barely keep up
with your projects as it is! Give us a break!" But we had no such luck.

Our car ride home was punctuated by his cell phone ringing out of its'
holster. When he paused to catch his breath, I borrowed his phone and called
Mark at City Hall to tell him the good news.

"Hoo-ra!" Mark yelled like the Marine that he was. In a second, all of City Hall knew that the city could finally, officially, begin construction on Campanelli Stadium.

Jack had been so optimistic that he'd already given the go-ahead to the contractor to begin laying out the actual ball field with the irrigation system underneath. The builder was two-and-a-half million dollars into the project without a guaranteed payback. But he and Jack both liked the idea of allowing the "field of dreams" to find its natural state before the stadium was built around it. Good thing the money came through—the press and other non-believers would have skewered Jack for that bold move if his considerable gamble hadn't paid off. But the way Jack thought, if the grant hadn't come through, Brockton would, at the very least, have "the best damn high school field in the country."

The following week, Jack won his fourth election with 82.2% of the vote. We were relieved to have another election behind us, even if Jack was disappointed to not have had a worthy opponent. He had so much to tell people about the positive changes happening in the city, but without debates and such, and with a newspaper that always wanted to emphasize the negatives, the opportunity bypassed him.

At the end of the week I tuned into radio station WBET in time to hear that there were a number of people who disliked the name Brockton Rox—chosen for the upcoming baseball team—and wanted the name changed. The editor of The Enterprise, Steve Damish, who was a guest on the show, said he hadn't met anyone who liked the name. He wanted people to start a letter-writing campaign to the paper to create a "grass roots movement so the people would have their say." I felt the blood rush to my face, and a familiar annoyance for that editor, because he preferred to criticize every new thing. He didn't even live in Brockton! But I took a deep, slow breath and called the station.

"You should open your eyes and ears," I mustered, my voice shaking a bit. "Lots of people like the name." Without letting them know who I was I said that the owners conducted a survey for the new team's name and "Rox" won the most votes from the age group of 14 years and younger. That was important to the owners.

The radio host, Bill Carpenter, told me he wouldn't buy any of their merchandise.

I told him I'd already bought season tickets and that my husband had a new Rox sweatshirt.

He retorted: "These non-locals come into our city saying they'll keep in line with Brockton pride and sports history and they let everyone down."

"You don't think the word "Rox" somehow ties in with Rocky Marciano?" I asked. "Not to mention that the kids like the name because it infers that Brockton "rocks," as in "we're cool"—isn't that a fun play on words?"

"No," he said. "It should have been "The Rockies" then." Oh, okay.

"But what happens if after you've put all that energy into finding a new name, you decide you don't like the next one?" I asked. Neither he, nor Steve, had an answer for that.

Finally, switching the subject, I was asked if I'd be watching the New England Patriots football team during Sunday's Super Bowl. "Of course," I said, and Bill asked me to predict the score.

"24-17 Patriots," I guessed.

He was surprised I picked the Patriots to win. Apparently they weren't favored.

But they did! They won! They beat the St. Louis Rams, 20-17, with a field goal by Adam Vinatieri in the last few seconds. The triumph was New England's first Super Bowl title and the state's first sports championship since 1986, when the Celtics basketball team last won the NBA finals.

Conor was studying in Ireland for a semester abroad by then and watched the Super Bowl on TV at a large pub in Dublin. He told me the American students painted "Go Pats!" on each other's faces and soon every Irish patron in the bar also sported the red, white and blue look.

For New England it was an intoxicating victory. Breck made it to the celebratory parade in Boston a few days later along with fifty B.C. High boys and more than a million other revelers. He said there was a spectacular sea of people. He and his friends climbed over rooftops to get closer to City Hall and at one point Breck saw fifteen kids hanging from a single tree.

I was at work and the white boom box in my little upstairs office was all shaky as excited announcers described the parade passing by. Patriots' quarterback, Tom Brady, the youngest quarterback ever to win the Super Bowl, received such intense applause the crescendo of energy sounded like a rocket ship blastoff.

A week later I received an anonymous email saying that the "ratio was 20-1 against the name Brockton Rox." It continued: "A better name would be the Brockton Fielders, named after the D.W. Field Park." I also heard over the next few days, names like the Brockton Shoemakers and the Brockton Knock-Outs. But you can't please everyone, and the Brockton Rox name stuck. The following day the steel frame for the stadium infrastructure went up.

Shortly thereafter, in Boston, Jack met with Congressman Stephen Lynch and several union leaders. Mark drove in with Jack because the officials had let it be known they were quite angry about the allocation of jobs for the stadium.

But Jack never let the men start up against him. He spelled out the situation as it was; that he'd given the unions plenty of work over the years and when they couldn't guarantee keeping the cost of the stadium to $17 million, he had to look elsewhere for an additional workforce and the entire process, he pointed out, was legal.

Mark said it was something else to see Jack. By the time the meeting was over, everyone was shaking hands and understood what was going on. On the drive home, Jack could breathe again.

Later that month, during U.S. Senator Ted Kennedy's 70th birthday party at the John F. Kennedy Library, people from all over the room came up to Jack wanting the latest updates about Brockton. There was lots of excitement about the pending baseball field.

Springfield Mayor Mike Albano sidled up to me singing "Take Me out to the Ballgame." His city never did get a stadium, by the way, after negotiating for eight years.

At the annual 21st Century Corporation's luncheon, which that year united the Brockton business community with the new Brockton Rox people, we met Ed Nottle, the new Brockton Rox manager. Ed once managed the Paw Sox, the farm team associated with the Boston Red Sox, which is located in Pawtucket, Rhode Island.

Ed had been living in his home state of Indiana of late and emphasized that although everyone out there was terrific and wonderful and decent, the difference was that he could walk into a bar any place in Massachusetts or Rhode Island and someone would know him. There was a communal atmosphere in our part of the country, he said, that doesn't exist elsewhere. I knew what he meant.

The other quality that Ed brought to the table was his exquisite voice. Ed entertained the crowd with his natural, effortless vibrato, vis-à-vis Frank Sinatra, and mesmerized the room with his rendition of "Welcome to My World." Ed is as superb a singer as I've ever known in my life. I couldn't believe Brockton's good fortune. We were getting baseball and adding to our musical talent pool.

Mike Veeck, (rhymes with check) the keynote speaker at the luncheon and a principal owner of the team, had us rolling in the aisles with stories about his one-legged father, the late Bill Veeck, who once owned the Chicago White Sox. He also brought up some interesting facts about Brockton, telling us the catcher's mitt was invented here and that the first stitched baseball was sewn together in a Brockton shoe factory.

Jack was then presented with a framed copy of a bar napkin from Thorny Lea Golf Club where the original conversation about the stadium had taken place a few years earlier. The framed napkin featured Jack's hand-drawn diagram showing the population centers in Massachusetts and why locating the stadium in Brockton made good economic sense. At the top of the napkin was scribbled Jack's birth date, January 24, 1952, along with "Mayor Yunits, Happy 50th thanks for everything" scrawled across the bottom.

I hung the gift where I hang everything of importance, in our little round bathroom tucked under the stairs. We affectionately refer to this location as the Oval Office.

"Now that it is over I realize that my dad being mayor was the best experience for me. I was challenged to become a better person and I was exposed to politicians who inspired me."
— *Mairi S. Yunits*

CHAPTER 26

"It is in the shelter of each other that the people live"
—*Irish* Proverb

The soft-spoken, lovely daughter-in-law of our friends, Suzanne and O.D., Lauren O'Donnell, was having supper at her kitchen table with her two young daughters, Elisabeth and Grace, ages 4 and 2, when they noticed a spider on the wall about the size of a nickel. The four-year-old asked if they should capture the spider and let it loose outside or leave it alone.

"Maybe we'll leave it alone because then the spider will eat all of the other bugs in the house," Lauren said, lifting a forkful of macaroni and cheese to her mouth.

"What if a ladybug gets in the house? Will it eat a ladybug?" Elisabeth asked.

"Well, I don't know if they eat ladybugs," her mother replied, wiping her lips with a napkin.

Elisabeth took a long sip of milk and put her sippy cup down. " Let's call the mayor," she suggested. "He'll know if spiders eat ladybugs."

The traditional St. Patrick's Day Breakfast, held in South Boston, is an annual Irish gathering, which brings together the top Massachusetts political officials for a morning of good-humored backstabbing. The late Congressman Joe Moakley began the tradition, followed by former Speaker of the House

William Bulger. From there, Congressman Stephen Lynch ran the show, and now the duty of the 50th annual had fallen to State Senator Jack Hart. Through Hart's association with Jack, I was asked to sing an Irish song that year, which was a privilege beyond any gig I'd ever played.

The air was crisp and cold and when Jack and I pulled up to the Ironworkers Local Seven building, preparations were underway for the St. Patty's Day parade, which usually followed the breakfast. We were ushered through the "Elected Officials" entrance, and an attendant motioned for me to take a seat by the stage. Jack stood behind me on a raised platform, shoulder-to-shoulder with hundreds of other people who didn't have seats. For the first time since Jack became mayor, I experienced privileges that he didn't. Scrambled eggs, served with Boston baked beans on a Styrofoam plate and a glass of orange juice were served to me. The people standing received nothing.

My prime spot was next to Wacko Hurley—the man who'd been running the St. Patrick's Day parade for years. I peered up at his weathered Irish face and decided to spare him any small talk. His darting eyes inferred 'twould be best if I kept to meself.

One of the first speakers at the podium was Republican Governor Jane Swift, who informed the huge crowd that businessman Mitt Romney was back in Massachusetts after having spent three years in Salt Lake City chairing the Olympics. The crowd knew Romney was considering running for Governor and that the Republican Party had been openly fawning over him, rather than supporting Mrs. Swift. Jane was a good sport, though, joking that Mitt had come at a bad time. What with the drought, it would be hard for him to "walk on water."

Democratic candidate for Governor, State Treasurer Shannon O'Brien, used the recent Olympics as her theme also, showing a picture of Jane Swift skiing downhill. "Gee, she's going really, really fast," Shannon pointed out, to much laughter and applause.

After several other speakers made their jabs my name was announced. I had to wrangle out of my chair and through the tight crowd before a woman took my hand and pulled me up the short stairs to the stage. I was handed a guitar and once the instrument was strapped over my shoulder, I turned to face a mass of green and blonde seated at long tables. I could feel the heat from the TV lights; saw cameras lining the back of the room. People were wedged into every available inch of the facility. In one of those random surprises of life, I looked down and seated right in front of the stage was one of Conor's best friends, Jared Fitzgibbon. His wide smile gave me a boost like an Irish good luck charm. I began the first verse of "Fields of Athenry," a lovely Irish ballad. When I got to the chorus, I knew without a doubt that I was in South Boston because every person in the room joined in. The moment was as significant to me as almost any other in my life.

When I was singing the verses, I tried looking for Jack to my right, where he'd been standing, only to learn later that he'd moved to the other side. When I finished, I saw Brockton State Senator Rob Creedon giving everyone a high five. His wife, State Representative Geri Creedon, congratulated me as I came off the stage and I felt extra grand about being Brockton's representative at the famous St. Patty's Day breakfast.

By then several Boston Bruins hockey team players had filed into the room and I brushed by them on my way out. They were so much taller in person than I would have thought. As they paraded onto the stage, Jack and I skirted out the door to drive to Mairi's majorette competition.

Two days later, Governor Swift announced that she would not run for election in the fall. Mitt Romney and the Republican Party had succeeded in squeezing her from the race. Still Brockton is forever grateful for Jane Swift's brief stint as Governor because it was she who awarded Brockton the grant Jack needed to get the stadium built.

By the end of March 2002, the roof was going on above the concourse at Campanelli Stadium, and in mid-April Shaw's Supermarkets donated $1 million dollars for naming rights to the stadium's attached conference center. It would soon be known as The Shaw's Center.

Over the next few weeks, I continued getting emails and phone calls from people saying they had seen me on TV singing at the St. Patrick's Day breakfast. One night in late April, at Joe Angelo's Cafe, a Vietnam Veteran sitting at the bar mentioned he watched the Irish event. He said it made him so proud. "You were one of us!" he declared.

Two weeks later, Sovereign Bank opened in Brockton and Jack said the President of the bank let him know that even two years earlier, he wouldn't have made the move to Brockton. But things kept looking increasingly better in the city, which prompted the president to seal the deal.

CHAPTER 27

"Baseball will take our people out-of-doors,
fill them with oxygen, give them a larger
physical stoicism. Tend to relieve us from
being a nervous, dyspeptic set. Repair these
losses, and be a blessing to us."
—*Walt Whitman*

On Saturday, April 27, 2002, as the city anxiously awaited our own opening day, Boston Red Sox pitcher Derek Lowe pitched a no-hitter at Fenway Park. That was the first no-hitter pitched there in 37 years, and added to the overall baseball fever.

As the days went by, Brockton's first Starbucks opened on the west side and a Super Stop and Shop signed on to build a store on North Montello Street. A few days later, Jack cut the ribbon in front of the new Dr. William Arnone Elementary School, a state-of-the art educational facility surrounded by a tree-filled park.

In downtown Brockton, construction began on a Dunkin' Donuts regional bakery, capable of making 9,600 donuts an hour. My mouth watered thinking about the bakery. Next to Black Russians, donuts are my favorite food.

Maybe I had one Black Russian too many one night in celebration of all the success, but I dreamt Jack was sitting on the couch naked as a jaybird watching TV. I kept telling him to get dressed because his behavior wasn't proper, and then I noticed something unusual. His testicles were enormous. "Like a buffalo's!" I told him.

Two days later, as God is my witness, a radio talk show host, Ron Van Dam, told the listening audience that the single most important reason for Brockton's great resurgence was, "The little guy, Mayor Yunits. Jack never backs down from a challenge because he has Big B's! It's Jack's Big B's that are driving this city forward, people!"

That same morning, Jack tripped on a pothole and fell during his morning run, skinning his knee and palm. I told him his constituents might not be sympathetic since their streets were probably full of potholes. Then he had an early meeting with the Building Superintendent Bob Finnegan to resolve another looming battle about the stadium signage and construction codes. Tensions were high as opening day approached, but Jack found time to squeeze in a visit to the hospital to pay a call on a former Brockton City Councilor. The man was seriously ill, and his wife told Jack he'd "gone to the hospital to die." The next day, Jack got a call from the wife.

"Thank you! Thank you! Thank you!" she said. Her husband had had a complete change of attitude. She said he was up having breakfast telling her, "I can't go now. The mayor needs me!" Jack had given him Rox tickets and now he was packing his clothes.

Conor returned home from Ireland in time to be hired by the Rox to run the promotions between innings. The job required long days and nights and the pay was minimal, but Conor couldn't wait to start. I was beginning to see a trend in this family for accepting low wages.

One afternoon Jack and I drove over to the ballpark. The day was a glorious one and industrious men were painting lines on the VIP parking lot when we pulled in. Jack went walking off as usual, leaving me to fend for myself. I spotted my friends, Andrea and Rick Bates, finishing one of the souvenir stands they were building. Walking toward them I heard Conor's voice.

"Ma! Do you want to be a human bowling ball?" he yelled.

I didn't really understand what he said, but answered, "Okay." The next thing I knew I was standing in left field removing my high heels and stepping into a deflated ring of clear synthetic. Conor used an air-pumping machine to inflate the droopy stuff into a large bubble and sealed me inside.

"Now run down the foul line and knock over the large bowling pins by third base!" he directed, pointing his arm away.

I rolled like a gerbil across the field. "Go faster!" random people in the stands hollered with glee. I couldn't believe how hard it was, or how out of shape I felt.

I hit the giant bowling pins, knocked them over, and toppled to the ground. My hair barrette crunched into my skull.

"Okay, ma, roll back!" Conor called, motioning with his hands. Oh, yeah, right, uh huh, no sweat.

Meanwhile, Jack was in the car honking at me to hurry up. I had to rotate all the way back, get out from the ball, find my shoes and purse, fix my hair, climb up into the bleachers, wipe the mud from my feet and the sweat from my eye sockets, put my shoes back on and gallop to his car. It was a great way to make an appearance at the appreciation party for Al Campanelli—the man whose $2 million donation helped set the ballpark in motion.

When Jack and I drove over to the field early the next afternoon the stadium was one busy place. The atmosphere resembled Santa's workshop. Employees were hosing down the seats, testing the sound system, hanging banners, and folding T-shirts. Giant Sumo wrestler costumes made their way past me as Conor directed the interns where to store them. Half of the leather couches had come in for the luxury boxes upstairs and were still wrapped in plastic; TV sets were being delivered and an artist named Andy Nelson was touching up figures of Rocky Marciano and Marvin Hagler in the men's room. Andy had a sense of humor- he'd also created a clown likeness of Jack in the ladies room.

Jack reported to me that Bob Finnegan was "hanging in there," and that the occupancy permit was due to come through any minute.

The Rox general manager, Dave Echols, figured on the evening being a "wild night" because severe thunderstorms were predicted. But I sensed from his calm nature that he could handle anything.

Jack was hustled down to the field for the opening ceremony as thousands of eager fans streamed into the park. The minute our family and friends got to our seats and the officials were ready to kick off the long awaited ceremony, dark clouds gathered overhead. There was a loud crash of thunder, a few bolts of lightning, another boom, and soon, a huge deluge.

My friend, Kim Tilas, pushed open her umbrella, which turned inside out immediately, and we couldn't stop laughing. It was opening day! Nothing could squelch the crowd's excitement or ours.

More than a dozen workers, including Conor, hurriedly heaved and rolled the giant silver tarp over the infield as five thousand drenched people cheered for them. The rain stopped suddenly and in that silence, the tarp toilers dragged the canvas back off. The crowd roared in anticipation.

The entire opening ceremony was staged during that brief storm pause. The song God Bless America was sung, by Andrea Bates, and the Brockton High School marching band played the national anthem. Awards were presented, Rox jerseys distributed, and finally it was Jack's turn to throw out the first pitch.

Our kids had begged Jack to loosen up his arm in the backyard beforehand, but he didn't. So when he threw the ball to the celebrity catcher, Bill Murray—the actor, a part owner of the team— the ball hit the dirt in front of the bag. Bill caught it, did a funny twist with his body, and threw the souvenir into the audience.

"You need lessons, Jack!" someone hollered out.

"Arm's not the same is it?" another teased.

Jack told me he threw it that way on purpose because if he'd thrown a simple strike, no one would have talked about it!

Unfortunately, the sky couldn't hold back the rain anymore and soon the celebrities were scrambling up into the stands. The longest, loudest thunderstorm let loose over the beautiful field, causing the game to ultimately be canceled. Yet, thousands of smiling soaked people crowding onto the steamy concourse wanted to extend the party. Officials were mystified as to what to do next when suddenly out of nowhere, into the mobbed concourse marched the Brockton High School band with Bill Murray leading the way. His arms were pumping and the band playing "Louie, Louie" as proudly as could be. What a great sport Bill was. His gesture made the event, allowing opening day to become one helluva unique memory for the city.

"As Mayor, Jack Yunits initiated a period of unprecedented growth for the City of Brockton, reversing a period of decline and stagnation. With his wife Lees at his side, the Mayor brought a wave of great optimism; his enthusiasm was infectious and was the driving force behind support for such projects as Campanelli Stadium- home of the Brockton Rox, the solar Brightfields, and the construction of the Plouffe, Angelo and Arnone Elementary Schools. I had the privilege of working with Jack while he was Mayor and saw firsthand the unyielding optimism and determination of a dedicated public servant who genuinely loved the families of the city he represented. "

—Congressman Stephen F. Lynch

CHAPTER 28

"I always like to look on the optimistic side of life, but I am realistic enough to know that life is a complex matter."
—Walt Disney

Regardless of the stadium's popularity and the accompanying good will, however, a ghastly batch of murders plagued the city that summer. The deadly spree began with a drive-by shooting near downtown, followed by another, and soon after that a young woman was gunned down in the parking lot of Guido O'Shea's, the restaurant that once hosted our victory parties.

Jack met with every city official and called an emergency meeting of the licensing commission to roll back Guido's license from 2 a.m. to midnight, while seeking to close the place down permanently. He warned the other 2 a.m. bars to put more police details on and to brace for the overflow from Guido's. He also suggested to the bar owners that they play Country Western or Irish songs on their jukeboxes. Maybe a change of music might keep the patrons more peaceable.

But then The Enterprise did the unthinkable—they accused Jack of contributing to the death of the woman killed at Guido O'Shea's, saying his association with the owners— who gave money to his first campaign— made him responsible!

Jack was absolutely ready to throw in the towel at that point. I may have said this before, but Jack's integrity is everything to him. From the beginning he had met with the editors, encouraging them to work with him in the advancement of Brockton, allowing them full disclosure on all issues, but they had chosen not to cooperate. I had to assume they were jealous of the city's success. Why else would they glorify these murders, time and again, and now place the blame on Jack?

In mid-August, when there was another killing, the papers and TV called the house, but Jack wouldn't talk to them. He was working with the police, the families of the slain, and the social workers—everyone but the press—to resolve the violence. Fox 25 from Boston phoned over and over. Jack told the reporters to meet him at the stadium and he'd talk with them there. But they didn't show up.

An additional slaying occurred. The unrelated deaths were a mix of bad drug deals and domestic violence and affected a tiny portion of the population. Why the murders had to happen during the summer when baseball came to Brockton I'll never know. It was a sad development. A woman reporter called one afternoon and I told her Jack was at the stadium.

"What stadium?" she asked, further evidence that the press was clueless when it came to good news about Brockton. It was like they wanted Brockton to fail by emphasizing the negative.

Finally, though, little by little, Boston writers and cameramen began turning up. Several spent an entire weekend interviewing spectators and taking in the ambience at the ballpark. You could see them munching hot dogs while directing their cameras toward the lush green outfield. TV station New England Cable News (NECN) did a nice piece about the Rox on their Sunday night show.

A friend of Jack's, Michael Baskauskas, who was raised in the "Lithuanian village" area of Brockton, but who had since moved to an exclusive neighborhood in California, spoke with Jack on the phone and confessed that he lived in a "perfect place." But, he added, California wasn't "real." Brockton was real enough. I just wished the maggots that caused all the trouble had used nerf guns instead of real bullets. They would have saved society, and Jack, a lot of distress.

Near the end of summer, Mairi, Jack and I drove Breck to North Carolina, to enroll in Duke University. Our car sailed through the picturesque Shenandoah Valley and the Blue Ridge Mountains on the way there.

Our last morning together, Breck drove off to get himself a haircut and when he came back into the hotel room, his hair looked shorter, and there was something else about his face that I couldn't figure out. His forehead looked swollen.

"Breck, have you been crying?" I asked, thinking, "How precious, he's going to miss us!"

But that wasn't it. He had his eyebrows waxed! Evidently, the cute girl who cut his hair suggested he get his thick brows waxed and he couldn't say no to her. I smiled, but my heart skipped a forlorn beat. It wasn't easy letting go of another child to the outside world.

We helped Breck move into his dorm room and with hugs, kisses, and money in his pocket Jack and I left our third child at college and drove home to Brockton.

Before the final Rox game, Mary Waldron, Jack's former chief of staff, arranged for dozens of people to hold thank you signs at both entrances to the stadium—thanking Jack for a wonderful summer. The wind was blowing a bit cooler that late August afternoon as more than sixty people showed up for a touching demonstration. Sixty people holding signs take up a lot of space curbside.

"Thanks Jack!" the waving signs read. Horns honked and people gave the thumbs up sign. The Enterprise, however, gave a "thumbs down" to Jack in their weekly column! Some editor degraded the "clique of political insiders" for holding thank you signs at the final Rox game! Even if the number of "political insiders" barely tallied five. The editors misunderstood the effect of Jack's positive administration and what a hearty "thank you" implied.

At least the new Governor, Mitt Romney, recognized Jack's leadership qualities, because he appointed him to his transition team. Better yet, The

Wall Street Transcript quoted Douglas H. Philipsen, the president of Rockland
Trust Company saying, "As a result of the cooperation between the mayor,
City Council and private interests, there has been more business revitalization
projects undertaken in the city of Brockton than virtually any city in New
England." He also said this about the Rox Stadium: "I can tell you that the mayor
of the city of Brockton has incredible vision. The Rox had an incredible year by
any standards . . . they exceeded all expectations."

CHAPTER 29

"Great is the guilt of an unnecessary war."
—*John Adams*

By the time Mairi started eighth grade at North Junior High and Conor was in his final year at George Washington University, Casey had moved to Perth, Australia, for a semester abroad. During her stay, she traveled to Broome, located in the Northwest bush country, with several other students and lived in a tent for a week. Though it appeared as if no one had ever set foot in the area, she told me the aborigines had lived there for a hundred thousand years. One native tribesman taught her to spear a stingray. Another offered her a guitar the night of the chief's birthday party and Casey played and sang his favorite song for him, Amazing Grace.

She resumed her studies at Catholic University in Washington during the winter of 2003, and the hot-button topic of the day was the pending war with Iraq. Her first political philosophy class provoked a discussion wherein Casey expressed that she wanted peace not war. The onslaught of insults she received absolutely appalled her. Her eyes stung when she told me she'd never felt such hatred from people in her whole life. Even from the professor! The group of them alleged that Casey was "uneducated and wrong." The entire class wanted to just "blow the Iraqis up and be done with it." That was a pro-life, Catholic college and the point of view totally baffled me.

We met up with Casey when Jack and I flew down for the annual mayors' conference and I told her I was proud of her for standing up for her beliefs. I suggested that maybe her fellow students should be reminded that the "peace be with you" phrase shared with a hand shake during every Catholic mass was an important part of their religion. Jack told her to go into the next lesson and say to the kids, "You're right, let's all go down and enlist." Then one could see who really had the guts.

"Those that talk the loudest, act the least," he said.

One of the nights Jack and I were in D.C. he took a taxi to U.S. Senator John Kerry's home for a cocktail reception. I'd been to Kerry's townhouse before (it is exquisite) but the day happened to be Jack's 51st birthday, so instead of accompanying him I rode the Metro to Union Station to buy some presents.

Jack was going to love his gifts. The thigh-high black stockings and sequined scarf I bought for myself would make him so happy. I felt sexy and confident riding down in the elevator to meet him later until one of the stockings started slipping down my leg. The elevator door opened to a lobby full of men. The stocking seriously started to slide off now. Halfway to the hotel lounge it was screaming, "I'm falling! I'm falling!" Mortified, I walked with a pronounced tilt to my gait. Thank God for the sequined scarf, which I wrapped around me in my best glamour girl imitation to distract from the malfunction. What was a girl to do? The stocking was a lemon! I waved weakly to a familiar face. Fortunately, the elevator was empty and so was the hallway to our room. I slid in through the door just as the nylon bunched around my ankle.

The next day, in Alexandria, VA, Jack had an important meeting with a colleague from Brockton, Ed Jacoubs, and with former U.S. Senator Harris Wofford. Along with Sargent Shriver, Senator Wofford had helped develop the Peace Corps. Senator Wofford was now the Chairman of "America's Promise," an organization started by General Colin Powell. Jack would be negotiating with the Senator and others for a substantial grant to link "America's Promise" to the youth of Brockton.

For some background, shortly after he became mayor, in 1996, Jack had assembled all of Brockton's Health and Human Service Providers—from welfare workers to educators to law enforcement personnel and job force trainers. At that meeting, the groups realized that more than a quarter of a billion dollars was being delivered to Brockton, for which there was little accountability. Those groups together formed Jack's "Blueprints Committee" and began to meet on a monthly basis. Data analysis began, and service refinement took shape through this new source of shared information. Now, Jack and Ed—who represented the Blueprints Committee—were in D.C. with hopes of demonstrating their successful collaboration, thereby convincing Senator Wofford that Brockton was worthy of obtaining this youth grant.

When I met up with Jack at Murphy's Irish Pub afterwards, Ed kept saying: "Jack was unbelievable, unbelievable." He said that as Jack was speaking Senator Wofford motioned to people outside the room to come in and listen. He apparently was convinced by Jack's ideas because shortly after we returned to Brockton the Youth Opportunity Grant was awarded and thus began "Brockton's Promise."

Once home, the pending war with Iraq overwhelmed all other news stories. The U.S. Government began putting out warnings that people should stock up on duct tape, sheets of plastic, bottled water and enough food for three days. To my knowledge, that meant preparing for radiation fallout.

Stores ran low on these supplies as people's imaginations took hold. My friend, Ellie Casieri, entered B.J.'s Wholesale Club to buy a case of bottled water, when an alarm sounded. The noise was deafening. A voice came over the loud speaker to vacate the store immediately.

"This is it!" everyone thought, leaving their shopping carts and running out of the building. My poor friend, who is 5'8" and maybe 110 pounds, shivered in the sub-zero temperature outside. Finally the store manager admitted to a false alarm and let the patrons back in.

In another instance, Casey called home from her job at Pizzeria Uno's in D.C. to tell us that Union Station had been evacuated. It turned out to be a fire in the popcorn machine at the theatre. But the unrest was indicative of the times.

The news stations reported that the inspectors in Iraq weren't finding the weapons of mass destruction we'd heard so much about. Yet President Bush and Prime Minister Tony Blair from England seemed intent on going to war. You could feel the momentum escalating. Americans wanted revenge for the atrocities of 9/11, although it was fair to say half the country—most likely the Democrats—didn't believe Iraq was the enemy.

Senator Ted Kennedy's office called our house inquiring as to how much money Brockton had received for Homeland Security. Nothing, nada.

There were demonstrations against the war in more than 600 cities worldwide. A million people marched in Paris and Berlin. Several hundred thousand marched in New York City.

I tuned in to a local radio talk show one Friday afternoon and the refreshing banter was about baseball. Two longtime Brocktonians—Peter Marciano, Jr. and Hank Tartaglia—were hosting a hilarious two hours of sports talk. I listened, grateful for the diversion from all the anxiety over war.

That night, on the way over to Ellie's for a "Turkey Fry" party, Jack and I stopped at Blanchard's liquor store up by Westgate Mall. The store has an extensive collection of wines, and sometimes even hosts wine tastings. Jack waited in the car while I went in. I passed a counter and a young woman asked if I'd like to try a new brand of wine. I said yes. I smelled, sipped, and swirled the wine around in my mouth. I liked what I tasted so I picked up a bottle and made my way to the register. The cashier promptly asked for my I.D.

"Wow you made my day! I'm almost 50!" I laughed. Then I fumbled around in my purse unable to locate my license.

"That's okay, ma'm, we'll catch you next time," the store manager said.

I carried my packages out to the parking lot thinking I must look okay for my age, heaved myself into the Nissan and slammed the door.

"Wrong car, sweetheart," a young man said. I twisted my head quickly and saw a stranger where Jack should be. I held my breath for a mini-second. The guy was cute and the interior smelled good, as if the man was on a hot date. I briefly wondered who was in the store buying his liquor for him, hoping that it was a woman. "Oops! What do you know?" I finally blurted, looking up at the ceiling, down to the floor, around to the backseat. "Our cars are just so, so similar!" He just stared. "Well, have a good night!" I said, pushing open the door and getting myself out. Jack missed the whole thing, thank God.

He was President of the Mass. Mayors' Association that year, and in that capacity had organized a summit between the mayors and Governor Mitt Romney. Thirty-nine of the state's 40 mayors attended the summit and were in an uproar about the latest budget cuts. Brockton alone was losing three and a half million dollars that would have gone to its police and fire departments.

Romney showed up at the meeting accompanied by six uniformed state police officers. Six! He had no idea how ironic that looked to the mayors whose police and fire budgets he was planning on slashing. At one point, the meeting became laden with hostility and verbal assaults. The Governor threw up his hands.

"What is this? I don't know what you call this!" he sputtered, his lacquered hair-do almost coming undone.

"This is democracy, Governor," Jack said.

The Enterprise greeted Jack the same day with a demeaning editorial, saying his "tired, old ways of tax and spend are nonsense," forgetting to mention that Romney's tax cuts had caused multiple police and firefighter lay-offs, severe deficits in the education budget and escalating misery for Brockton's less-fortunate residents. City Hall was already inundated with deranged men whose medications had been cut by the state. One homeless guy came in, crapped in his pants and left his mess on the floor of the basement. Another locked himself in the bathroom brandishing a steak knife. These were small examples of what mayors of economically strapped cities have to deal with.

On St. Patrick's Day, March 17, 2003, President Bush issued an ultimatum for Saddam Hussein to leave Iraq in 48 hours or the U.S. would go to war.

On March 19, the U.S. started bombing Iraq.

I had a sick feeling inside. My cousin's son, Christian Ellis, was heading overseas. My brother-in-law, Major Garry Schwartz, was already there. So was Mark O'Reilly's son, Mark.

On April 9, Baghdad, the capital of Iraq, fell. When the enormous statue of Saddam Hussein toppled the shared belief was that it was "the beginning of the end" of the war. What a miracle it would have been if that were so. Bush could have been a hero. As I write this, however, the war still rages six years later. More than 4,000 American troops as well as countless Iraqis, mostly civilians, have perished. The numbers are still climbing.

One day, as Jack lay sleeping, the full moon shone in through the bedroom window, accenting his silver hair. He had aged so much since taking office I felt a shiver. Tonight though he looked peaceful and I was glad he was getting a chance to rest.

Despite the war and the economic uncertainty, progress continued in Brockton. Filene's Department Store debuted at the Westgate Mall, as did a Texas Roadhouse Restaurant and a luxury day spa, Tranquil Escapes.

Hundreds of Jack's supporters packed the brand new Shaw's Center for his annual fundraiser. The Shaw's Center is attached to the ballpark and is a function hall that can hold as many as four hundred people. The large windows look out over the baseball field yielding a wonderful view. Jack gave a short speech reassuring the crowd that the city was in better shape financially than it was when he first became mayor. He said that he was in a fight for our budget though and wasn't afraid to "get bloodied."

We ended up with several of our friends and supporters at Thorny Lea for a nightcap, until Mairi called Jack's cell phone in a panic. She had seen "a flash," she said, that scared her and she wanted us right home. When we got there Mairi's face was crumpled and her eyes red—a complete change from her appearance an hour earlier. People at the fundraiser had commented how beautiful she looked. Now, Mairi was terrified that someone might be taking pictures of her, even though all the curtains were closed.

Fortunately, the "flash" turned out to be a light bulb that sparked out in the kitchen while Mairi was watching TV. But I believed that Mairi's jitters were indicative of the overall atmosphere concerning the Iraqi war.

I began having my own manifestations. One night I dreamt I was in a dance studio in Brockton, which had a coffin displayed inside. The owner, Denise Buote, told me that Little Richard, the rhythm and blues singer, was in the coffin. "It's true," she said. "Little Richard. People are paying their respects to him at our house." As the dream continued, there was a disruption and someone handed me a gun. I dropped it on the ground and cried, "I'm a musician! I don't want to be involved in this!"

Jack had his own dream. He met the captain of a ship in a bar and they spent several months together on a cargo vessel going around the world. It was the greatest feeling of freedom Jack had ever known. The two of them sailed everywhere and on the long voyages spoke together about philosophy, history, and literature. The captain was well read and had a rich lifetime of experiences to share. One night the man asked Jack, "Have you ever been married?"

"Holy shit!" Jack responded, " I forgot to tell Lees that I was leaving!"

"For the past year or so it seems like wherever I go in Brockton there are changes ... our Mayor, Jack Yunits, has been performing miracles on our very streets...a beautiful new Courthouse, beautiful huge schools with play yards we could never have imagined having... breaking ground for a beautiful new park on White Ave. This is only to mention a few of his magical tricks ... we are getting ready for his best yet, something close to my heart ... a Stadium and Conference Center. I know in a few years we'll look back with pride on this CITY THAT JACK BUILT. We're not only the City of Champions, but we have a heavyweight leading us ... our Mayor, Jack Yunits."

—Paul (Red) Sullivan

CHAPTER 30

"Every man's life ends the same way. It is only the details of how he lived and how he died that distinguish one man from another."
—Ernest Hemingway

Hands down, my favorite perk to being the mayor's wife were the dinners we often attended. Being culinarily challenged in the kitchen, I lapped up every chicken and green beans plate with aplomb. One night in particular, Jack and I were invited to share a private meal with Boston Mayor Tom Menino and his wife. I knew this one would be extra scrumptious because we were going to an Italian restaurant in Roslindale—an area of Boston where the Meninos' home is. We were also joining the President of Stonehill College, Father Mark Cregan, who loves fine cooking, and his assistant, Sr. Jean Gribaudo. Dressing for the evening was tricky. The rain outside threatened to become snow, so I pulled on black leather boots, added a knee-length skirt, a camisole, and a black jacket, before going down the stairs to catch up with Jack. "Too much," he said immediately.

"Which part?" I asked, looking over my shoulder.

"The top. Remember, Mrs. Menino is a grandmother."

"Should I dress like a grandmother?" I asked, toying with the satin camisole.

"No. Just tone it down," he said. Jack has a nice eye for women's attire, so I didn't object; I just changed the camisole to a black sweater, but kept the leather boots on.

I actually felt like I was about to attend a mafia meeting when we entered the restaurant. The room was small and narrow and several male waiters wearing white aprons stood around. Of course, the service was splendid, and Mayor Menino did the ordering. I especially enjoyed talking with Boston's First Lady, Angela Menino. Her husband had been mayor forever. I wondered how she coped. She said her approach to being the mayor's wife was to "go with the flow." She also said that she was appreciative of the opportunities she'd had like meeting the Pope and having dinner at the White House. I agreed, and shared with her that I met the actor, "Markie Mark" Wahlberg—from "The Perfect Storm" and "The Departed." "He has a body that doesn't quit," I said, dipping freshly made bread sticks in garlic oil. "Mark visited Brockton to see the results of a large donation he made to a Catholic school. When he entered the church hall and the girls in Catholic uniforms started shrieking all I could remember was his role in "Boogie Nights" as a male prostitute." Jack eyed me from across the table, wondering what I was sharing this time. I stopped talking and munched my bread stick. But Mrs. Menino was good-natured and smiled. She's a grandmother, after all.

The two mayors agreed that they didn't like to go out on Sunday nights— usually the only night they could stay home. Our time together was humorous and relaxing. I gave Angela a big hug in the rain and handed over her doggie bag with the leftover veal parmigiana. We were home by 7:30.

The day after, I was soaking in the bathtub when Jack came in and sat down on the closed toilet seat.

"Finny," is all he said.

"What about him?" I asked, soaping up. He was referring to Brockton's Building Superintendent Bob Finnegan.

"Heart attack."

"What do you mean?" I asked, stopping before I was done.

He didn't answer. The silence reverberated. Jack hung his head.

"Dead?" I asked, feeling a terrible rumble in my heart. He walked out of the bathroom. "Jack! Dead??" I yelled, jumping out of the tub. Couldn't be. Bob Finnegan was only 47 years old.

I wrapped a chenille bathrobe around myself and found Jack standing at the window in our bedroom staring out at the pond. He told me Bob's sister, Liz, called with the news that Bob died on vacation in the Dominican Republic. Jack was in a trance; my mind was swirling. Didn't Bob just run in a marathon? Wasn't that Bob mowing the lawn at the senior center the other day? The tears began to gather in my eyes as reality set in. Jack continued staring, and then collected himself enough to walk to my nightstand, pick up the phone and call Mary Waldron. I could hear her scream all the way across the room. It was just the beginning of the most painful week we had had in a long time.

City workers were in shock. Women bawled when they found out. Bob's devoted friends were heartsick. In the building department there were so many projects going on. Bob's secretary, April, was having a tough time. Besides fending off her own grief, she said business hadn't slowed down at all and she was trying to do what Bob would have wanted. Customers were getting nasty, but she didn't want to lower herself to their level. Since she and Bob started working under Jack's administration there hadn't been a workday that either one of them wasn't in the office.

Bob's brother, Jack Finnegan, asked Jack to be a pallbearer and to give the eulogy, saying that there were plenty of "Finny stories," but that he felt it was important for people to hear how Bob contributed to Brockton.

"I don't want to do a eulogy," Jack moaned from across the bed, waking me one night. He was lying on his back unable to sleep, his arms tucked under his head. I rolled over next to him and lay my hand across his chest. The reality that Bob was no longer present, no longer guiding the physical rebirth of Brockton, had knocked the life out of Jack. "I spent more time with Finny than with you," he told me, looking at the ceiling. "We talked two, three, four times a day."

Bob's bereaved mother, Joyce, visited Bob's office at City Hall to return his office keys and to give Jack the cigars Bob had bought for him. It was something Bob did for Jack whenever he went away, which wasn't often. We used to joke that Bob always got lost the minute he left Brockton.

She told Jack that Bob had a good vacation and the night he died he'd been on a stage dancing with showgirls. After that, he went up to his room, turned on the TV and collapsed on the floor, the remote still in his hand.

"He ate too much, drank too much, and dropped dead," his mother recalled, steadying herself by placing her hand on the back of a chair. "My heart is broken. He was very good to his mother."

The day of the funeral, knowing how much Bob loved women, I tweezed and shaved and dressed and smelled as beautiful as I possibly could.

At the family's request, I sang my song "The Very Best of You" on the altar. The words felt as strong to me as when I first wrote the song for Jack's father— who also died from a sudden heart attack.

"All the love that we had could not save you. All the tears that we cried would not do. As the time gets away, it's not over. There is still so very much of you."

My fingers felt numb trying to pick the strings.

"For the world has never known such a man as you. Giving more than any man's required to. And the loss that we bear is a difficult thing. But the gain is the very best of you. Yes the loss that we bear is a difficult thing. But the gain is the very best of you."

When I finished, Bob's mother jumped up in the front row applauding. The congregation followed, which took me by surprise. I was a bit nervous afterwards and got a little tangled up in the guitar strap while trying to put the guitar down. When Jack stood up to give the eulogy, he passed in front of Finn's Irish-green casket. "That hen's a keeper," he winked, nodding at me. He was referring to Bob's playful way of describing women.

Jack ascended to the pulpit to give the eulogy. He adjusted the microphone downward.

"We had a great run at it," he said with determination, barely looking at his scribbled notes. "Bobby was relentless. Rebuilding our city started with the wrecking ball." People chuckled, moving ever so slightly in the pews.

"I call this period Bobby's demo stage," Jack continued. "Finny never saw an abandoned property that he liked. And in his first 30 months, hundreds met his wrath.

"Then Bobby's building stage. Under Bobby's watch more than $300M dollars was invested in construction permits in our city. Three times the value of the seven years prior. Three new schools—on time and on budget—the DPW facility, 26 schools renovated, BB Russell School converted to alternative High School, the Paine School to the Adult Learning Center. Every city building made handicapped accessible; War Memorial rehabbed using a boiler Bob recycled; the new library about to open, the Council on Aging is a gem. And finally our jewel—City Hall—won state and federal historical architecture awards under Bob's direction."

Jack took a step back and cleared his throat. "There is no place you can look and not think of Finn. His effort was inexorable. He is still ubiquitous. He asked one thing of every applicant. Do it right. We met every day. We argued, we disagreed and even when we agreed to disagree, I still lost.

"Politicians love the gray area, that abyss between rules in which you can maneuver to achieve an end. Finny never saw gray. It was black or white. It was wrong or right. But it was the same for all, friend and foe.

"On a personal note, I know what he did for others, countless others. Little stories, little people in the city he loved, in the job he loved, and was committed to. And when I think of Finn, I see that devilish Finn grin. Dinner for 8 at Finny's with a 20-lb ham, two turkeys, 10 pounds of pork roast, and Bobby's own venison chili for digestive purposes. And, of course, some beverage."

"My last walk with Bobby was that Friday before he left for vacation. We were at Crescent and Montello, the old Merritt Gas lot. The state funding to make it a park was zapped by the budget crunch. Finny reassured me. He had a plan, he said. He and his guys would do it. Cheap. 'Don't bid it,' he told me."

"Folks, we are going to do it for Finny. On the site we will build Skinny Finny Park. We owe it to him because if the shoe were on the other foot he wouldn't rest until he did it for us." [Jack was true to his word and the Robert Finnegan Park, complete with a cement fountain, was built and dedicated in late December 2005.]

"In closing, let me say I have 8 years of Jesuit education and a philosophy degree from Boston College. I try to figure it out, too, but I haven't a clue why Bob died so young. But this I know. If life is to have purpose, the measure of the person is this—When the world in which he lived is better today for others because of his efforts, that life was a life of quality, no matter how long or how short."

At the cemetery on Cape Cod, the priest intoned his prayers and when he finished nobody moved for the longest time. The sun beat down and a slight breeze stirred the women's skirts. We seemed unable, unwilling to walk away, to leave our friend there alone. Someone whispered they'd never seen so many grown men cry. "We're at that age," another added. "We're too young!" I countered.

Jack couldn't stop staring at the coffin and my heart ached for the desolation he was feeling. Finally, quietly, people began taking flowers as memorials. Mrs. Finnegan plucked a green and white carnation and walked over to where Jack and I were standing. She appeared as if she was going to give the flower to Jack, but then held the fragrant carnation up for me. I let out a sob I didn't know was there.

After a time she said, "Come on, let's go get a drink," and slowly people drifted over to their cars.

Dozens convened later at a friend's home near the water. We were helping ourselves to drinks when Jack removed a cigar from a plastic bag. It was from the Dominican Republic, only this one had been half-smoked by Bob. Jack lit it up and passed it around.

When the cigar came back to him, he carried the stogie with him out the door. He was gone so long I began to worry. The sun had long since set. Finally, he returned, hair wind blown, cheeks ablaze, and told me that he was standing on a dock overlooking the inlet when a gust of wind whisked the stub out of his hand and sent it sailing about 30 feet into the water. He swears he heard Finny's voice say, "Heh!" in his usual way, so Jack whipped his empty glass in after the cigar, releasing some angst.

Later, upstairs in the guest room, I was about to crawl into bed when Jack grabbed me tight. Holding on to my shoulders he pulled me toward him and began to break down, slowly at first, then his sobs came in convulsions as he released the tears he'd held in all week. My shoulder was wet, and I was crying along with him now for his deep sorrow. "He was such a good guy. He was such a good guy!" he lamented.

When we were finally under the quilt, strains of my song rolled around in my brain. "All the flowers that you grew still are blooming. And the presents that you bought, still arrive. Just today, someone else said they miss you. I believe we will miss you all our lives."

Rest in peace Finny. Thank you for everything you did for Brockton.

"As mayor of Somerville, Massachusetts, for 9 years, I came to know every mayor in Massachusetts and many more throughout the country. No one has impressed me more with his warm personality, sharp intellect, professional tenacity and caring heart than Jack Yunits. Any mayor of a large, older, urban city knows how to fight—few can stop fighting long enough to govern and lead their city into the future. Fewer still can do it and maintain their character and commitment to what's right. Jack Yunits is such a leader and man. Even having left office several years ago, Jack still cares deeply about his city and neighbors. I am proud to call him a friend."

—Congressman Michael Capuano

CHAPTER 31

"I'd rather watch a good leader than hear one any day."
—*Anonymous*

As if Finny were giving commands from above, the summer of 2003 was far more peaceful in Brockton than the previous year and citizens saw a 20 % drop in crime. Come September, a new bar, "Mulligan's Pub," attached to the smaller Joe Angelo's Café, opened on Main Street. One of the first smoke-free places in town, the spacious room with exposed brick walls included a mahogany bar that stretched three car lengths long.

Conor worked for the owner, Joe Angelo, that summer and on the night of Mulligan's grand opening he was stacking beer cases. A sizeable crowd was on hand and one of the highlights of the evening was that the Brockton Rox baseball team was about to clinch a play-off spot. Conor was keeping the crowd abreast of their progress, as well as the Red Sox/Yankees game coming through on the radio.

"Rox—two nothing! Red Sox—three nothing!" Conor yelled out and the crowd responded with whoops and whistles. At the end of the night the final results were two checks in the win column.

The next evening, four thousand people crowded Campanelli stadium waving white towels. The atmosphere was electrified and the Rox won again.

At the game, Jack talked with a man from Weymouth who had spent the day in Brockton.

"God, I love Brockton!" he told Jack, shaking his hand. "I played golf today at Thorny Lea, I've just seen the greatest baseball game and now I'm going to the Foxy Lady! Is this heaven or what?" That would be one more check in the win column for Jack. I wanted to thumb my nose at Mike Barnicle, the columnist who declared us a dying city.

On September 11, 2003, two years after the nation's tragedy, and one year after the Rox came to Brockton, the crowd had everything you could ask for in a ballgame—a warm night, a full moon rising over the outfield, a few homeruns and the championship! The Rox beat the North Shore Spirit 4-1, to sweep the series. Ed Nottle, the singing manager, was thrilled beyond all imagination. Champagne corks popped and the team members drenched one another. Trophies and speeches were presented. The crowd stayed and stayed, chanting, "Brock-ton Rox! Brock-ton Rox!" People on the concourse told me Brockton was truly the City of Champions and that it was because Jack believed in its citizens.

At Mulligan's Pub later, everyone was celebrating like we'd won the World Series. The D.J. was playing full tilt and the bouncers kept moving the tables aside to create a bigger dance floor. Every Rox player attended and one could hardly move through the crowd.

When Ed Nottle arrived he got on the microphone and took the crowd to an even higher plane with his gratitude and his singing. We stayed until 1 a.m., a crazy hour for a school night, but times like that were worth every minute of unplanned joy. Mairi had just started high school, but I let her sleep late the next day. She was grateful for the diversion.

Freshman homework, in particular, at Cardinal Spellman was making her extremely antsy. She had little patience for learning Spanish and was struggling with a current events piece about President George Bush and his plans to fight terrorism. From the kitchen Later that week I could see her staring at her computer monitor, nervously chewing on the antenna of her cell phone, and huffing her way to a full-blown anxiety attack. I finally suggested that taking a shower might help calm her nerves, which she readily agreed to, and raced up the stairs. Physical activity always worked for Mairi. She was much better afterwards and able to concentrate.

Like many freshmen, she had her doubts about high school, socially as well as academically. She made the cheerleading squad, but commented that she felt the cheerleaders were "too white," referring to the fact that her junior high had been largely made up of Cape Verdeans, African-Americans, and Haitians. Cardinal Spellman draws mostly Caucasian students from towns and suburbs surrounding Brockton. So her individual fashion sense was in flux, also. She'd recently bought a Los Angeles Raiders jersey.

"Isn't this gang-related?" I asked, tugging at the sleeve. She got mad at me, but was still going to wear it. Then Conor said the same thing. The next night, a friend of hers came over and braided Mairi's hair into cornrows. After looking at Mairi a few times, I asked if that style was allowed at Spellman. She said yes. Later, I asked again because the look was so radical. There were wide white lines of her scalp showing between rows of dark braids. I said I didn't think Spellman, a conservative Catholic high school, would approve. Without too much argument, thankfully, she unraveled them.

A steadily increasing growth of non-whites in Brockton has the city in a state of flux as people learn to adjust. Similar changes are happening in other cities like Lowell, MA—which has a large population of Cambodian immigrants; and Quincy, MA, whose Chinese population is soaring. The Cape Verdean population in Brockton exceeds more than a third of the school's 16,000 students. I watch this advent of new cultures with interest and a touch of reservation because the lack of attention to learning the English language and/or American customs makes me question where the loyalty of these new immigrants lies.

But I believe the more we interact with each other to develop friendships and understanding through sports, music, and hopefully, politics, the more sharing of positive attributes will occur.

That is why, in October, Jack and I traveled to Cape Verde, an island nation
to the west of Africa. At the time, the only American politician to have visited
the islands of Cape Verde was Massachusetts Congressman Barney Frank.
Secondly, Jack's Procurement Officer, Michael Morris, an adorable Tiger Woods
look-alike, was going to be married on the island of Sal, and had invited us to
his wedding. For the record, I paid for all my own expenses.

Several Cape Verdean officials met us on the tarmac when we deplaned.
Jack and I were ushered away from the wedding group and escorted to a VIP
room located in a private section of the small airport. A wonderful aroma
permeated the air—some particular wood, I guessed, used to build the coffee
tables. Jack gave out Rox hats and Brockton pens to those who greeted us and
they were delighted.

Mostly Jack and I spent time in professional situations, meeting other mayors
and dignitaries and being marshaled between formalities like TV interviews,
question and answer opportunities, gift presentations, and formal dinners. One
particular incident during our first night, however, was totally unmatched.

A handful of us flew to the volcanic island of Fogo. Men in African-print
shirts met us at the teeny airport and soon had us buckled in to two SUVs that
went bumping over rocky roads.

Through fog and quickening twilight, we climbed a dangerously steep,
breathtakingly beautiful mountain path until finally passing through miles of
disfigured rock resembling settings from the movie "Lord of the Rings." No one,
I imagined, could possibly live in so desolate a place. Just then, out of the gloom
there appeared a smattering of concrete houses, an illuminated restaurant and
a tiny store.

By then, however, it was way too dark to view the actual crater of the
volcano, so the jeeps began the descent downward. A heavy downpour added
to the scary situation. Our translator told us Jack's presence had brought the
island good luck. Until Jack came, the interpreter said, the island had been
experiencing a drought. Figures.

After a lengthy and bumpy ride, four of us were dropped off at a darkened building by the ocean. We could hear waves breaking, but we couldn't see them. We lugged our suitcases up chalky cement stairs, over a water-covered concrete floor and into our rooms. Jack and I were given the owner's suite, because he was back in Brockton tending to his furniture store. The electricity stayed on long enough for us to see the way into our room, then went out and stayed out.

Our room contained two leather couches, a TV, a stereo, and a refrigerator. There was a separate bedroom with a shower and one set of towels, which had been used. The room also had two tall ceramic lamps depicting shiny Victorian ladies and gents wearing white wigs and holding stringed instruments. Huh? It was all so bizarre I felt like we had walked into the song "Hotel California."

Did I mention it was our 26th wedding anniversary?

If there were ever a "dark and stormy night," this was the quintessential. Jack fell asleep instantly on our double bed while I swatted little no-see-ums away from my face. The lack of screens on the open windows caused the yellow nylon curtains to whip about inside the room. One enormous bolt of thunder made me jump off the bed. I ran to the window several times thinking rain was pouring in, and was certain that Count Dracula was going to reach in and pull me out into the abyss.

When I finally fell asleep, I dreamt I was at my friend, Ginny's, house in Brockton where it was raining torrents. I was holding a large tub of shoes and when I reached for a red one, the tub slipped away and down an embankment. My other shoes started spilling everywhere. "Okay, I can do this," I thought as I tried to grab the shoes. But the river started carrying me down the road. "Help! Help me! Hehhh-lp!" I yelled, all the while wondering if people really screamed like that anymore.

In the morning, when we looked out the window we could see that the unfinished hotel was situated on an expanse of black lava that went down to the ocean. The sea looked bleak in the distance and unapproachable because of the rough terrain. Jack let me take the first shower. Bless him; there was just enough hot water for one. He also started calling me "Joan Wilder," from the movie "Romancing the Stone," with Kathleen Turner and Michael Douglas. "Yep, that's me," I joked, twirling my wet hair into a bun. Off in the distance, a rooster crowed good morning.

Later, he and I met the Minister of Economic Solidarity and his wife for lunch. Over a meal of salmon, followed by a scrumptious ice cream pie called Romantica, Jack told the Minister that he should consider marketing Cape Verde for travelers, not tourists—in other words, those who appreciate adventure as opposed to predictable routines or habitats like air-conditioned hotels.

Back on the island of Sal, we had an hour of downtime between the wedding ceremony and reception. A group of us went to one of the air-conditioned hotel rooms for a cold beverage. Someone turned on the TV and there on the screen, in full color, was Jack at the Shaw's Center where he was officiating at the previous week's Cape Verdean dinner. Everyone hooted in unison, and abruptly the power went off, again.

Cape Verde is perhaps one of the world's last frontiers. On certain islands, roads are still being built. The topography is unique and beautiful, including the volcanic terrain on Fogo, and the salt mines on Sal. The desperate poverty in several areas, however, prohibits quick economic growth. Plus, the oppressive heat on the islands could benefit from one or two Desalinization plants to increase their water supplies. But our trip opened my eyes to the (mostly) peace-loving Cape Verdean immigrants back in Brockton, as well as their loyalty to the mother country.

On the flight home, Jack was quiet. He seemed to have acquired a rare "bug," to put it nicely, and spent most of the ride in the men's room. When we finally got through customs, he helped load everyone's suitcases into the van and then gathered all the luggage carts that were in the parking lot, even those that weren't ours, and organized them into straight rows. He was ready to be in charge again, to do what had to be done, to make order out of chaos.

In November of 2003, Jack won his 5th election with 77% of the vote, to become the city's most elected mayor in its 100-plus-year history. Several supporters at the after-party asked me, "Can Jack be mayor forever?" It seemed that they wanted him to be.

The following day, Jack spoke to a history class at Brockton High School and was asked how long he intended to be mayor and if he'd ever run for higher office, like Governor. He answered that running statewide wasn't on his radar, but that he'd never close the door on an opportunity to help his city. When asked what the best advice would be for someone who wanted to run for mayor, he responded, "Read history. Nothing's going to happen that hasn't happened before. The colors may have changed, it's a different kind of paint, but it's still the same."

"One's time in office can be considered a success if they improved the quality of life not only for those who were there at the time, but also for future generations whom they will never meet. Jack Yunits has been very successful."

—North Adams Mayor John Barrett, III

CHAPTER 32

"To become a champion, fight one more round."
—James J. Corbett

"Eight years of hard work down the drain," Jack mumbled at four o'clock in the morning, waking me up. His foot was shaking vigorously. He added, "I've been awake for hours I'm so mad." Through my sleepy haze, I remembered that the day before he'd been in Boston testifying at the State House in favor of the desalinization plant to solve Brockton's water problems.

"What's the matter, honey?" I asked, placing my fingers on his pulsing leg.

"The lack of aggression from Brockton's state delegation frustrates me to no end!" he said, adding that, "if a city isn't growing, it's dying. And now it is so apparent that some officials prefer doing nothing! I want out. This is a terrible business and I've had enough." He started the choking, wheezing cough he always got when he was under too much stress, and my heart winced. I could sympathize with his frustration. After the hearing, which had gone well—with support from State Representative Tom Kennedy—Jack and I had slipped off to the nearly empty 9 Park, a cozy bar near the State House. Jack was in a good mood, satisfied that work could finally begin on the desalinization plant. He ordered a martini. I ordered a pomegranate Cosmopolitan. The bartender mixed my concoction right in front of us. Seeing him add real pomegranate juice to the blender was rather soothing to watch.

Jack's cell phone rang and he almost didn't answer it. The bartender placed my drink on a square napkin. "Should I?" Jack asked me, weighing the phone in his hand. I shrugged, leaning forward to sip. Of course he answered. It was the city solicitor, Tom Plouffe. Jack was caught completely off guard when he heard that the desalinization bill had been "tabled." He closed his eyes, scrunching up a napkin. The project had somehow lost favor in the short time since the completion of Jack's testimony and our arrival at 9 Park. The result was that the professional water company would not receive the financing it needed to get going until after a follow-up hearing in the spring. That set the whole construction phase way back.

Now, Jack's foot was making the bed shake again. I swung my leg on top of his.

Things took a turn for the better, however, when Jack drove back to Boston later that day to meet with Governor Romney for a ceremony honoring Massachusetts' new mayors. While Jack was there, he ran into Senate President Bob Travaglini. After being informed of the latest fiasco, Travaglini responded that he would take another look at the bill because Jack had done "so much good for the people in Brockton." Later, Jack got a call that a special session about the issue had been scheduled. I was so thankful that there was some hope to what had seemed like a dire and hopeless situation.

Meanwhile, Jack and I traveled to Boston together on another day when he needed to testify again– this time in federal court. We were sitting side by side on a bench in the new John Joseph Moakley Federal Courthouse in Boston, when the judge came in to the room. "Please rise," an official said. We stood and I could see a handful of people, including the city's lawyers, were there. Brockton's Police Chief, Paul Studenski, who was also testifying, was there as well.

The police officer who had initiated a civil suit against Jack was standing on the other side of the room. I couldn't bear to look his way. Four years earlier the officer was transferred from a detective job to that of a patrolman. He claimed that the transfer occurred because he supported Martha Crowell for mayor over Jack. As a result he was so pissed that he sued the city, Jack and the Police Chief.

So here we were sitting in a near empty Boston courtroom. Jack was about to be called to the witness stand when he pulled a button off of his suit coat. He nudged me with his elbow. I saw what had happened and dug around in my purse. It just so happened I found a tiny sewing kit.

"No, no. I have to go up now," he whispered. But I had enough time to sew the button on before he stood up.

During his examination, Jack was asked a few questions, and everything he said substantiated that the transfer was not his decision. It was the police chief's. I was surprised how little interrogation there was. The court took a recess afterwards and Jack and I walked through the double doors and out to the hallway. When we got to the enormous glass windows that open to a breathtaking view of Boston Harbor, he was still talking to his attorney but slipped me the same button to the suit coat. So much for my sewing skills. Staring at the button in my hand I wondered how I was ever going to win the Miss Domestic Goddess award.

The court case was serious but Jack felt confident that he'd be acquitted. The next day he traveled alone by train to Boston for the final day of the trial. I couldn't go and didn't hear from him all day, so I was a bit nervous. When I returned home after dropping Mairi off at gymnastics, Jack's car was in the driveway. The house was dark. I walked in and heard him coming down the main stairs. We met in the dim front hallway—an area large enough to be a room.

"How did it go?" I asked, trying to read his expression.

"Bad, very, very bad," he said, hugging me hard.

I froze in place. "What do you mean?"

"The jury found me guilty of violating the officer's civil rights."

"No!" For a minute I thought he was kidding. But the way he held me told me otherwise. We pulled apart. His face was stricken. I took him by the hand to lead him through the doorway into the den. We sat down on the couch.

After a long pause, and a swipe of his forehead, he said, "The penalty—at least to the city—is fifty thousand dollars."

"You're kidding!" I said, rubbing his arm. "Geez, that's a lot of money. What the heck was that jury thinking?"

"And to me," he could barely utter the words, but they slid off his tongue when he finally said them. "Three . . . Hundred . . . Thousand . . . Dollars!"

"Wha-at?" I exclaimed, my eyes opening wide.

"I'm sorry. I'm sorry. I don't like being weak," Jack said, beginning to lose his grip.

"Weak?" I said. "You did nothing wrong!" This was not happening! My mind was racing. My heart was picking up speed. Who, why, how, what?? We didn't have any money! We didn't have assets! We certainly weren't giving anything to that jerk!

Jack said there were many issues that the defense underestimated. He didn't blame his attorneys, but in hindsight saw there were many holes in the case. The team probably should have called character witnesses, he said, or other people who supported past candidates, but whom Jack continued to work with.

"All the good I've done for people," he anguished, his voice trailing off.

He said the officer whimpered like a baby on the stand saying he'd developed eating disorders as a result of the transfer. People who grew up with the policeman in Brockton said he always had eating disorders.

The guy wanted to be police chief and apparently had been promised as much by Martha Crowell—had she become mayor. When she lost the election, he was denied his personal ambition and couldn't handle the letdown. That's when he started carrying a tape recorder around the police station, watching his fellow officers, claiming there was corruption on the force. Jack authorized three separate investigations to rout out corruption if any, and the results always came back clean. *good* !

But the policeman was still pissed off at Jack and unfortunately for us, hired a well-known Boston lawyer to represent him in court. Unbelievably he had then succeeded in winning the suit.

"Those who love you will still love you, Jack," I said, rising to my feet. "The rest, who knows? Who cares? The majority of people understand who you are and what you've done for the city. They trust you," I added, flicking on the light switch. The TV came on, too, but I shut it off and sat back down next to Jack.

Jack mentioned there was an Iraqi-looking person on the jury who kept nodding during the opposing lawyer's closing arguments. The counselor had gone on and on about Baghdad and civil rights and translated all that to Jack's case.

"There's a slight chance that the judge will reconsider the enormity of the award," Jack said, rearranging a pillow, "but those kinds of reversals are rare." He would appeal the decision immediately he stated, slumping back on the couch, adding, "I just want to go out and hit somebody. Or play football."

Our phone was ringing. Neither Jack nor I wanted to speak to the press or anybody for that matter. Enough was enough. When I eventually checked the messages, one was from Tim Cruise.

"My wife and I wanted to make you a dinner but we had no food in the house, so I went to West Side Pizza and there's a bag outside your door," he said.

Like manna from heaven. Jack and I were famished. I brought the package in from the back hall and lifted out chicken lemon soup, Greek salad, pizza, and chicken kabobs with rice. Inside the bag was also a fake check made out to us for $350,000.00. On the face of the check Tim had written, "For faithful service to our city."

We called Tim, his cousin, Dave, and their wives, Donna and Tricia, to come over. After I got everyone a drink I was surprised to see that they were all so upset about what happened that they were ready to drive to New Hampshire, where the officer had retired, and "do some damage." They also said they'd easily find 30 people to give us $10,000.00 a piece! "Ri-ight," I said, stacking the used paper plates and carrying them into the kitchen.

Jack vowed he'd go to jail before giving the officer one nickel. I was sure he meant it. I pictured the kids and I staring out hungrily through the poorhouse bars.

Our friends left and the reality of the verdict settled in. Neither Jack nor I slept. We were restless all night wondering how Jack was going to continue to run the city, or, for that matter, if he should.

The jurors claimed Jack "misinterpreted the Constitution of the United States by violating the officer's right to support the candidate of his choice without fear of repercussions." I was so livid, I, too, wanted to hit somebody. But what I really wanted was to squash that officer's little you-know-what.

The headline in the newspaper the next day read, "Jury: Mayor Violated Cop's Civil Rights." Several of our friends came over after reading the afternoon paper—some brought food like when a family member dies. Dozens of people called, pledging 100% support. *nice*

One sweet friend, Andrea Gulezian, who'd organized the coffee hours during our campaigns, said: "You'll win the appeal and then I'm going to personally raise one million dollars for you guys because Jack is the best!" *nice*

Mary Waldron arrived with a casserole and a bottle of Kahlua. Ah, the woman knows me. She was sniffling as she placed the dish and bottle on the kitchen counter. "It's nothing to cry about," I said. But later, shoveling snow from the driveway, I cried, too. The enormity of the compensation was inconceivable.

"The truth will come out," friends reassured us. "That guy was always a tattle-tale and a crybaby," others said.

I thought of what public service had meant to us. How much we'd sacrificed in time and opportunities with our kids. Jack thought about Mairi's lot in life and all she'd dealt with because he'd been "doing the right thing."

In bed that night, I said to Jack that it would be our response to the aberration that counted, not the act itself. "Thank God I have you," he kept repeating, kissing my mouth and squeezing me tighter.

Jack was a zombie all the next day, walking from room to room in our house, unable to focus, finally going up to bed before seven o'clock. At 8:15, he was throwing up. I ran up to the bathroom, stroked his back and handed him tissues. Afterwards, he moved back to bed shivering madly. I put the electric blanket on, crawled in behind him and wrapped my body around his. He moaned from the pains in his stomach. I caressed his shoulders and arms. My face was wet thinking that a jury of eight strangers—who knew nothing *SAD* about what he'd done for Brockton, or the honesty and integrity that he stood for—had reduced him to this state. It wasn't their fault. The jurors saw letters of acclaim about the officer. Nothing was presented about Jack winning the "Man for Others" award at Boston College High School, or the honorary doctorate from Stonehill College, or the awards from New England School of Law, the United Way or the Massachusetts Bar Association. We decided in hindsight, that the city's lawyers recklessly assumed that the case would be a slam/dunk. It was a slam all right.

At 10 p.m., I was downstairs watching TV by myself waiting for Mairi to come home from babysitting, when the line at the bottom of the screen rolled by announcing that Mayor Yunits of Brockton had been found guilty of a civil rights charge. The words felt like a slipknot around my heart.

or sad

When I dressed for work the next day I needed to feel strong, which in my case means sexy. So I donned a pair of flashy blue high heels with an ankle strap, added a turquoise sweater, a short-ish black skirt and a bear medallion necklace from Arizona that Jack had given me.

The first encounter I had was in the reception area of the law office, where I greeted a man who claimed he worked for the city. I didn't recognize him, but he said his job was to inventory office computers and desks to make sure they were properly categorized for tax purposes. I took great umbrage at what I saw as an invasion of privacy. How did I know this stranger wasn't casing the joint? What if we got robbed the following week? The judicial system had betrayed us, who else would?

"No offense," I said, after looking at his business card, "and it's nothing personal, but I'm going to call the assessor's office to verify this." I strutted over to the receptionist's desk and picked up the phone.

START The City Assessor, Bernie Siegel, a humble man with a bushy moustache, who lives up the street from us, told me the inspector was legit, but that I didn't have to let him look around, so I didn't. I apologized to the young inspector. "We have nothing to hide, but this week I'm very leery of people and circumstances," I explained, handing him back his card.

The man was understanding, even cool. In fact, he was a bass player and we talked music for a moment. As he was about to leave, he added that he owned a similar bear medallion and asked if I knew what the bear stood for.

"Yes," I said, fingering the medal, "strength."

"I can see you are very strong today," he responded, turning away and resting his hand on the door handle to make his way out. He turned back. "Do you know who gives the bear his strength?" he asked.

"God?" I said, with a flick of my hand, knowing that's what he wanted to hear. I meant "the universe—life, legend."

Casting a quick glance at my cleavage he nodded and walked out the door.

When Jack spoke on the radio for his monthly broadcast, he answered people's questions about the case, telling me later that they had a right to know. He also said he had the right to stick up for himself.

Mayor John Barrett, from North Adams, who'd become a close confidante of Jack's, called him to show support. Other mayors phoned in wondering how they'd ever move employees around or fire anyone.

At a packed Chamber of Commerce breakfast at the Holiday Inn later during the week Jack was the keynote speaker. The M.C., Mark Linde, who had also once supported Marty Crowell for mayor, introduced Jack, saying, "Our next speaker is the one who has led Brockton with integrity and dedication."

Jack received a standing ovation when he walked to the podium. I felt a soothing reassurance that the Brockton community knew the kind of man Jack was. They are a wary bunch too—suspicious until an official has proven himself consistently. But once you're "in" you're in. Jack was in. Once the crowd settled, he began his address, which focused mainly on the positives in the city. During a question/answer period afterwards no one asked a single question about the court case. Instead they were curious as to where he stood on the gay marriage issue that was being hotly debated at the time. Jack said that the decision should be left to the elected officials; that it shouldn't be put on the ballot because the "mob mentality" ought not to rule. He said if that had been the case in the 1800's, today any civil rights, or women's votes, or desegregation, wouldn't exist.

Apparently his answer carried a special meaning to everyone because he couldn't get out the door for all the people telling him what an impassioned speech he gave. Maybe they were all just feeling sorry for the recent turn of events. But I sensed something stronger.

One woman, Gayle Kelley, whom Jack had recently hired as Brockton's newest Cultural Affairs director, said Jack's speech was exactly why she wanted to work for him. He was "the real deal" she said, a "rare bird."

A week after the verdict, an editorial came out in The Enterprise saying that the officer "got away with murder and that the jury sent a 'chilling message to management.'"

I left a phone message for the editors thanking them for telling the public what really happened. In a sense, their words exonerated Jack.

Several people asked how I'd been doing after the verdict. The funny thing was that after the initial wrenching disbelief, every day had gotten better. I was uplifted by the love and true concern we received from hundreds of people around the city. Our mailbox was filled every day with cards expressing support and allegiance. Jack had made a lasting, positive difference in people's lives. Brockton people had wrapped their arms around him, around us. That's what I wished the jury had been shown, that Jack was not only a man of substance, but he was also an honorable politician—a "rare bird."

We waited for a trial date for the appeal, and as the month of February wore on, Jack attended several grueling meetings in Boston regarding Brockton's water issue. The Environmental Protection Agency was now appealing some decisions Jack said it felt like he'd had to row back to England before America's colonial days and start over. That was how long and involved the process had become.

One night he dreamt he was on a boat with Governor Romney and could tell something dangerous was in the water coming at him. "Don't worry Jack, you've done this before," the Governor reassured Jack in the dream.

Jack also attended a meeting with a Harvard-educated professional woman, Lori Colombo, about the Brightfield grant. Brockton had been awarded a grant to begin construction of a solar panel field or "array," as its called, to be built on its east side. This would be the first solar panel field in New England. But a certain Romney official was hesitant to hand over the funds. Before the session ended, Lori approached him to say, "Sir, we've been granted this money and it's your legislative duty to disperse it to us."

"Up here we're not concerned with legislative duties," the Republican replied. She almost went at him. It seemed like everyone had to keep fighting.

"You could write an entire book on what's just happened these last two weeks," Brockton's CFO, Jay Condon, said to Jack.

During that time, I also experienced another of the unique advantages to being a mayor's wife. Jack took me to a luncheon at the waste water treatment plant on the outskirts of the city—the place where human "sludge" is treated, and where the salt and sand get stored for winter. P.U.! When we drove up my nose was assaulted immediately. I told Jack that every person aspiring to be a politician should visit the bowels of a city or town. That would open their minds to municipal complexities. Maybe even change their opinions about serving. The stench stayed in my nose for two days.

Finally, in late February 2004, Governor Romney signed the water bill, effectively giving Brockton the go-ahead to build the desalinization plant, and in mid-March, the Massachusetts Water Commission also voted in favor, 7-0.

Even better, on March 30, the judge who was overseeing Jack's federal case overturned the decision against Jack and cleared his name! According to the city's lawyer, the judge told him that Jack had been honest, "almost too honest," on the stand, and he felt the jury had been "misdirected." The officer would still get money for "emotional distress," but far less than the original amount, and from the insurance company, not us. Jack's absolution was a miraculous relief and helped restore my faith in positive, universal love, as well as in true justice in America. I yanked my children from the proverbial poor house and plowed on.

Since then, the Federal Courts in two separate districts have determined that the lateral transfer of a police officer to another position is not evidence of a civil rights violation and does not entitle an employee to compensatory damages. Hallelujah!

YES

"*Jack Yunits is the best thing that ever happened to this city of Brockton. This man did a great job following through with the plans that were started by the previous mayor and following them through completion. Such as Schools, The Senior Center, The Court House etc. When Mayor Yunits came into my store he complimented me on the great job I was doing along with the Campello Business Assoc. and nick named me "The Unofficial Mayor Of Campello" by planting 52 trees on Main St. in Campello. He lifted my spirits so high by saying "this is only the beginning." I need your help and the help from every citizen so we can make this city the best city to live, work and play in. I believe in this man. I am a very proud citizen to say "I live in Brockton and Jack Yunits is my mayor." I know when he sets his mind to something he has his heart and sole in it. We all need to pitch in and help him and one another keeping this the "City Of Champions."*

nice

—Ron Bethoney

nice

CHAPTER 33

"There is an alternative to war. It has been with us forever."
—*Sargent Shriver*

I switched on the TV one night to see a popular Boston TV show "Chronicle" broadcasting a full half hour of positive happenings going on in Brockton. The stadium was highlighted, as was the actor, Bill Murray, who owns a piece of the Brockton Rox, and our singing Rox manager, Ed Nottle. A reporter also spoke about the train to Boston, the Brockton Symphony Orchestra, the War Memorial Building, the renovation of the Thomas Edison Times Building, the improved Footjoy factory, and the strength of the Catholic churches. Jack was being interviewed and looked fit and proud. He spoke about the value of one's money in Brockton, and that citizens could live in the city and still work in Boston due to the easy train ride. *nice*

When the show paused for a commercial, I almost jumped out of my skin when I saw that Mike Barnicle, the reporter who slammed Brockton years earlier, was one of the news anchors. "Take that, Mike, you bum!" I yelled at the set. "A dying city? Huh!" I was stacking books on the coffee table when Jack walked in looking tired. He plopped down on the couch and I wrapped my arms around him. He was the real hero, who, like so many in the city, worked their tails off day after day after day, trying to make a positive difference and reclaim the Brockton, the America they loved. He was making it a place where kids could ride bikes and people could walk to the 7-ll's without fear; where a symphony orchestra entertained and kids got a first-rate education. The Chronicle program was a huge validation for everyone's efforts.

On the heels of that, the Democratic National Convention came to Boston and, in addition to several festivities that Jack and I attended I was invited to a luncheon at the Museum of Fine Arts. The lavish affair was being hosted by Senator Ted Kennedy's wife, Vicki, in honor of Teresa Heinz-Kerry, whose husband, John Kerry, was running for President of the United States.

It was an honor to attend, although by the time I got there after a hot subway ride and a lengthy walk to the museum, I felt somewhat wilted. My back was aching from all my recent engagements so I had elected to wear dressy flip-flops. Vicki Kennedy appeared radiant and fresh in a Kelly-green suit, her brown hair falling to her shoulders. She was ever graceful and smiling. She recognized me; I thanked her for the invite—curling my right foot behind me in embarrassment. The hall was filled with politician's wives, Congressmen's wives, even the actress, Glenn Close, was in attendance. I could see her across from our table. She had a new haircut and was sporting a contemporary look. One other mayor's wife, Sheila McGlynn, told me she'd been escorted to the event via a police car. I wanted to move to her city.

When Vicki spoke at the podium, the topics she brought up resonated with the guests in attendance—all women. She presented the guest of honor, Teresa (pronounced Ter-ay-za), with a beautifully framed replica of a letter that former First Lady Abigail Adams wrote to her husband, John, when he was in Philadelphia helping compose the Declaration of Independence. Through the letter, Abigail implored her husband to keep women in mind when he set the direction for the country. Good advice. I'd like one masseuse, a new pair of shoes and a police escort, thank you.

Teresa took her turn at the microphone, her voice low and resonant, and her theme rich with the idea that women needed less "rights" and more "value"—as in appreciating those of us who give birth, nurture and raise the world's future generations. I loved that message. She also introduced several of her women friends who accompanied her on the political trail. You could tell by her tone and the compliments she bestowed, that she obviously cherished them.

"Now, I wouldn't have thought she had girlfriends," a woman sitting next to me at the table said.

"I don't know where I'd be without my girlfriends," another whispered, replacing her napkin in her lap.

"Me, either," I said, conjuring up images of the girls I go to New York City with at Christmas, and my writing group, and my ever faithful Brockton chums. Heck, I'd have a multitude to pick from if ever Jack ran for President.

Those at my table knew of Teresa's contributions to women's health and financial issues, as well as her concern for the environment. I felt she was a woman of our time, and sincerely hoped she'd get a chance to be the country's First Lady.

During the same week, Jack and I hosted a B-52's music concert at the Rox Stadium and after the band performed "Love Shack," (is there a better song?) he and I rode the elevator up to a luxury box to watch John Kerry's speech on TV. It was the moment many Democrats had been waiting for and Kerry was what he needed to be—informed, experienced and presidential. We felt optimistic about his prospects. Even better, if he won the presidency, Congressman Stephen Lynch would probably run for Kerry's Senate seat. In that case, Jack might throw his hat in the ring for Congress with the hopes of representing Brockton at the federal level. I secretly hoped Jack would get the chance. He'd be good for Congress. They could use more workers, less talkers. But we had a few months to wait and see what happened.

Summer began winding down, and one rare night at home I was sitting on the couch next to Jack watching the opening ceremonies of the summer Olympics on TV. The games were being held in Greece. As throngs of international athletes paraded into the arena, we considered Casey's latest turn of events. Since graduating from Catholic University, she'd been accepted into the Peace Corps and would be moving to the country of Moldova—a small, poor nation, located between Romania and Ukraine. Casey was acting on her belief that peace was better than war. We continued watching the screen and to our surprise the word Moldova appeared. The solitary athlete, carrying the country's flag, waved to the crowd. Jack and I leaned toward the TV. The reality sunk in that our beautiful, peace-loving daughter would be going to a country represented by one single athlete. Jack was feeling the pain of missing so much time with our kids. He squeezed my hand. "I'm so proud of my Casey," he said.

CHAPTER 34

"Politics is not a game. It is an earnest business."
—*Winston Churchill*

"Jack, who would you rather see the Red Sox play in the World Series—St. Louis or Houston?" I asked. He was brushing his teeth. He swished his mouth, spit and ran his brush under the water. Placing the toothbrush in the holder, he grabbed a towel, wiped his face and said he'd prefer St. Louis. But wouldn't it be great, he added, for the Red Sox to play a Texas team and beat them, considering we were two weeks away from the Presidential election between a Texan—George W. Bush—and U.S. Senator John Kerry from Massachusetts.

The St. Louis Cardinals ended up facing the Red Sox, instead, and suddenly Boston was in the astounding and unlikely position of being three games up and on the brink of World Series stardom. It had been eighty-six agonizing years since they last won the title. In the fourth of seven games, Red Sox outfielder Johnny Damon hit a home run his first at bat. The Sox not only swept the Cardinals by winning all four games they shut them out 3-0!

Red Sox nation went ballistic. Radio stations, TV, the phone lines, print media and fans had waited for generations. Devotees had lived and died without ever seeing their beloved team do the impossible. The "Curse of the Bambino"—a phenomenon that haunted the Red Sox since Babe Ruth was traded to the Yankees in 1918—finally broke.

One great result of winning was that there is probably not a single person left in the Commonwealth who hasn't had his or her picture taken with the World Series trophy. Mairi had her opportunity at West Side Pizza, where she worked at the counter, when the "trophy team" stopped in for lunch after appearing at the Shaw's Center. The rest of us were at the center itself. Lots of trophy pictures decorated our refrigerator.

Shortly after the big win Jack walked into our bedroom to wake me up, placing a cup of coffee on the bedside table. "Today is the day that we elect a President of the United States who comes from Massachusetts," he said, straightening the covers. I opened my eyes halfway turning my head to the side as he tucked the down quilt into the space between the mattress and box spring. "You can say you hosted the First Lady in Brockton and that you've been to two of their homes," he added, pulling the blankets tight once more.

"Jack," I responded, barely able to raise my neck off the pillow. "How do you expect me to get out of here?"

That night we lit a fire in the fireplace, ordered pizzas and had political friends over to watch the election results. Tim was convinced John Kerry was going to win. Jack nodded but didn't say anything. We received a call from Chris Micklos, our former campaign manager in Wisconsin, who was also sure. I said, "I'll be surprised if Kerry wins, but I hope he does."

As the count wore on there were discrepancies in Florida due to the 60,000 people who never received their absentee ballots. Casey's absentee ballot had been sent in from Moldova by the Peace Corps, but according to the Registrar of Voters hadn't arrived as of the day before the election.

Long after our company left, and the pizza boxes had been thrown into the recycling bin, there was still no clear winner. We turned off the TV, trudged upstairs and just as my head nestled into the pillow Casey called from overseas. I reached out and pulled the phone to my ear.

"Who won?" she asked.

"Hi, honey!" I exclaimed, propping myself on an elbow. I filled her in and she was disappointed to learn the election didn't look good for Kerry.

"The Peace Corps isn't in the greatest financial shape since Bush became president," she told me.

In the end, the state of Ohio swung that election. Overall, Bush received the highest number of votes ever tallied in a presidential race. But to put it in perspective, John Kerry received the second highest.

Kerry conceded the election at 2 p.m. the next day. Having met Senator Kerry on several occasions, and been invited to his homes—one in Boston, one in D.C.—I felt that John was a sincere, hard-working politician and I was sorry for his, and our country's loss.

Yet after a refreshing walk with Jack on a sunny day and some comforting yoga, I rationalized that America would keep going and I still had my family. What we as a nation had lost, however, was the respect of the world for re-electing a president who didn't value the decisions of the United Nations, who lied to the American public about "weapons of mass destruction" being the reason we were at war in Iraq, and whose "No Child Left Behind Act" was just political speak.

The morning after the election I asked Jack if his juices were still going strong about running for higher office especially after seeing how the Republican right was dominating the country. "No," he said simply. "My throat hurts from too much small talk yesterday and I have a stomachache because I'm fighting with the unions again."

When we went outside for a walk he explained that negotiations with police, firefighters and teachers could get so nasty that some mayors caved in and gave the unions what they wanted, regardless of whether or not there was money in the budget. As time progressed, cities could go bankrupt trying to fulfill their financial obligations. Jack refused to let that happen. In my eyes his stance took balls, "buffalo balls," as it may be.

"The payoff will come," he said, "when cities like Brockton are still in the black, while others go into receivership and the state steps in." Of course, these benefits to Brockton would occur long after Jack was gone, and people wouldn't remember, or know, the effort he put in to keeping the union contracts affordable.

On November 8th, Jack told me he'd made up his mind and wouldn't seek re-election the following year. He'd been mulling the decision since the devastating civil rights trial with that disgruntled police officer. Plus, Jack's mother's debilitating Alzheimer's condition, as well as our concerns about Breck, who was having some personal issues, was weighing on us. It was a relief for me to think that someday Jack could spend more time with our family instead of being responsible to resolve snow plowing snafus, homicides, or kids throwing chairs at teachers.

One day I woke up from a solid night sleep remembering a dream about the two of us arranging a room of furniture. Jack had put up a crib and then there were two cribs, then three, and I lashed out saying, "Will you stop? What are you doing? We don't need cribs!"

Maybe having him around the house wasn't the best idea.

But the notion of him not running was beginning to take root. At the "Red, White and Black Ball" in late November, I was standing with a gentleman in a line at the cocktail bar. He offered to buy me a drink, which I readily accepted. He then asked, "Do you think Jack will be running for mayor again?" The question seemed to be popping up more often around town.

"He hasn't decided for sure," I answered, taking an icy Cosmo from the bartender. The drink spilled onto my gloved hand. My new friend dug in his pocket for dollar bills.

"I think it'll be a long time before we see the likes of you two again," he said, tossing a few bills on the wet bar. I acknowledged the compliment, while admiring the fact that the people in this city are good tippers.

"Thank you. I appreciate your comments very much," I said. "And thanks for the drink!" We smiled and he moved along. Ah, I would miss this attention. Catching up with Jack, I saw that he was in conversation with an editor from The Enterprise. Oh, boy. He, too, asked Jack the same question, whether he'd be running again, adding that the newspaper had lots of "good stories in the can," which they'd pull out in the event he didn't run.

"Why couldn't they have brought out a few more of those along the way?" Jack uttered to me as the editor slinked away. "It's been hard enough steering the ship of Brockton without The Enterprise shooting holes in it."

"Jack, I'm amazed you've been able to accomplish all you have in spite of the newspaper," I told him. He continued shaking hands with acquaintances as I sipped my drink.

Days later I was in a meeting of the Board of Trustees for the Good Samaritan Hospital—a position I was offered, I'm quite sure, because of my relation to the mayor—when Jack called my cell phone. I managed to pull the little device from my purse before the Caribbean ring tone stopped. Jack told me that Senator Ted Kennedy had secured another $2 million for Brockton's parking garage, and allotted $300K more for the new Joseph Moakley Center at the hospital. I was excited to share the information with the other board members. I would miss learning news of that nature firsthand when Jack was no longer in office.

On December 19, 2004, Jack stayed home all day working on his final State of the City speech to be delivered in January. On a pad of yellow legal paper, in longhand, he included words about stepping down when his fifth two-year term ended the following December.

The next morning he was awake at 4:30 to go swimming. Since injuring his back running, he'd been taking advantage of the high school's sizable pool to swim daily laps. He returned to the house at 7:15, showered and lay down on the bed. I thought he was just going to rest a minute, but he didn't wake up again until four o'clock in the afternoon. I kept checking on him between errands because that behavior was so out of character. Finally, I kissed his cheek and he stirred. He said his throat was so swollen he couldn't talk. Exhaustion, and maybe the relief he felt from his decision to not run again, had finally worn him out.

Within an hour, though, he was dressed and downstairs. He gathered kindling to start a fire in the fireplace, read the paper from front to back and returned fourteen phone messages. One was from Medford Mayor Mike McGlynn. "Jack! You can't leave now!" Mike said.

Jack made plans to sit with his staff and tell them he was moving on. He was proud that when the next mayor was sworn in, there'd be money in the bank. Not to mention two more new schools on the way, as well as plans and funding for a five-story Brockton Neighborhood Health Center on Main Street, in the heart of downtown. Interestingly enough, it would be located where Jack's first law office was, in the same lot where the former Bessie Baker Building had stood. Perhaps most important to Jack were the highly qualified individuals who now held the city's department head positions. The new school superintendent, Basan "Buzz" Nembirkow, who delivered hope to Brockton's youth, was one of those.

For Christmas I gave Jack a golf-bag cart along with several golf shirts and sweaters. He had played golf sporadically in the past nine years and I knew he was salivating at the thought of more golf in his future.

One of his gifts to me was a book on Feng Shui, the art of placing your household items "just so" in order to improve your life—spiritually and economically. I said we should enhance the "career" section of the home to ensure success when he was no longer mayor.

Before he relinquished his mayor title, however, several issues still required his full attention. One was the Brightfield's bill—the solar panel "array" still pending for the east side of Brockton.

The bill had been delayed in the State House, again, but was presented on the last day of the session. Representative Tom Kennedy led the, albeit delayed,

charge with Sarah Connors, his Chief of Staff, and Conor, who now worked for
Representative Kennedy. Sarah was also Conor's new girlfriend. The three were
able to get the bill approved by the House. When the papers were delivered to
the Senate, however, the political body had closed early and the referendum
died, just like that.

The Brightfield's coordinator, Lori Colombo, the woman from Harvard, was
in tears and stormed over to State Senator Rob Creedon's law office in Brockton,
only to find that it, too, had closed. The Senator and his staff and friends were at
The Pub watching a football game. The woman was livid and called Jack to vent
her emotions. He called me afterwards.

"How many meetings did I attend in Ward 5, listening to everyone over and
over?" He anguished, sitting at his desk in City Hall, ready to punch the phone
buttons, poised to make more calls, appalled that the State House had let him
down again. "How many times did I drive to Boston for meeting after meeting
to get this through? Years!!" he exclaimed. "I gotta go," and he was off calling
someone else to try and remedy the situation.

I had a mix of feelings when Jack and I went to The Pub several days later.
Incidents over the years, including the countless times Jack had been harassed
while trying to unwind over a cold beer, had marred our enthusiasm for the
place. The Pub hadn't changed one bit since Jack took office. The décor was the
same dark paneling with black vinyl booth cushions. The chef, Haikal Haikal,
however, still made the best hummus and tabouli and patrons told jokes while
standing at the long bar. The owner, Joe, was still the only bartender, his wife,
Debbie, the only waitress, and politicians and lawyers drank cocktails together
alongside Enterprise truck drivers. Like in the sitcom "Cheers," everyone at The
Pub really does know your name. And in cities like Brockton, or Pittsfield, or
Gloucester, having places like The Pub can be sweetly comforting. It's easy
enough to let go of grudges, forget past failings. When, for instance, Rob Creedon,
the Senator, gave a little whistle to call me over to hear his latest Irish joke,
how could I resist? Someone bought me a "short one"—a small glass of beer,
a "pony," a "tulip"—and I sidled up next to Rob to hear the funny quip in his
practiced Irish brogue. That was what I liked about being in an interwoven,

deeply entrenched community. No one stays mad at one another for long. You're bound to run into them at a wake or funeral or a ball game or at The Pub, so what's the point?

Jack's phone began ringing off the cradle when word got out that he might be stepping down. Most of his calls were from businessmen telling him they'd invested a lot of money in Brockton and didn't want him to leave.

One of Jack's first supporters, our good friend, George Baldwin, called while vacationing in Florida to tell Jack to be aware that he would be treated differently when he was no longer mayor. "The pedestal you're on, pal—that will be removed," our friend warned, with a laugh. "You might have a tough transition."

"Especially with the women," I joked. Several of his female admirers would be sorry not to be able to pop in on him at City Hall so frequently.

Days before Jack was to give his State of the City speech, a number of colleagues approached him. "If you intend to not run again, this speech must be your best," one said. "You must tell everyone how much progress Brockton has made under your leadership. People need to be reminded."

So, together with Mark, Tim, and others, the group hammered out a new address—on a Saturday, no less, freezing their butts off inside City Hall because the heat had been turned way down.

Mark brought the written speech over to our house that afternoon. He tried to brush the snow off his boots, finally decided they were too wet to wear in the house and removed them. Padding over the kitchen floor in his socks he said the group worked together for hours. I poured him a scotch on the rocks as he told me they included the names of the buildings and schools that had been built, the businesses that had flocked to Brockton, and the lives that had been improved. "It's a whole different speech than the one Jack started," Mark said, taking a sip from the glass I kept in the pantry just for him. Jack had told me the speech he had written was probably too technical anyway. But I made him leave in the parts about "Black Fiber," the stuff that runs through cable lines, and enhancing the Wifi technology so that people could use their laptop computers without having to plug in to an electrical outlet.

The day of the speech I drove to the law office to interview three potential legal secretaries. By the time I got home at 6 p.m., the family had a quick bite of salad and ziti with red sauce while Jack read his speech through.

After loading the dishwasher, I yelled upstairs to see if Breck and Mairi were ready. Mairi said she thought Breck was in the shower, but I didn't hear the water running. I hurried upstairs to check on him and found him lying face down on his bed with his clothes and shoes on. I approached him and heard sniffling.

"Breck, are you sleeping? Are you sick? What's the matter?" I asked, my hand smoothing the back of his wrinkled shirt.

"I can't go," he said, his words muffled by his pillow.

"Oh, sweetie. What's going on?"

He shifted his face so I could hear him better. "My friends are calling from Duke. They're talking about getting together after the holidays. I won't be there." His words were shaking from his mouth. "I can't bear to explain myself tonight."

And like that, "Bam!" It hit me how much my kids had sacrificed.

Everything our family had done over the past nine years had been shared with the public. Countless events and conversations too numerous to calculate had infiltrated the most basic right of life—privacy. We had obliged the public's curiosity by being friendly and upbeat. But sometimes, life's issues were best kept to oneself. Breck was having a private, debilitating time and couldn't subject himself to scrutiny that night. I covered Breck with blankets and lay down beside him. Speaking softly in his ear, I reassured him that everything would be all right. "Your setback is just a bump in the road, a blip on the screen," I said, stroking his damp cheek. "You'll get through." Then I tucked him in, kissed him, told him I loved him and raced to refresh my makeup.

Conor drove Mairi, Jack and I to City Hall for Jack's final State of the City speech. The people who'd been with us from the beginning were standing around the conference table in Jack's office. I bent over to hug the diminutive Mary Waldron, Jack's first Chief of Staff, for the longest time. We all understood what the day meant. Jack had led the city through the most productive time in a hundred years. He led Brockton into the 21st Century like he said he would. We survived Y2K, 9/11 and record-breaking snowstorms. He oversaw the removal of 400 abandoned buildings, the construction of three new schools, three train stations, a new District Courthouse, a revamped waste water treatment plant, the restoration of the War Memorial Building and the rise of the Brockton Rox. He had had wonderful, loyal help. I kissed and hugged the City Solicitor, Tom Plouffe; the current Chief of Staff, Mark O'Reilly; Veteran's Services director, Bob Gayle; Human Services Administrator Bob Martin; Jack's Communications Director, David Farrell; his secretaries, the lovely Lillian Pilalas and Sylvia Carvalho; and our close friend and advisor, Tim Cruise. It was fitting and appropriate that they were there with Jack.

"We owe it all to you, Mairi," Tim joked, patting her dark hair, "because of the publicity Jack received when you were hospitalized right before the first primary." She smiled, embarrassed. He said, "What's that on your shirt?" When she looked down, he clipped her chin with his index finger. "Gotcha!" Tim laughed. Tim makes everyone around him smile.

We walked up the wide marble staircase to the City Council Chamber and when we got there I requested the audio technicians to please make sure Jack's microphone was turned up. Jack never quite got the hang of microphones. He was always too far away, or moving back and forth too much. But tonight his words were too important to go unheard. When Jack's name was announced, the standing ovation, whistling, and clapping went on and on as he walked to the podium shaking hands along the way. Mark and I took our places next to Conor and Mairi on the long bench in the front row and sat down in unison. Several tears rolled down my nose, dropping onto my folded hands.

Jack delivered the speech his friends prepared for him, and then took a deep breath. Everyone in the room knew what was coming. The walls were lined with people standing. Several older women were scrunched into the pews, some sucking on Altoids.

In his own words he began. "The task of running any great city knows little rest," he said, his voice a bit subdued. Pulling himself taller, he ramped it up. "A duty that constantly drives the spirit of the leader can sometimes drain the leader of spirit. And a good leader must know that at that moment the task is complete—his duty fulfilled. And he must have the confidence in his accomplishments to know that the city is great enough to stand on its own."

Jack unconsciously turned from side to side slowly as he addressed the room. His voice went in and out of the mike. "It has been the greatest honor to serve and, although I hope to be remembered as a good mayor who led with heart, integrity and grit, I would rather be remembered as a great dad *nice* and husband, who fulfilled his duty at home. It is the nature of the job to give of yourself to others and that means nights, weekends and days away. Kids' games, competitions, plays and simple moments best spent with loved ones are sacrificed for duty. My family understood this and never wavered in their support for me and the task at hand. Now it is time for me to commit wholly to them. It is without reservation that I have decided not to seek re-election." *SA D*

Someone murmured, as more people slipped into the back of the warm room. "It is not easy to leave this job I love. But it is made easier knowing that, thanks to the commitment and help I have had from our great city employees and citizen volunteers, Brockton is again a city of pride . . . I am moving on, but I am not moving out. I remain committed to doing whatever is required of me to move our city forward." He hesitated and his shoulders relaxed. Taking a deep breath he continued. "To every elected official, to you the City Council, and to each and every citizen of this great city who has given more than asked, I humbly and graciously say thank you and good night." The audience rose to its feet. Cameras flashed. Applause filled the chamber. *nice*

I found Ginny and Frank, our wonderful neighbors, in the vast hallway outside as we slowly made our way through the thick crowd. We hugged and I told them how happy I was to see them. They are like family to us, and Brockton has a core of people just like them—hundreds and hundreds of citizens who dish out money and time for the charities and clubs and road races and fundraisers that keep the city going. In a broader sense I pictured every manufacturing city in the country that might be having similar setbacks or comebacks and knew that the first most important ingredient for success was leadership. The second was a willing citizenry.

At home afterwards there were several phone messages. One was from my friend, Ellie, who said, "[Sniff] I wanted to be the first one to call [sniff] and say I have never, ever in my life been prouder [sniff] to be a Brocktonian than right now. [Laughing]. My mother and I held hands and cried the entire speech. Jack you were FABULOUS. Lees you looked beautiful. Mairi you looked gorgeous. I mean, oh my God, it was so overwhelming. I can't tell you how proud I am right now on one point and how sad I am that Jack's not going to run again because there's never going to be a better mayor than him. But, Lees and Jack, God bless you both, you've done such a great job for this city and we love you so much. Goodnight."

Suzanne and O.D. called from Florida. "We love you! Say it ain't so!" they pleaded.

Another message from our friend, Dave Cruise, said: "Congratulations. I think politics is like buying a boat. Buying it is the best day of your life and selling it is the second best day."

My sister, Cynthia, simply said, "Wow!"

Jack took a call from Congressman Stephen Lynch who implored, "Jack you can't do this to me!"

A week later, there was a message at our house from Senator Ted Kennedy: "It's Ted Kennedy in Washington calling Jack. Say it isn't so Jack! I mean, how can you not be there when we need you as our leader? I send him my best wishes, warm regards, and I look forward to talking to him sometime. All the best. Bye."

CHAPTER 35

"There's always the motivation of wanting to win. Everybody has that. But a champion needs, in his attitude, a motivation above and beyond winning."
—Pat Riley *read this*

Jack seemed lost in thought on the plane ride down to D.C. for our final U.S. Conference of Mayors. When the stewardess brought our tomato juice, he and I clinked our glasses together before sipping. "To our last conference," I said. He didn't say anything. "What's on your mind?" I asked, handing him the pretzel package, which was impossible to open. He shook his head, handed back the opened pretzels, swirled his ice around, and turned his head to look out the small window.

Finally, he told me he had a vivid dream earlier that morning. He leaned closer, his mouth grazing my shoulder. "I was fighting in WWII, and got captured by the Germans."

"Uh-huh," I said, munching.

"But I led an escape and made my way to Italy, where I met and married a beautiful Italian woman."

"Naturally."

"But the Germans executed her."

"Oh, too bad," I mumbled.

"I couldn't return to the war because I was being tried for desertion, so I traveled to Cape Verde and became mayor under the name of Tony Delgado."

"Hmm," I said, remembering a lady I met in Cape Verde. She owned the same microwave as me.

"And I started a fishing business. But I was always sad and felt I was a man without a country because I wasn't allowed back to America." He took his napkin, wiped down his tray, scrunched the napkin and stuffed it inside the plastic cup.

"Maybe leaving your post as mayor is affecting you on a deeper level than you know," I said. He turned away to again stare at the passing clouds. The stewardess retrieved our cups and the empty pretzel bag.

The mayors' conference definitely lacked the energy it had in previous years. Few Massachusetts mayors attended, when in past years our state practically dominated. The fun and singing we once enjoyed seemed long over.

On the last night, Jack and I, together with a group of mayors, went to Archibald's strip club, of all places. It was across the street from the Capitol Hilton. We entered the bar sometime around midnight.

A round of drinks was delivered and a svelte dancer came over to a row of tables where a group of us were sitting. She was about to flirt with one particularly handsome mayor, but instead engaged my eyes, then reached forward to take my hand in hers. The gesture was surprisingly gentle.

"Go, Lees!" someone yelled over the music.

"Thank you all for coming!" the bartender said, to indicate the night was about over. But the young woman pulled me up and out of my seat. The thought crossed my mind that if I were a Congressman's wife I probably wouldn't be in this predicament. So what was I doing? Feeling saucy because Jack was getting out of politics? Maybe. And we were out of town so there were no cameras, no judgment waiting to be passed. I mean I wasn't going to strip or anything. I was just following this persistent girl somewhere—to the stage it turned out. I was handed a dollar bill as I passed the cute mayor. "I want to watch you put it in the stripper's garter," he said. Jack wasn't visible through the darkness, but I was quite sure he was amused by the situation. Strobe lights throbbed as the young woman stepped onto the low stage, then swiveled around and began fluctuating her body my way. I moved along with the loud rock music—my purple suede boots stepping to the rhythm. Her eyes were on me. I looked at the floor, glanced around the room. The men whistled—their tongues wagged. Men are so simple. The cash in my hand felt damp. The bartender was watching, smiling. I drummed up a bit more courage and, after several more catcalls from the guys, slid the bill up the woman's thigh under the strap of the lacy garter. The place erupted in hollers and hoots. I spun around laughing as the bartender brightened the lights for our departure. Jack winked at me from across the room. There. I'd done it—I'd crossed some barrier—morphed from political correctness to resuming my love of life.

We left D.C. the next day. Overall, we were a more somber group than when we arrived in 1996. Back then there seemed such promise for America under President Clinton. He was funding cities and social programs—listening to the mayors, interacting with them regularly. And there was a jovial atmosphere around town. The difference now was that George Bush spoke at the mayors not with them. America was involved in a futile war, and the President's tax cuts seemed to help no one. Still, I would miss the conferences, the politics, the men and women, Washington, D.C.

Several more things I knew I'd miss when Jack stepped down were first off, the intellectual stimulation from being in the heart of the political world. Politics is often thrilling and definitely has its exalted moments. I loved being on the arm of a man whose politics I admired, a man who worked hard for others.

I would miss meeting important people like President and Mrs. Clinton, Senator and Mrs. Ted Kennedy, and going to the White House and the Kennedy Compound. I would miss the many surprising encounters, too, like the time

President Clinton flirted with me during Congressman Joe Moakley's funeral. The church in South Boston that day was full of dignitaries, including Al Gore and President Bush, and I was returning from receiving communion at the altar when my eyes looked over to where Clinton was sitting. He was checking me out, up and down. I was so startled I blushed and turned away. When I looked back again, he was smiling. I love that guy.

Likewise, I came to know the actor, Bill Murray; had lunch with former middleweight champion Marvelous Marvin Hagler (who trained in Brockton); watched a Red Sox game from the owner's box; and traveled to conferences in Las Vegas and New Orleans. I even had a conversation with singer/songwriter Willie Nelson once and slipped a cassette with two of my songs into his pocket! I would miss those perks.

Above all, however, I would miss having Jack as Brockton's mayor because he brought class and dignity to the city. He made everyone work harder than we thought possible. He helped us believe that we were all champions and that we could rise to any challenge. He lifted Brockton's spirit up from defeat.

Back home, Jack drove his car into a "truck farm" as he called the area, to make sure that the plows were ready for a pending blizzard. The trucks were warming up all right—one of them had exploded! Flames were everywhere. Jack called the fire department from his cell phone, and then found the drivers, who were inside the building staying warm and watching a Patriots football game. "What'll they do without me?" he asked when he returned home, throwing his car keys into the drawer.

In the 113 years for which records have been kept, four out of the five worst snowstorms in Massachusetts happened during Jack's administration. Thankfully, during this latest storm the electricity stayed on and we were able to watch the Patriots not only win the contest against the Pittsburgh Steelers, but they also went on to beat the Philadelphia Eagles to win their third Super Bowl in four years! New England dominated sports while Jack was mayor, including Brockton's own football team—Division I Champions three times.

And in a different arena close to the heart of many Brocktonians, the city gained another boxing champ, Kevin McBride, a lad originally from Ireland. Kevin had been training with the Brockton-based Petronelli brothers, known for training middleweight champion "Marvelous Marvin Hagler." Kevin's lifelong dream was to fight Mike Tyson, a former heavyweight champion. One day in June, at the MCI Center in Washington, D.C., Kevin got his chance.

The newspapers, including The Boston Globe, The Enterprise, and USA Today, all pegged Tyson as the sure winner. Jack and I, along with Suzanne and O.D., were there for the event. Jack guessed that Goody Petronelli would instruct McBride to lay low the first four rounds so that when Tyson tired McBride could go in and destroy him. That was pretty much what happened, except that Mike tried to break Kevin's arm and head butted him several times in the interim. During the 6th round, Tyson fell down on his rear end. The referee didn't count. Mike got up, the bell rang, and he slumped to his corner. He never answered the seventh round bell. Kevin McBride won in a 6th round TKO.

Later we met up with the boxing professionals at the Wyndham hotel. Goody and his corner man, Chick, were walking into the hotel lobby, dodging a tall indoor tree as we walked toward one another. Goody was so surprised to see Jack.

"I can't believe you're here!" he said, squeezing Jack's shoulder. Nearly 80 years old, Goody looked trim in blue jeans and a white tee shirt that read "Team McBride." He reminded us of Clint Eastwood from the movie "Million Dollar Baby." Only there was no press nearby for these two men—no groupies for these old timers holding buckets, whose winner tonight had beaten former champ Mike Tyson.

"I can't believe you're here, Jack," Goody said again. Then, with a twinkle in his eye added, "We got you another champion."

"If I may speak on behalf of the family, Dad, we are all so proud to call you our father. You have given us more than any child can expect. We've witnessed first hand so many trials, struggles, and achievements, and we are better people because of it. Thank you."

—Casey A. Yunits

LEES YUNITS   *263*

CHAPTER 36

"Have a vision. Be demanding."
—Colin Powell

Two more "champions" added to Brockton's rising trajectory during Jack's last few months—U.S. Senator Hillary Rodham Clinton and Brockton born-and-raised Attorney Kenneth Feinberg, one of the key players in the Victim Compensation Fund set up to compensate the victims of 9/11.

When Mrs. Clinton arrived in Brockton the atmosphere among the hundreds of onlookers on the steps of the War Memorial Building was electric. Brockton had reached the big league—Mrs. Clinton was here! She alighted from an SUV, dressed in a peachy red pantsuit and came straight towards Jack and me. I was humbled beyond belief to meet her and could hardly contain my excitement.

Later, Ken Feinberg told us that Hillary Clinton was the "go to" person after 9/11. He couldn't praise her handling of the situation enough. Once inside the building, in her speech, Senator Clinton often likened Brockton to several cities she represented in the state of New York—old manufacturing cities rebounding from tough times. She then talked about the 9/11 Compensation Fund and told us that in order for the fund to work, there had to be just one person in charge of deciding the amounts awarded to all victims. The person chosen was Attorney Kenneth R. Feinberg.

During a quiet second, someone in the balcony yelled "2008!" and everyone clapped, knowing the presidential race was coming up. Hillary gave much of herself when she spoke from the heart. We were united in our love of Brockton and another of our native sons, Ken Feinberg, who had rendered exceptional service. The wind ensemble from Brockton High played their hearts out and received the longest standing ovation I'd ever heard. "That's the beauty of a big city," my friend, Marti Nover, whispered to me at our table. "You have enough students to form an orchestra like this." I was struck by her words. It had been a long time since I'd heard the words 'Brockton' and 'beauty' together in the same sentence.

It felt great to be part of a city that was poised for growth. Because of the expertise of Jack's Cultural Affairs Director, Gayle Kelley, and the hundreds of volunteers, that event put Brockton on par with Boston. We were able to entertain celebrities by hosting a fabulous luncheon, drive the honorees for tours around the city in our new trolleys, and end with a lobster dinner at the Shaw's Center with Senator Ted Kennedy in attendance.

As the black-tie dinner drew to a close, Ken Feinberg stood at the podium and re-iterated that his passion for life and justice all stemmed from growing up in Brockton. His love for the city was evident and his speech was the biggest plug for Brockton anyone will ever give. He mulled over his nostalgic feelings again and again, saying Brockton was a "state of mind," one that gave him his strong family values and lifelong friendships. There was no question that Brockton had been his biggest positive influence.

You would think that big event studded with dignitaries would have made the "top of the fold" of The Enterprise the next day. It didn't. Instead of Hillary's or Ken's or Ted's picture, was a picture of an ugly man, temporarily living in Brockton, who had allegedly murdered a family member. Aaaaaaagghhhh! I was absolutely despondent when Jack brought the paper into the house. "Jack! What the fuck is wrong with this paper?" I asked, throwing it down on the kitchen table.

"Calm down, wifey," Jack said, although his eyes were weary. He, too, had had enough of the newspaper's small-mindedness.

"I mean, what do they gain from this?" I asked. "Thousands of people turn out for this extraordinary event and this is what they print? I swear this paper is the single most destructive force in the city. A murder such as this—if it needs to be mentioned at all—does not take precedence over the memorable event we have just witnessed in the city. How unconscionable to dismiss true heroes like Mrs. Clinton and Attorney Ken Feinberg," I said.

In the fall, Jack stuck a shovel in the dirt and officially launched work on the desalinization plant. Brockton's water solution was finally on its way to becoming a reality.

However, one nagging issue continued to cast a shadow over Jack's last few months. It was the residency clause in the firefighters' contract—which mandated every working fireman must live in Brockton. Jack had agreed to reduce a lifetime commitment down to seven years, but the City Council refused to sign the contract during an election year. The atmosphere around town was threatening to bring all Jack's hard-earned community building to a grinding halt. People were taking sides. The firefighters even picketed our house in August when Jack wasn't home and I had to deal with their walking back and forth carrying signs.

Now, in October, our family was busy getting dressed up to attend an event honoring Jack. He would be accepting the Historic Citizen's Award from the Brockton Historical Society. I was upstairs ironing his tuxedo shirt when Conor and Sarah came in the house. I met them downstairs; they looked polished in a tux and a long black gown. Mark O'Reilly arrived unexpectedly, grazing his head against the duck ornament that hangs in the kitchen. He then stopped to pull the string that makes the duck's wings go up and down. "I love this thing," I heard him say.

"Mark, what are you doing here?" I asked from across the kitchen. He stepped further in and we shared a hug. His coat smelled like wet canvas, alerting me to the fact that it was raining outside, but his grip was warm.

"I felt it was necessary to warn you that the firemen's union members are demonstrating again," he said. "This time they've brought along a giant, inflatable rat, which is sitting near the main entrance to the Shaw's Center."

"Oh, gross!" I shrugged.

Jack joined us too and told me, "The unions use the rat whenever they're having trouble in contract negotiations. It is effective."

"I guess so," I said, not wanting to believe that the firefighters were going to ruin Jack's night. They were the highest paid force in Massachusetts, for one thing, and because of Jack's support over the years had state-of-the-art trucks and night vision apparatus. Up until the point that they put Jack's life through a living hell I had respected the union probably more than any other.

Conor drove the family to the Shaw's Center in the pouring rain and pointed out the rat through the gloom. My stomach clenched. The creepy apparition stood about twenty feet tall and had little ratty claws and a snout.

I emerged from the car hurrying to keep from getting too wet, but there was no avoiding the fifty nameless people dressed in hooded sweatshirts yelling and booing. I smiled and waved just to spite them. How could they? The demonstrators got louder as we ran to the door and I half expected something to hit me in the back. I was so mad I could hardly breathe. What happened to those guys? The union president, Archie Gormley, said it was a small group of younger men causing the trouble. They certainly had organized the others well.

Jack lit up when he saw the Brockton High School wind ensemble and easily put the protesters out of his mind. I couldn't. The moment was so heavy with contradictory feelings that my eyes teared up. The band was playing the Notre Dame Fight Song and I was a mess. A friend took my coat and another handed me a Kleenex. I'd barely used the tissue when we were ushered into the hall where hundreds of elegantly dressed men and women were standing and applauding Jack. The musicians played continuously. I was so happy and so hurt at the same time. Thankfully, I had Mairi with me for support as Jack made the rounds. At 16, she had grown into a confident young lady. Her long, silky brown hair hung straight and her smile warmed people. Everyone apologized to the two of us for the shenanigans outside, telling us to forget about it. My friend, Yiannis Davos, asked us what we wanted from the bar and then handed us a cool white wine and a Pepsi.

The M.C. for the evening, Attorney Paul Finn, got up to speak before dinner was served. "Are the firefighters protesting because they don't want to live here in Brockton?" he bellowed into the microphone. "Then let's take up a collection and get them the hell out!" His words broke the ice and everyone laughed. The night continued in good fun along those lines with one speaker, Mike Veeck, wondering if it was "Protest Night" at the Rox when he saw the rally outside.

After dinner Paul returned to the podium. Honoring Jack's request to avoid long speeches, he rapidly read through letters of tribute. "Here's one from so and so and he says blah, blah, blah and we thank him and let's move on." The crowd was bent over laughing. It was just what Jack and I wanted. We had both sat through enough long- winded speeches. Paul did, however, allow a heartfelt video tribute from Senator John Kerry to play on the giant screen. Senator Kerry was ebullient in his praise of Jack. The protesters were beginning to fade from my mind.

The award-winning music director from the high school, Vinnie Macrina, brought the student musicians to the dance floor and said, "If it weren't for Jack's devotion to kids, kids, kids the music program wouldn't exist." The Brockton High musicians are some of the finest in Massachusetts. That night they soared.

Afterwards, Conor pushed back his chair and walked up to the podium. His voice was confident as he began to speak and I was filled with love. I had no idea he was going to speak. After his introduction he talked about how hard it had been over the years to have regular family dinners. "As you can imagine, between school committee meetings, football games, majorette practices and Peace Corps missions, this hasn't always been easy.

"But on the rare occasions when my mother can take the 6-8 hours she needs to prepare a meal, [hearty har har] the whole family sits down to enjoy each other's company…for about five minutes. At this point, my father, having already polished off his plate, gets up and starts clearing the table.

"Over the years this has become a running joke in our family. Five of us tell stories and jokes and generally have a great time, while my father is in the kitchen loading the dishwasher. Of course, the question you all have is, is it us? Are our conversations that boring? If you have spent anytime with Mairi you know that's not the case. No, what it really comes down to is my father's mindset. He believes that talk is great, but if everyone spends all night chatting, no work will get done, and at the end of the night we are still going to have a pile of dirty dishes waiting to be cleaned.

"In many ways, this mannerism has defined his career over the last decade. Now that we are a little older and wiser, it's only fair that the rest of us push back our chairs and pick up our plates.

"Dad, on behalf of Casey, Breck, Mairi and myself, I want to say thank you for doing our dishes.

"And on behalf of all of us in this room who are working for a better Brockton, I want to assure you that on January 1st, when you have run that dishwasher for the last time, the rest of us won't let the dirty dishes pile up. All of us together will continue the hard work of the past decade. So that many years from now, in a Brockton of "Education, Industry and Progress," [the slogan our forefathers granted Brockton one hundred years ago] the Historical Society will gather our children and grandchildren together on a night like this and let them know that these past ten years were when the comeback began. Thank you."

Conor received sustained applause as he returned to his seat. Jack rose
from his chair, shook Conor's hand, and patted him on the back. What splendid
children Jack gave me. People around our table, including Congressman
Stephen Lynch, who had left a family wedding to be there, were beaming
and clapping.

The President of the Brockton Historical Society, Attorney Larry Siskind,
called me up to the stage and handed over a dozen white roses. I bent my head
to take in the delicate scent and Larry asked me to say something. Caught off
guard I walked to the microphone and said, "Well, it's been quite a ride. Thanks
for being on my . . . sled. Jack has always promoted team effort and together
we've all been quite a team. Thank you so much." Sled? Toboggan more like it.
Locomotive. Before I could be too embarrassed, the bandleader encouraged me
to sing "Sentimental Journey." At least I remembered the words to the song.

On Election Day in November, Jack received an early morning email from
Breck, who had re-enrolled at Duke and was on his way to obtaining a degree in
Economics. "I just realized that they're going to elect a new mayor's son today!
I've had that title for 10 years!" That evening, as the tallies came in Brockton
voted James Harrington into office as the city's newest mayor.

People often voice that being a mayor is a thankless job. That is true in
many ways, especially during contract negotiations or the early morning phone
calls about snow. But I have to admit that more often than not Jack received
gestures of thanks on a regular basis. Marching in our final Veteran's Day parade
was no exception.

"We'll miss you Jack!" spectators yelled. "Thanks for your service!" Little
kids of every race and color sat on a curb in front of the new Arnone elementary
school watching the parade pass. "We love Brock-ton! We love Brock-ton!" they
chanted, while stamping their feet in unison.

When the parade ended, Jack and I walked a mile back to our car. He
refused several offers for a ride. "Thanks, honey," I said, "these boots don't hurt

a bit." We stopped in to see Conor and Sarah, who, coincidentally, were now renting the same apartment our family occupied for a while after the house fire. Climbing the long staircase up to the apartment, we noticed flower petals decorating every step. They traced a path to the living room where the two of them stood with arms around each other. Sarah held out her hand and on her finger was a glittering diamond engagement ring. Conor had proposed and Sarah accepted. I guess there would be life after politics after all.

CHAPTER 37

*"A good compromise, a good piece of
legislation, is like a good sentence; or a good
piece of music. Everybody can recognize it.
They say, 'Huh. It works. It makes sense."*
—Barack Obama

The GAR room in City Hall, named for the Grand Army of the Republic, is a
large oval-shaped public meeting room, and over the years has experienced
its share of wear and tear. Gayle Kelley, Jack's new Cultural Affairs director,
suggested to me that, as a parting gift to Brockton, maybe I'd consider leading
a restoration project. So, with Jim Casieri, from the building department,
coordinating the effort, we chose new ceiling tiles, a red and gold star-studded
rug, navy leather-look chairs, long white drapes, valences with a New England
lighthouse theme, and a large brass chandelier. Jim refinished the existing
oak table and we exchanged hundreds of ugly spectator chairs for handsome,
comfortable ones.

A cocktail reception was organized to unveil the room, and included a
martini bar courtesy of the recently opened Tamboo restaurant, as well as a
wine tasting set up by 1666 Liquors. After I thanked the audience for coming,
several photographs were snapped and the double doors to the GAR room were
ceremoniously opened.

Although a "No Food or Drink" sign had been placed in a visible spot and
everyone was respectful of that request, I was standing inside speaking with
a gentleman, when my friend, Denise Lindquist, handed my friend and me a
chocolate martini and a green appletini. He and I clicked our glasses together

in a toast, but his hand had a tremor and the liquid from both our cups spilled over onto the new rug. "Oh shoot!" I said, hurrying out of the room to the safety of the tile floor. First Lady spills first drink.

After that event, which was on December 1st, Jack's and my hectic pace continued through the holidays, and one night, after waking up every few hours to eat a TUMS, guzzle more water, or swallow a Motrin I said to Jack, "We're too old for this." He agreed.

He'd also been holding his hand to his heart fairly often saying, "It's too much, too much." There were so many lists in his head and as was often the case, too much information pounded in his skull." Yet, despite all the advice that it would kill him politically, Jack figured out how to settle matters with regard to the firefighters without putting the City Council on the spot.

One morning, as he was standing at the sink shaving, Jack had an "ah-ha!" moment. I was in the tub soaking as he arrived at his solution. He decided to create two contracts instead of just one. The first included a residency modification, meaning the residency requirement would be reduced to a seven-year commitment to live in Brockton, not a lifetime. However, that contract offered no money concessions, such as sick time or pay raises. The City Council, whose role was limited to voting on money issues, couldn't approve the first contract, but Jack and the firefighters could and did. The second contract contained better concessions financially for the taxpayers and the Council voted in favor.

Although some of the councilors killed Jack in the press, privately they loved him for getting the matter settled. After all it was a compromise with a win-win factor.

Shortly thereafter, the policemen's union agreed to the same terms. Several policemen told Mairi at West Side Pizza that her father was a hero—that he "took the bullet" so that Brockton could go forward peacefully.

During the final week of Jack's administration, the Brightfield's bill finally passed in the legislature. That ensured that a solar panel array would be built in Brockton–the first of its kind in New England. Jack said it was "a nice project to influence our youth, knowing that the future will necessitate alternative power resources."

The Environmental Protection Agency also dropped its appeals allowing the desalinization plant to continue construction again, and Brockton's bond rating upgraded to A2, the highest the city had ever had. That achievement had taken several years, as Brockton CFO Jay Condon, and others, including Jack, had made several trips to Wall Street in order to obtain lower interest rates for the Pension Obligation Fund, saving taxpayers forty-two millions dollars over the next twenty years. That money pays all the pensions for retired employees.

A municipal bond expert—Bob Harding, a round faced man—asked an Enterprise reporter, Jennifer Kovalich, if she understood the significance of the A2 upgrade. "Did you know this is very big news in financial circles? Why haven't you written about it?"

"My hands are tied," she said. She had been instructed by the editors to ask Jack only three questions regarding his time as mayor. The first was about his taking a pay raise eight years earlier, the second about the way the Rox stadium was financed. I forget the third.

"I'm not wasting my breath," Jack said.

Years earlier, our friend, John Buckley, had said that the true test of Jack's leadership would be measured by his success in saving the Rocky Marciano homestead. Tellingly, a relative of the famous boxer restored the home and made the first floor open to the public.

Shortly past midnight on New Year's Eve, 2005, Jack coaxed me onto the couch to watch the movie "Sleepless in Seattle." It was the wee hours of his last official day in office. By now the snow had been falling for some time. A truck noise disturbed the otherwise peaceful moment.

"Was that a plow?" I asked, rising from his arms.

"Sander," he said. A few minutes later, we heard something else. "That's the plow," he said. I smiled. Jack knew his city trucks.

The Enterprise wrote several articles about Jack on New Year's Day, under the headline "Mayor Yunits: Mission Accomplished" and gave him a "thumbs up" in a column. Finally.

That same New Year's Day, I begged Jack to drive me around the city so I could make a note of all that had changed under his watch. Because a Patriots game was on, he only grudgingly obliged. But we brushed the snow off the silver Ford Taurus he'd been driving for nine years and eased out of the driveway. Traffic was more than we bargained for. Still, the game was on the radio and it kept him amused, especially when then quarterback, Doug Flutie, threw an exceptional pass.

Quickly Jack rattled off four, five, six businesses all at once. He drove down streets, around corners, and through side roads knowing every shortcut like they were the most familiar territory. I knew he just wanted to get this over with. All the while I scribbled away. Driving from west to south to east to north and circling back to west, we ventured down streets I'd never been on. I learned more about businesses, bars, schools, parks, golf courses and people, than I had room for in my brain. He got impatient when I asked him to slow down because there were cars on his tail.

"That itself is a testament to your work, honey," I said, "traffic jams! Everyone wants to be in Brockton!"

The Patriots lost the game and we kept driving. It was dark when we finally pulled into our driveway. Jack started recalling more details, including the Campanelli Stadium, and the new soccer fields behind the high school. The transformation of Brockton filled fifteen pages.

The next day Jack and I were at the Inaugural luncheon for Mayor Harrington when Jack leaned over and whispered to me that he felt like a blow-up doll that had been pierced and which was slowly being deflated. My hand slid across his shoulders and I planted a kiss on his cheek.

Afterwards, he and I enjoyed several relaxing cocktails with friends and family at the member's bar. We shared stories, remembering Jack's first year in office when the snow wouldn't stop. All the storms earned Jack the label Brockton's weather mayor. The sun was beginning to set as the two of us walked slowly by the beautiful mahogany bar, stopping for a few words with Tim Cruise's Irish clan, our faithful supporters through all of Jack's ups and downs. "Jack? What? You're leaving a place early? Geez, I guess we are going to see changes around here," Tim laughed. As we left the club waving to those who were still drinking we were given a lengthy applause. It felt like a standing ovation, although later I wondered if maybe they were happy to see us go!

It was a tribute to Jack and his focus on bettering Brockton that the transition between mayors was a smooth one. Jack even allowed James Harrington's people to paint the mayor's office before they officially moved in. When Jack took office he was presented no such cordiality.

The next morning school was canceled due to snow. Jack shook his head calling the new mayor a wimp, even though the decision is usually made between the School Superintendent and the mayor. The snow accumulation only amounted to four inches, which in a terrible twist of irony was practically all that fell on Brockton the entire year.

I sat at my computer with a cup of coffee and found an email that Casey had sent from Poland where she was spending the holiday with friends. She wrote:

"I just wanted to share this moment with you all . . .we did it!!! I think we'd all agree that the past ten years were completely unpredictable, and probably a lot more so than your average family. Remember that first campaign? When it was all about fundraisers and door to door? Then the first few years when it was Papa Gino's and Mairi screaming every night? It wasn't easy for any of us, especially mom and dad. I can't even imagine how liberated you both feel today. You raised our city to a higher level. You set such a good example for how people should live."

I called Jack over to read the letter, which continued, "If I may speak on behalf of the family, Dad, we are all so proud to call you our father. You have given us more than any child can expect. We've witnessed first hand so many trials, struggles, and achievements, and we are better people because of it. Thank you."

Jack kissed the top of my head. "Isn't that great?" he said. I kept reading. "And mom, how you ever took time away from your busy singing career we will never know. [These kids are always picking on me.] Just think, now you can finish your book!"

Mairi wrote about her feelings in a college essay saying that her dad being the mayor was the "best experience," and that she was "challenged to become a better person" because of his efforts. She added that she was "confident, determined and responsible. I am who I am because I was a mayor's daughter."

That night my dream had me at my alma mater, Berklee College of Music. I was walking over to where some musicians were jamming on a bright green grassy knoll when a flash flood quickly filled the streets. Jack pulled up in a car and I jumped in, but the water was seeping in through the doors. I swirled my head around to look at Jack. "He'll take care of it," I thought, as the water began pulsing around the floor mat. The level was rising. Why wasn't he doing anything? It was his job to do something! The water rose to my thighs, covering the seat, soaking us both. Jack seemed oblivious. The long road was open before us; his freedom waited. Staring straight ahead, he began to inch the car forward through the rising waves, peacefully driving us to safety. Problems with the weather were no longer his responsibility. Now I knew that Jack's work here was done. *At least for the time being.*

buried at Arlington National Cemetery; Jack's late father, John, who, along with Jack's mother, Sylvia, now deceased, gave Jack his lifelong values; Jack's and my extended families for their help; our four beloved children, Conor, Casey, Breck, and Mairi, who had no choice but to hang on and keep moving forward—I am profoundly blessed by having their wonderful souls in my life; our amazing new family members, Sarah Yunits and Derek Smith, who married Conor and Casey respectively; my original freelance editor, author Susan K. Perry from California, whose expertise made the initial process of creating this book so joyful; my friends Jan Brogan, Andrea Bates, Beth Masterman, Paul Finn, Claire Cronin, Linda Smith and Jane Condon who read early drafts and helped direct the book's focus; Poornima Ranganathan, the official editor; Linda Smith, for her keen eyes and welcome suggestions; who offered to print my book and whose enthusiasm and expertise re-ignited my dream; Betsy Gold, for her original and uplifting book design, and all the good people of Brockton who gave in big and small ways to help restore Brockton. If ever there were a force behind, and a reason for naming a book "We, the Mayor," these people I've mentioned are all that reason. I believe they would agree that the ten years spent under the leadership of Jack Yunits will be long remembered. I hope so. Thank you to each and every one. Thanks also, to the countless volunteers and supporters who voted for Jack and who called me by name in the supermarket or at a Rox game. I am forever grateful for your love and support.

A heartfelt apology to all people who may have gone unmentioned in the story. You are still included in my thoughts and considerations. Thank you for everything.

Finally, this book wouldn't have been created were it not for my unwavering belief in my husband and best pal in the world, Jack Yunits. Being married to a man who desired nothing more than to improve the quality of life for thousands of city-dwellers was an amazing lifetime experience. Thank you great citizens and friends of Brockton for all the love, respect and support you gave to Jack, to me, and to our family during the ten years that encompassed the turn of the 21st century. We love you. We will never forget you.

About the Author

As a twenty-three year old singer-songwriter playing guitar in coffee houses and pubs in the Boston area, the last image in Lees Breckinridge Dunn Yunits dream portfolio was that of serving for ten years as the mayor's wife in Brockton, a blue collar city and one of Massachusetts largest old industrial towns.

Although she was from a family steeped in American history dating back to her great-grandfather five times removed, John Witherspoon, signer of the Declaration of Independence; a Vice-President and Confederate war general, John C. Breckinridge, whose own grandson and namesake was a Marine Commandant; a family who graced public service in the medical world with Mary Breckinridge, the Founder of The Frontier Nursing Service, as well as her own father, a Lt. Colonel in the Air Force, her dream was centered on music and entertainment. As a devoted mother of four children, raising kids slowed her music career but didn't stop it as she produced her first two CD's.

Now, two decades after she departed the Berklee College of Music in Boston, on the verge of producing her third CD, her dream popped and morphed into a decade of public commitment in a world she previously respected from a distance and had no desire to pursue. But things changed and Lees' new creative venture was to become a chronicler of the daily challenge of being a mayor's wife in a city that most people had given up on, but that her husband stood committed to fighting for until the end. This is a story of that struggle from an artist and mother's perspective.

Lees is a graduate of the Berklee College of Music with a degree in Composition, has produced three CD's of her own compositions, and is a yoga Instructor and Reiki Master.